The
Shahids

The Shahids

Islam and Suicide Attacks

Shaul Shay

With a foreword by
Aharon Ze'evi Farkash

Translated by Rachel Lieberman

The Interdisciplinary Center, Herzliya

The International Policy Institute for Counter-Terrorism

Transaction Publishers
New Brunswick (U.S.A.) and London (U.K.)

This book is printed on acid-free paper that meets the American National Standard for Permanence of Paper for Printed Library Materials.

Library of Congress Catalog Number: 2003067190
ISBN: 0-7658-0250-3
Printed in Canada

Library of Congress Cataloging-in-Publication Data

Shay, Shaul.
    The shahids : Islam and suicide attacks / Shaul Shay ; with a foreword by
    Aharon Ze'evi Farkash ; translated by Rachel Lieberman.
        p. cm.
    "The Interdisciplinary Center, Herzliya. The International Policy Institute
    for Counter-Terrorism."
    Includes bibliographical references and index.
    ISBN 0-7658-0250-3 (cloth : alk. paper)
        1. Suicide bombers. 2. Suicide bombings. 3. Islam and terrorism. I.
    International Policy Institute for Counter-Terrorism (Israel). II. Title.

HV6431.S4659   2004
303.6'25—dc22   2003067190

This book is dedicated to the memory of my teacher,
the leading expert on terror,
the late Professor Ehud Sprinzak

Contents

Glossary of Terms

ALF—Arab Liberation Front (A pro-Iraqi Palestinian terror organization)

BKI—Babbar Khalsa International

Defense Shield—IDF campaign against terror entities and the Palestinian Authority following the wave of terror perpetrated in March 2002

DFLP—Democratic Front for the Liberation of Palestine (a secular Palestinian terror organization)

Determined Path—IDF campaign against terror entities and the Palestinian Authority during the months of July-August 2002

Ebb and Flow—Term the Israeli Defense Force (IDF) uses to refer to the Al-Aksa Intifada

Fatwa—Islamic religious ruling

GIA—Armed Islamic Front in Algeria

Global Islamic Jihad—Confederation of radical Islamic terror organizations headed by Bin-Laden and Al-Qaida

IDF—Israeli Defense Force

Jihad—Holy war waged by Islam against heretics, enemies of Islam

LTTE—The Tamil Tigers

Palestinian Islamic Jihad—Islamic terror organization

PFLP—Popular Front for the Liberation of Palestine

PKK—The Workers' Party of Kurdistan

Sharia—Islamic law

Foreword

Since September 2000, the State of Israel has been fighting for its home. This war constitutes a violent clash with the Palestinian Authority and Palestinian terror organizations stemming from a strategic decision on Yasser Arafat's part to attempt to attain by the force of terror those strategic objectives that he was unable to achieve at the negotiation table. In the course of this conflict, the Palestinians have made extensive use of suicide attacks, which they regard as "a strategic weapon" in their confrontation with Israel.

Since the beginning of the violent incidents, the Palestinians have perpetrated over 100 suicide attacks; scores of other suicide attacks were thwarted by the IDF and Israeli security forces. Although suicide attacks constitute less than 1 percent of all of the attacks perpetrated by the Palestinians (123 out of approximately 20,000 attacks), in their grave consequences they account for over 50 percent of the Israeli fatalities, the majority of whom were civilians (900 victims). Since the Oslo Agreements, Palestinian suicide attacks have been carried out by Islamic terror organizations and the Palestinian Islamic Jihad. Since October 2001, the trend has shifted and currently secular terror organizations such as the Popular Front and the Fatah's "Martyrs of the Al-Aksa Brigades" are also joining the ranks of suicide attack perpetrators.

Terror, including suicide attacks, constitutes a strategic problem not only for the State of Israel; it threatens the well-being and security of the entire Free World. The Al-Qaida Organization and additional Islamic terror organizations have adopted suicide attacks as a modus operandi in their struggle against their adversaries all over the world. The September 11 attacks represent a historical milestone in the threat that terror poses against global security, and took the heaviest toll in bloodshed in the annals of terror.

The terror campaign operated by the Palestinian Authority, including suicide terror, thus constitutes part of a growing trend, particularly in radical Islamic circles, to turn this modus operandi into a strategic weapon that Islam wields against its foes. This was expressed in the attack campaign sponsored by radical Islamic entities during October-November 2002, in which, starting from Yemen (the attack against the French oil tanker), through Bali, Indonesia, and finally in Moscow where Chechen terrorists took over a theater, use was made of Islamic suicide attackers.

The Shahids: Islam and Suicide Attacks analyzes the roots of the phenomenon of Islamic suicide attacks, the modi operandi of various organizations
worldwide, and offers a series of recommendations regarding how to contend
with the phenomenon. This volume constitutes a unique contribution to professional literature pertaining to the area of terror in general, and suicide
terror in particular, and the ways to contend with them.

Aharon Ze'evi Farkash, Major General
Director of Military Intelligence, IDF
January 2003

Introduction

Suicide terror is not a new phenomenon. Nevertheless, the intensive use of suicide bombers and the lethal consequences of this activity have turned suicide terror into a strategic threat against the security and stability of Western society, and perhaps against the security of human society as a whole.

This volume was written against the background of the September 11, 2001 attacks perpetrated in the United States, and in light of the unprecedented suicide terror campaign being carried on by the Palestinians since September 28, 2000, the beginning of the Al-Aksa Intifada. It focuses on the phenomenon of Islamic suicide attackers because Islamic terror organizations, spearheaded by Al-Qaida, have turned suicide terror into a "strategic weapon" in the cultural conflict between radical Islam and its adversaries, with Western culture (including Israel and Zionism) at the top of its list. While it does indeed focus on Islamic suicide terror, it also addresses secular terror organizations functioning in Muslim states or within national/ethnic conflicts, where one of the sides to the conflict is Islamic (for example, secular organizations in the Arab-Israeli conflict, the PKK [The Workers' Party of Kurdistan] in Turkey, and more).

Despite the above-mentioned areas, this book also addresses the "Tamil Tigers" in Sri Lanka, an organization that does not meet any of these criteria but is included in this study as a basis for comparison, due to its reputation as the leading organization in the area of suicide attacks in the past twenty years.

Chapter 1 of *The Shahids* deals with the definition and description of the suicide terror phenomenon and with historical precedents involving Islamic suicide terror. Chapter 2 provides an in-depth description and analysis of the suicide terror phenomenon in the Israel-Arab conflict, in the Lebanese arena and in the Palestinian arena. Chapter 3 provides a description and analysis of suicide terror perpetrated by Islamic and secular terror organizations worldwide, and chapter 4 presents a comparative view of the suicide terror phenomenon and offers recommendations regarding ways to contend with this phenomenon.

Although the phenomenon of suicide terror characterizes the activities of the majority of Islamic terror organizations, and it is possible to identify similar characteristics in the definition of their goals and modus operandi, nevertheless each conflict and every organization has unique attributes that necessitate the search for a focused and relevant solution to the problem. This volume focuses mainly on the issue of suicide terror in the Israel-Arab conflict; thus most of the recommendations for ways to contend with it are formulated with an emphasis placed on this connection. However, there are many aspects that are relevant to the international handling of this phenomenon. Several examples are given in each chapter to illustrate characteristics of suicide terror and the terror organizations. The intention is not to present all of the data regarding these attacks, but as stated above, to provide the reader with examples for illustration.

This book surveys the development of the suicide terror phenomenon both from the historical perspective, starting with the days of the *Hashashins* (Assassins) in the tenth century AD up to Bin-Laden, and from the aspect of an organizational and territorial cross-section in the modern era. The data regarding suicide attacks are updated to the year 2003 and are generally based on official records or research published in this connection. The attacks of September 11, 2001 were undoubtedly the most important suicide attacks in history. The extensive description of the attacks in this book is based on a chapter addressing this matter in *The Globalization of Terror*,[1] a book I co-authored with Yoram Schweitzer.

The U.S. offensive in Iraq has ended successfully; it achieved the decimation of Sadam Hussein's army and toppled his regime, but terror activities and guerrilla warfare against the coalition forces in Iraq are just beginning. To date several suicide attacks have taken their toll among the coalition soldiers, and additional attacks have taken place in Saudi Arabia, Morocco, and Turkey. It would appear that Iraq serves as another illustration that suicide attacks continue to constitute a central strategic tool in the asymmetric war between Islamic entities and the West. The handling of this challenge necessitates the introduction of solutions that are fundamentally different than the methods used to contend with challenges posed by regular forces, such as the Iraqi army, which was easily defeated by the United States and the coalition forces.

The Shahids provides a comprehensive and comparative description of the phenomenon of Islamic suicide terror and was written in the hope that it may help the State of Israel and the Free World to contend with the strategic threat posed by suicide attacks to their security.

Note

1.   Yoram Shweitzer and Shaul Shay, *The Globalization of Terror: The Challenge of Al-Qaida and the Response of the International Community*, Transaction Publishers, New Brunswick, NJ, 2003.

1

Definitions and a Historical Review of the Phenomenon of Suicide Attacks[1]

Suicide terrorists are not a new phenomenon in human history. Many terrorists have already proven their willingness to die while perpetrating attacks for their political cause, by making the ultimate sacrifice that culminates in their death by choice.

Suicide terror can be found as early as the tenth century in the *Hashashin* (Assassins) sect. From the beginning of the eighteenth century, the pattern of suicide attacks was adopted by Moslems waging their battle against Western colonialism in Asia. However, the "modern" manifestations of the suicide terror phenomenon surfaced with the appearance of the first suicide terrorists in Lebanon about twenty years ago. Modern suicide terror has certain unique characteristics that distinguish it from those inherent to suicide terror in earlier periods. From the early 1980s, terror organizations began to carry out suicide attacks while using one or more individuals who constituted a "guided human missile." The suicide bomber carries explosives on his body or on a platform that he is driving, and out of his own conscious choice moves towards a predetermined target and executes an act of self-killing. The suicide bomber determines the site and timing of the attack, and he can navigate himself and decide on the spot, in keeping with the circumstances and surrounding environment, about the execution of the attack so that it will cause maximum damage to the chosen target. The definition of a terror attack as a suicide bombing thus depends primarily on the perpetrator's death. Therefore, a "modern suicide terror attack" can be defined as "a violent, politically motivated action executed consciously, actively, and with prior intent by a single individual (or individuals) who kills himself in the course of the operation together with his chosen target. The guaranteed and preplanned death of the perpetrator is a prerequisite for the operation's success."[2]

The choice of the suicide weapon as an instrument in the hands of the terrorists derives from the fact that it is available and "cheap," and the damage caused to the morale of the rival population is grave. A suicide attack, like all other terror attacks in the modern era, is primarily meant to provide its perpetrators with maximum media coverage, thus magnifying "a powerful self-image." Terror organizations do indeed exploit the multitude of media means to further their interests.

Suicide attacks in the modern era began in Lebanon in 1983, at the instigation of the Lebanese-Shiite terror organization, Hizballah. During the 1980s, Lebanon served as a central arena for the "development" of the suicide attack method. These attacks continued into the 1990s, but with less frequency. Today suicide attacks in Lebanon are rare. A total of about fifty terror attacks were carried out in Lebanon by six organizations. About half of the suicide attacks were perpetrated by Hizballah and Amal (a Lebanese Shiite organization) and the rest were executed by secular organizations, some communist and others nationalist, including the Lebanese Communist Party, the Socialist Naserist Organization, the PPS—The National Syrian Party (also called "The Syrian Socialist Nationalist Party"). The Hizballah also perpetrated suicide attacks against Israeli and Jewish targets in Argentina in 1992 and in 1994.

The use of suicide attackers stimulated considerable prestige for the Hizballah and turned it into a symbol of sacrifice and a source of inspiration for terror organizations worldwide that adopted and even "refined" the suicide attacks. Among the organizations in the world that adopted this method, the most prominent is the isolationist Tamil organization, "The Tamil Tigers" (LTTE), which is involved in a struggle for independence of the Tamil minority from the Sinhalese majority in Sri Lanka.

The "Black Tigers" unit began perpetrating terror attacks in 1987, and since then has initiated over one hundred and sixty terror attacks carried out by over two hundred suicide attackers; in several of the incidents, more than one suicide terrorist participated in the attacks. These attacks were particularly vicious and caused many hundreds of deaths. This organization, which focused its suicide attacks on senior leaders in Sri Lanka's political and military establishment, is the only one in the world to succeed in assassinating two heads of state. The first, Sri Lanka President Primadasa, was assassinated in an attack in which twenty-two additional victims met their deaths (May 1993), and the second, former prime minister of India, Rajiv Gandhi, who at that time was involved in a reelection campaign in Madras. This attack claimed the lives of a total of eighteen people (May 21, 1991). On December 17, 1999, the organization attempted to assassinate Sri Lanka's President Chandrika Kumaratunga, via a female suicide terrorist who detonated herself at the president's front door. The president lost an eye in the attack, but survived.

The organization also acted against politicians affiliated with the Singhalese majority as well as pragmatic politicians from the Tamil minority, senior military personnel, boats, command headquarters, and economic facilities such as oil centers. In the attacks, the LTTE demonstrated indifference to the killing of innocent bystanders and showed no compassion for anyone who happened to be in the vicinity of their target. The main motivating factors behind the Tamil suicide attackers are an aspiration for national independence, blind obedience to the charismatic leadership of the organization's leader, and strong peer and social pressures.

Another "secular" organization that perpetrated suicide attacks in Turkey is the Marxist, separatist Kurd PKK, although its members are Muslims. The organization was active mainly during the years 1996-99 and carried out sixteen suicide attacks (another five were thwarted), which caused about twenty fatalities and scores of casualties. PKK's suicide campaign did not induce the Turkish government to allow Kurdish autonomy. The PKK suicide operations of male and female terrorists were carried out under the command and inspiration of the charismatic and central leader Ocalan, who was perceived by the members of his organization as a "sun onto the nations." Following his arrest and the death sentence passed in 1999, the suicide attacks of his members ceased. A female member of a left-wing Turkish terror organization carried out a suicide attack in 2002 in protest against the treatment of her friends in prison.

Egyptian organizations, the "Jama'a al-Islamiya" and the "Egyptian Jihad," which were affiliated with Bin-Laden's "Islamic Front," carried out two suicide attacks, in Croatia (October 1995) and at the Egyptian Embassy in Karachi, Pakistan (November, 1995).

Under Bin-Laden's direct command, Al-Qaida had carried out three suicide attacks before September 11, 2001, and it has "assisted" in the perpetration of four additional attacks. Al-Qaida's first attack was carried out by suicide drivers who detonated car bombs near the American Embassies in Kenya and Tanzania (September 7, 1998), killing 214 and wounding about 5,000. The second attack was against the *USS Cole* at the Aden port (October 12, 2000), in which seventeen American sailors were killed and thirty-five were wounded. The terror attacks perpetrated in the United States on September 11, 2001 obviously constituted the apex of suicide attack operations in the annals of terror in general, and suicide terrorism in particular.

Since September 2001, additional suicide operations carried out by terror cells supported by Al-Qaida are:

1. The assassination of Massoud Sh'ah, military leader of the "Northern Alliance" in Afghanistan, which presented the main opposition to the Taliban regime in that country. Sh'ah was terminated two days before the terror attack in the United States by a team that was apparently affiliated with the Algerian GSPC (the Salafi Group for Propaganda and Combat), acting according to the instructions of the Al-Qaida headquarters. The attack was meant to neutralize the Taliban's main adversary prior to the

perpetration of the terror attack in the United States. It was carried out by two terrorists masquerading as press photographers who asked to interview Sh'ah. One of the two detonated himself, killing Sh'ah in the process, and the second was terminated by his bodyguards.

2. The attempt by Richard Reed to cause an explosion on the American Airlines flight from Paris to Miami on December 22, 2001. The attempt was made by Richard Colvin Reed, a suicide terrorist who hid the explosives in his shoe.

3. The detonation of the oil tanker near the synagogue in Djerba, Tunisia, by a suicide driver, causing nineteen deaths, including fourteen German tourists, who were inside or near the synagogue.

4. A suicide driver detonated his car and hit a bus driving foreign workers to the Karachi shipyards. The death toll was fourteen, including eleven French workers.

5. The detonation of a boat bomb near a French oil tanker opposite the shores of Yemen.

6. Suicide bombings on the Island of Bali, Indonesia, that killed over 200 people.

7. A suicide attack against Israeli tourists in Mombassa, Kenya.

8. Suicide attacks perpetrated in Riyadh, Saudi Arabia.

9. Suicide attacks against Jewish targets in Morocco.

10. Suicide attacks against Jewish and British targets in Istanbul, Turkey.

In recent years, the circle of suicide attackers has been expanded by Chechen and Indian terrorists. Chechen organizations executed about twenty suicide attacks beginning in 2000. The culmination of these attacks was the combined overtaking of a theater in the heart of Moscow by terrorists wearing explosive belts.

Indian organizations carried out several suicide attacks in car bombs driven by suicide bombers; one of the most prominent attacks was the joint assault of the Jeish Muhammad and Lashkar e-Toiba organizations on the Indian Parliament in December 2001.

The Palestinian terror organizations, Hamas and the Palestinian Islamic Jihad, also adopted suicide attacks, based on the active assistance and inspiration of the Hizballah and with Iranian backing. Palestinian terrorists started carrying out suicide missions in 1993. Between the years 1994 and September 2000, they perpetrated some twenty-five attacks.

September 28, 2000 marked the beginning of violent activity known as the "Al-Aksa Intifada," instigated by the Palestinian Authority. Since that date, Palestinian terror organizations have perpetrated some 123 suicide attacks (in addition to 255 suicide bombings that were thwarted).[3] These attacks were initially carried out by "religious" Palestinian terror organizations, such as the Hamas and Islamic Jihad, but since the end of 2001 the "secular" terrorist organizations of the Fatah/Tanzim have joined the activities under the cover name of the "Al-Aksa Brigades," in addition to the "Popular Front for the Liberation of Palestine." Five Palestinian women perpetrated suicide bombings, and several other women were caught while planning or en route to an attack. Most of the women were affiliated with the Tanzim/Al-Aksa Brigades of the Fatah organization (one was from the Islamic Jihad).

Journalist Thomas Friedman published an article called "Lies of the Suicide" in which he stated:[4]

> The consequences of the war currently being waged between the Israelis and the Palestinians will have a crucial impact on the security of every American and also, I believe—on the security of civilization as a whole.
>
> Why? Because the Palestinians are currently checking out a new form of combat, based on suicide bombers wearing explosive belts and dressed as Israelis, meant to achieve their political goals, and it works.
>
> Let it be clearly stated: The Palestinians have adopted the suicide attacks as a strategic choice, not out of desperation, and this phenomenon threatens all of civilization. Because if they let it "succeed" in Israel—then just as in the case of airplane hijackings, the method will spread and culminate with a suicide bomber detonating himself at a nuclear facility.
>
> This is why the whole world must ensure that this strategy is defeated.
>
> "...during the Spanish Civil War, the superpowers tested their new weapons prior to the world war," claims political science professor Yaron Ezrahi of Hebrew University. Today, in the framework of the Israeli-Palestinian conflict, a wide scale experiment in the use of suicide terror as a type of liberation strategy is taking place. We must vanquish them, but this necessitates other steps aside from military strategy. The Palestinians have been so completely blinded by their narcissism that they have forgotten the basic truth upon which civilization is based; the sanctity of life of every human being, starting with themselves. If America does not channel all of its energy to stop this madness, it will spread. The devil is dancing in the Middle East, and he is whirling in our direction.

Terms Related to Suicide and Suicide Attacks

The suicide attack or martyrdom (*estishad* in Islamic terminology) constitutes a specific instance in the suicide phenomenon that has been granted religious and social legitimacy, while suicide for personal reasons is conceived by Islam as a grievous sin whose punishment is banishment to hell.

The Western world regards the phenomenon of suicide from a totally different viewpoint, both from the aspect of understanding the phenomenon and from the aspect of its philosophical and cultural impact.

Yoram Yovel addresses this issue in his book *An Emotional Storm*:[5]

> Man is apparently the only living creature who is well aware that death awaits him. He cannot elude death, but he can bring it on himself with his own two hands: Man can commit suicide, and many do so. In the United States one out of fifty individuals will end his days in this manner. The choice of life is an ongoing decision to which most people dedicate little thought. But sometimes every additional day of life is the result of a renewed choice, perhaps the ultimate choice; "See I have set before thee this day life and good, and death and evil." (Deut. 30: 15)

In the beginning of his book, *The Myth of Sisyphus*, Albert Camus writes:

There is only one serious philosophical question, and that is suicide. To judge whether life is or is not worthy of living, effectively means to answer one of the basic questions of philosophy.

Suicide is a form of response to this existential dilemma, a response that chooses death. But is suicide a free choice? This question is currently a topic for public discussion that is being held on several levels: legal, moral, philosophical, theological, and psychological. The response of psychiatry to the question of free will vis-à-vis suicide is straightforward and clear: No, suicide is not the result of free choice, although the subjective experience of a suicide victim often resembles a free choice experience, which is accompanied by profound relief. Life is too hard to bear at that moment and death is perceived as an escape from these difficulties.

There is no more isolated individual than someone who is about to commit suicide. He is overcome by feelings of failure and desperation, and he dies with a sharp awareness of his isolation. The psychologist Kay Redfield Jamison, one of the leading researchers of bi-polar disorders, also studied the issue of suicide, a matter close to her heart as she herself attempted suicide. In her book *Night is Falling Quickly* she writes:[6]

Suicide is an especially terrible way to die. The emotional suffering leading to it is in most cases prolonged, sharp and hard. There is no morphine capable of alleviating the anguish, and often death is violent and gloomy. The suicide's suffering is personal and unexpressed, and he leaves behind him relatives, friends and associates who carry the pain of loss which is almost indescribable together with a sense of guilt. Suicide carries a level of confusion and a feeling of destruction which in most cases cannot be expressed in words.

As noted above, there is a critical disparity between the perception of human life as a supreme value in Western society and the Islamic view of the Muslim's commitment to the values of Islam and to martyrdom as an emissary of Islam.

Suicide Attacks—Definition of the Phenomenon

The phenomenon of suicide attacks is nothing new. Examples of these attacks can be found in the tenth century AD. Throughout history it was always possible to recruit people willing to sacrifice their lives for society, religion, ideology, and national interests. Our definition earlier of the modern suicide attack stated as follows: "A violent, politically motivated action executed consciously, actively and with prior intent by a single individual (or individuals) who kills himself in the course of the operation together with his chosen target. The guaranteed and preplanned death of the perpetrator is a prerequisite for the operation's success." Here follows another definition of the suicide attack: "A mode of operation whereby the act of assault depends on the terrorist's death. The terrorist is fully aware of the fact that if he does not commit suicide, the assault plan will not take place."[7]

The central component, which makes the suicide attack unique, is the attacker's knowledge that his death is a prerequisite for the very occurrence of the attack.[8] Suicide attacks are considered a preferred means by terror organizations for the following reasons:[9]

- Suicide attacks cause grave damage to property and multiple deaths.
- Suicide attacks receive broad media coverage. A suicide attack is a "media event," as it necessitates determination and martyrdom on the terrorist's part.
- Although a suicide attack is essentially uncomplicated, it can be perpetrated at the time and place that the attacker chooses.
- The control over timing and venue enables its direction so that it will cause maximum damage, more so than other techniques like detonating an explosive charge using a clock or remote control. The suicide attacker is a kind of sophisticated guided missile that knows how to launch the explosive charge at the target exactly at the optimal timing.
- Once the suicide attacker has set out on his mission his success is almost ensured because it is very hard to prevent the attack. Even if the security forces prevent his advancement towards the planned target he can always change the target or detonate himself among the security forces.
- A suicide mission does not necessitate the preparation of escape routes, which constitutes a complex stage in other types of attacks.
- In a suicide mission the attacker is killed during the attack so there is no fear that he will fall into the hands of the enemy and divulge information about the organization (although there have been cases when the perpetrator was apprehended before detonating the charge or reconsidered and was arrested by security forces).

Encouragement received from the immediate vicinity, and from society in general, contributes greatly to the motivation and willingness of the suicide attacker.

The suicide terrorist is involved in an inner conflict until the very moment of the act of suicide; thus, his environment has a significant impact on the degree of determination to perpetrate the act. This is why terror organization activists that recruit and prepare the terrorist for the act of suicide must launch him on the path of preparation and action that propels him to the point of "no return." The suicide attacker enjoys acts of religious and social reinforcement and undergoes "ceremonial activities" that generate a commitment within him to fulfill his mission.

As stated above, the suicide attacker is embroiled in perpetual inner conflict until the last minute. The role of his operators is to ensure that all of the stages and steps leading to the perpetration of the act pass smoothly, in order to minimize the possibility that the suicide bomber will have second thoughts or refrain from carrying out the attack.

Attacks Involving Sacrifice

At various arenas of conflict worldwide, terror organizations carried out attacks in the past characterized by a high level of probability that the attacker would forfeit his life. However, these attacks cannot be described as "textbook" or classic suicide missions. During the Al-Aksa Intifada, aside from textbook suicide attacks, other attacks were also perpetrated that are referred to as "acts of self-sacrifice" (*amaliyat estashahidiya*) by the Palestinians. These are attacks with low chances of survival, and the attackers themselves are aware of this fact and regard it as a kind of suicide attack.[10]

In anticipation of the perpetration of these acts, most of the terrorists prepare written or taped wills in which they express their willingness to die in the course of the attack and become *shahids*. (The shahid [martyr] is a Muslim who falls in the holy war [Jihad] and is promised a haven.) Therefore, in most of these attacks no escape route is planned for the perpetrators.

The main difference between "attacks involving sacrifice" and "suicide attacks" lies in the method of operation. In the classic suicide attack explosives are used; the attacker detonates himself at his chosen site. Through his death, the suicide bomber ensures the mission's success. But in attacks involving sacrifice, the attack is carried out by shooting or lobbing grenades, and the attacker dies at the hands of the enemy (i.e., there is a slight chance that he will survive or surrender). Nevertheless, it is very difficult to classify attacks in this category because the definition is somewhat ambiguous. It is to be noted that the secular Palestinian terror organizations, as well as the Indian and Pakistani terror organizations, do not actually differentiate between "classic" suicide attacks and those involving sacrifice.

During the Al-Aksa Intifada several scores of attacks have been perpetrated that can be included within the definition of attacks involving sacrifice. In most of the attacks, the modus operandi involves one or two terrorists who penetrate an Israeli town or IDF outpost, fire weapons and cast grenades with the intention of causing as many casualties as possible before being terminated by the Israeli security forces.

Similar attacks have been conducted in Kashmir, Chechnya, and the Philippines, in the course of which one terrorist or small cells penetrated compounds or structures belonging to the security forces or government authorities, and attempted to cause massive casualties.

Another type of attack involving sacrifice, which was identified in the arena of Palestinian terror, is the kind that is executed by a lone terrorist who is unaffiliated with any organization and decides independently to perpetrate an attack. This type of attack cannot be classified as a suicide attack, because weapons other than firearms are usually employed (a knife, an ax, etc.) and therefore its characteristics are comparable to those of an attack involving sacrifice. Many such attacks were carried out in the framework of the Intifada during the years 1987 and 1993.

Ehud Sprinzak described this period and its characteristics as "pre-suicide terrorism."[11] He expressed the opinion that during this period "the road was paved" for the adoption of the suicide attack pattern by Islamic Palestinian organizations.

Religious Legitimization for Suicide Attacks

The first individuals to pass a religious ruling permitting self-sacrifice on behalf of Islam were the Imam Khomeini and other Shiite clerics, who encouraged the Shiites in Iran (in the war against Iraq during the years 1980-1988) and in the Lebanese arena to sacrifice themselves in their struggle against their enemies, thus winning the title of shahid, along with all of its implications regarding life in the world to come.

As a result of the entry of radical Sunni organizations within the circle of suicide attacks, Sunni clerics were also asked to grant religious rulings permitting self-sacrifice as emissaries of Islam. The dispute that arose regarding the legitimization and justification of suicide attacks was finally resolved in favor of those who supported suicide attacks. On March 6, 1995, Hamas leader Sheikh Ahmad Yassin stated that in any case where a suicide bomber received the blessings of a certified Muslim cleric, he was not to be considered a suicide for personal reasons, but rather a shahid who fell in the Jihad.[12] In March 1996, Sheikh al-Kardawi, one of the clerical leaders of the Muslim world, addressed the issue of the suicide attacks in a sermon aired over Qatar television. In his sermon Kardawi stated that the suicide raids conducted by the Hamas in Jerusalem, Ashkelon, and Tel Aviv at the end of February and the beginning of March 1996, attacks in which scores of Israelis were killed, were to be considered "Jihad for Allah" and not terror. According to Kardawi, the suicide attackers who were killed in these raids acted "in order to protect the land and honor against the Israelis who stole Palestine." Thus, they are not suicides but rather "shahids' who fell in the Jihad.[13]

The disputes in this regard became sharper in the wake of the attacks of September 11, 2001, but the "hawkish" line, whose prominent spokesman Kardawi published several ruling *fatwas* in favor of suicide attacks, is currently the dominant policy. The more moderate Islamic religious establishment has been forced to change its stand from total opposition to qualified support.

Kardawi claims that the suicide attacks were the supreme expression of the Jihad in the name of Allah and a model of terror permitted by the Sharia. He quotes verses from the Koran according to which the Muslim must be prepared to spread fear among Allah's foes. He claims that the term "suicide mission" is incorrect and even misleading, because this is a heroic act of martyrdom that has no connection whatsoever to suicide. He explains that the mentality of the martyr is totally different than that of a suicide.[14]

In an interview given to an Egyptian newspaper Kardawi explained his conceptions regarding the issue of suicide attacks.[15]

According to his opinion, a suicide puts an end to his life out of selfish considerations, while someone who sacrifices himself does so for his religion and nation. The suicide is motivated by loss of faith in himself and Allah, whereas the person involved in martyrdom (*mujhad*) is brimming with belief in Allah and his mercy. He fights his enemies and the enemies of Allah with this new weapon, which fate has placed in the hands of the weak so that they can fight and defeat the arrogant and stronger adversary. The mujhad becomes a human bomb detonating in the heart of the enemies of Allah, leaving them helpless vis-à-vis the brave shahid who lays down his life for Allah and is granted *shuhada*.

Kardawi claims that these actions are legitimate even if the victims are civilians, as Israeli society is militaristic in character. Men and women serve in the army and can be mobilized for military service at any time. On the other hand, if a child or elderly person is hurt in a terror attack, this is not a premeditated act, but rather an error or the unpreventable consequence of a military campaign. Necessity justifies the act. In connection to the dispute about the suicide attacks, Kardawi states that those who oppose the suicide attacks are religious clerics who are really the agents of secular regimes, and they do not constitute a binding religious authority.[16]

Abed Alaziz Rantisi, one of the leaders of the Hamas, has averred that if a person kills himself due to the fact that he is tired of living then it is suicide, but if he chooses to sacrifice his soul he will become a shahid and Allah will reward him for this, all in the interest of striking the enemy a blow. He stresses that the Hamas has no doubt that those who perpetrate suicide attacks are shahids.[17]

The Sheikh Hamid al-Bitawi, director of the Palestinian Islamic Researchers' Association, has declared that according to the Sharia the Jihad is a collective duty, but if infidels invade Muslim land (Dar al-Islam), as is the case in Palestine, then the commandment of Jihad becomes the duty of each and every individual, and therefore the suicide attacks are legitimate.[18] Sheikh Muhammad Ismail al-Jamal, the mufti of Jericho, published a fatwa of his own in the daily *Al-Hayat Al-Jadida*, in which he elaborated on the main difference between self-sacrifice, which is permissible and even desirable according to Islam, and suicide, which brings the punishment of hellfire on Judgment Day down upon the individual committing suicide.[19] Researchers of the Al-Azhar Center for Islamic Studies in Cairo published their own stance vis-à-vis the issue of suicide attacks:[20]

A person who sacrifices himself (*fadaai*) does so in order to achieve greater closeness to Allah and out of an aspiration to protect the rights, honor, and land of the Muslims. On the other hand, a suicide loses his soul due to desperation and a desire to end his life, not for any lofty, religious or national purpose, or to liberate his stolen lands. When Muslims are attacked in their homes and their land is stolen, the Jihad becomes the duty of every Muslim (a personal duty). In this state, self-sacrifice becomes the highest duty of the Muslim and the supreme expression of the Jihad. The Al-Azhar researchers believe that the participation of Palestinian children is a type of Jihad. When the Jihad becomes the personal obligation of each Muslim, then everyone is obligated to join the Jihad, including children, even without requesting their parents' permission.

Sheikh Al-Azhar Muhammad Sayyid Tantawi also expressed his opinion vis-à-vis the issue of suicide attacks, and claimed that the suicide bombings are an act of self-defense and self-sacrifice, as long as the intention is to kill enemy soldiers, but not women and children.[21] In an earlier discussion, following the attacks on the American Embassies in Kenya and Tanzania, Tantawi stated that any explosion that causes the death of women and children is to be considered a criminal act of cowardice, as a brave and sane person would never commit acts of this kind.[22] As mentioned earlier, his stance vis-à-vis Palestinian suicide attacks is more aggressive, but his approach is still more moderate than that of Kardawi and other Palestinian clerics, and even other Islamic researchers at Al Azhar.

It would be accurate to say that today there exists a consensus in Palestinian society regarding religious legitimization of suicide attacks, which are defined as acts of martyrdom. The Palestinian leadership regards suicide attacks as a strategic weapon that provides a deterrence effect and a strategic balance in relationship to Israel. Suicide bombings are not a marginal phenomenon in Palestinian society, but rather a reflection of a new social norm that has the encouragement and support of the general public. Expressions of the latter are to be found in the joyful reactions after every attack, at suicide bombers' funerals, on every street corner where the bombers' pictures are on display, in the glory attributed to them in the Palestinian media, and even in Palestinian public opinion polls. An expression of the normative dimension of the suicide bombings can be found in the words of Salah Shekhada, a leader of the Hamas, who stated the following in an interview for the organization's Internet site:[23]

> The flow of people who want to become suicide bombers indicates emotional health and does not imply escape from a feeling of desperation and frustration.

Shekhada mentions four principles in the process of choosing the suicide attacker:[24]

1. The candidate is religiously observant—he says his prayers, gives charity and does good deeds. Regarding his family, the preferred candidate must ensure his parents' concurrence.
2. He must not be the sole breadwinner; the organization does not accept a potential attacker who is an only son.
3. He must have the capability to perpetrate the act assigned to him.
4. Most important, the attack must encourage additional suicide attacks and promote the Jihad in the general public.

Palestinian suicide attacks are also given religious and moral legitimacy by the spiritual leader of the Hizballah, Sheikh Fadallah. In an interview that Fadallah granted to the *Daily Star* in May 2001, he said,

> Suicide attacks, including those perpetrated by the Palestinians against Israel, are permitted according to Islam. It is the duty of all Muslims to participate in the Jihad which serves a just cause, and in its framework we must generate as many fatalities as possible among our enemy." [25]

In another interview, which he gave a year later (June 2002) to the same newspaper, Fadallah discussed the issue of sanctioning suicide attacks at length:[26]

> ...the suicide attacks are legitimate opposition in view of the dangers of escalation. The killing of one's self is exactly like killing another human being and this requires permission. A person must have Allah's approval to kill himself or someone else. Basically, these two acts are prohibited according to the Koran, but in the case of Jihad, which is a defensive or preventive war according to Islam, they is allowed, because the Jihad is conceived as an extraordinary situation. Allah does not define a clear procedure regarding how to combat the enemy and protect the nation's rights (the community of the believers). If in the interests of victory there is a need to cross through a minefield and it is clear that many will die in the process, we will cross that minefield. The Palestinian suicide bombers do not aim their attacks against civilians; their goal is to protect their people by striking out at and causing damage and fatalities to the Israeli side, thus achieving a sort of balance vis-à-vis the sophisticated arsenal of weapons in the hands of the Israeli military.

Edward Sa'id noted in this connection in May 2002:[27]

> (Suicide attacks) have distorted and undermined the basis of the Palestinian struggle. Every liberation movement throughout history has stressed that its struggle is for life and not for death. Why should ours be different? The faster we educate our Zionist enemies and show them that our opposition offers coexistence and peace, the chances that they will be able to claim victims among us at their whim and treat us only as terrorists will be reduced.

Suicide is perceived as a crime from the religious point of view. Life is not the private property of an individual and therefore it is forbidden for him to end to it. Human life is the property of Allah and therefore it is forbidden to take a life. He who takes his own life or the lives of others without permission will be sentenced by God to suffering in hell. But things are very different when a person sacrifices his soul in a mission for Allah. While the inclination among Islamic clerics is to unequivocally adopt the radical line justifying suicide attacks, among academics and politicians in Muslim states there are other approaches. For example, at the summit meeting of Muslim countries that convened in Malaysia in May 2002, the issue of Islamic suicide attacks was a subject for dispute among the participants. In his opening speech at the conference, the deputy prime minister of Malaysia Abdallah Ahmad Badawi declared that a Holy War cannot be won with violence (suicide attacks) because this does not achieve a thing aside from reinforcing the Palestinians' image as terrorists. He expressed his opposition to violence in the name of Islam and called for the recognition of any attack against civilians as terror. Badawi's positions came up against widespread opposition from the conference's other participants. The Saudi foreign minister Sheikh Salah Abd Al-Aziz Muhammad Al-Sheikh claimed that suicide attacks are permissible and the death of a suicide attacker is to be considered the demise of a martyr.[28]

In subsequent discussions, Badawi called for the Islamic states to act to remove Islam from the hands of those who do not understand it properly and march under the banner of militarism. He expressed the opinion that action should be taken against the belief that the meaning of Jihad is a military confrontation. "There is a need to tear down the conceptual barrier that we have created and adopt knowledge and innovations. If Islam is equated with the deeds of marginal elements that appropriate our religion, the world will continue to loath Islam."[29]

The conference participants did not reach a joint, universally accepted position regarding suicide attacks; therefore, it is possible to say that the Muslim world remains divided about the question of the legitimization and desirability vis-à-vis the use of suicide attacks in connection to the Arab-Israeli conflict, and also in connection to the wider connotation of the phenomenon as expressed in the attack on September 11, 2001 and at additional focal points worldwide.

The positions adopted by representatives and leaders of Muslim countries spring from the political interests of their countries, both in the internal arena related to the stability and security of their regimes, and from foreign policy considerations. Thus, in contrast to the religious clerics and leaders, whose approach stems almost exclusively from their religious and conceptual understanding of suicide attacks, in the political arena the positions adopted by Muslim states are far more complex and are influenced by a combination of interests and considerations which form their policy in this matter (see further elaboration subsequently in the chapter discussing the positions of Muslim countries vis-à-vis the suicide attacks).

The Characteristics of Suicide Attacks

There are four main characteristics of suicide attacks, which are distinguishable from each other according to their modus operandi:[30]

1. A suicide attack using an explosive charge or explosive belt carried by the suicide bomber.
2. A suicide attack using transportation means on land or via animals.
3. An aerial suicide attack using an aerial platform.
4. A maritime suicide attack using a floating vessel.

The common denominator of all these modi operandi is the suicide terrorist who perpetrates the terror attack using one of these methods.

Portable Explosive Belts and Explosive Charges

Explosive belts and explosive charges carried by the suicide terrorist constitute the most common means used in suicide attacks in the Israeli arena and in other focal points worldwide. Explosive belts, or explosive charges, carried on the body of the terrorist are characterized by a relatively small amount of explosives (from a few kilograms up to about 20 kg. explosives). The suicide attacker attaches the explosive device to his body with the help of strips, bandages or tape. The device is generally hidden under clothing to enable movement towards the target in an innocent guise. In some cases, use is made of bags, knapsacks, or suitcases to carry the explosive device. The explosive devices are made up of standard or improvised explosives, which are often supplemented by nails or metal balls to augment the dispersal effect. The suicide attacker detonates the explosive belt, generally by closing an electrical circuit through the pressing of a switch or by connecting electrical wires to a battery. The attacker will aspire to move towards his target in an innocent manner up to the moment that he detonates the device, although there have been instances when the suicide bomber stormed the target, thus revealing his intentions.

In the arena of the Arab-Israeli confrontation, explosive belts were already used by the Palestinian organizations in the early 1970s, although the attacks themselves characteristically involved killing and bargaining or hijackings, rather than typical suicide attacks. Several examples follow:

- In the hijacking of the Sabena aircraft from Brussels to Lod Airport in 1972, the hijackers wore "girdles" whose pockets contained about two kilos of a plastic explosive called Semtex. The explosives served as a threat to the lives of the hostages, as a factor impeding any rescue attempt by Israeli forces, and if all else failed, would enable the perpetration of a suicide operation.

- In several killing and bargaining attacks, Kiryat Shmona (April 1974), Kibbutz Shamir (June 1974), Metulla (June 1975) and others, the terrorists were equipped with explosive belts. In these attacks the terrorists perpetrated mass killings and/or the taking of hostages, and in addition in some of the cases they detonated themselves with the explosive belt, thus inflicting additional damage on the hostages and the Israeli rescue forces.

Explosive belts prepared by Palestinian terrorists were also discovered during the "Peace for Galilee" War, although there are no known cases of the terrorists using these belts against the IDF forces.

The Hizballah Organization was the first to begin perpetrating bona fide suicide attacks in the Middle East arena. The first attacks were committed by suicide bombers driving car bombs, but subsequently the organization also perpetrated suicide attacks through the use of suicide attackers wearing explosive belts. This modus operandi was adopted, in 1985, by other Lebanese organizations, and beginning with the 1990s by Palestinian terror organizations. Most of the Palestinian suicide attacks from 1993 to date have been conducted through the use of explosive belts. Islamic terror organizations have also made extensive use of explosive belts in places like India (Jammu-Kashmir), Chechnya, Turkey (by the PKK secular Kurdish organization), and Sri Lanka (by the Tamil Tigers).

Car Bombs

The car bomb is an extremely widespread means of attack although it follows the pattern of an explosive device rather a suicide attack. The Hizballah was the first organization to perpetrate a suicide attack via a car bomb driven to its target by a suicide terrorist.

The use of a car bomb for a terrorist attack has several prominent advantages:

- A relatively large amount of explosives can be transported in the car to the target, thus inflicting greater damage.
- A car offers many opportunities to conceal the explosives in order to prevent early detection.
- The vehicle offers the attackers mobility and flexibility in choosing the target and reaching it.
- The vehicle itself serves as part of the outer spray layer and enhances the lethal effect of the attack.
- The vehicle enables arrival at the target under an innocent guise.

In order to prepare a car bomb, any type of vehicle can be used: sedans, vans and trucks. The preparation of a car bomb does not require any special infrastructure; any repair shop or garage can be used for these preparations. The car bombs generally contain large amounts of standard or improvised explosives; the terrorists sometimes add gas balloons in order to enhance the effect of the device. The device is generally triggered by the driver from inside the car through the use of an electrical switch or by bringing two electrical wires in contact. When the device is concealed in a vehicle, the operating system can be installed and hidden among the car's operating switches. There is also the possibility of providing the suicide driver with a "backup system" through a remote control mechanism, in the event that the terrorist reconsiders or if the operating system malfunctions. In such cases another terrorist located at an observation and supervision point may activate the bomb.

There are several scenarios for activating a car bomb driven by a suicide attacker:

- Attacking a secured or protected facility by parking the vehicle nearby or storming the site (the American Embassy and the Marines Headquarters in Beirut in 1983, the Israeli Embassy in Argentina in 1992, the U.S. Embassy in Kenya in 1998, among others).
- Attacking a crowded civilian target.
- Attacking a vehicle or a military convoy by using a car bomb manned by a suicide attacker who detonates himself after pulling up next to the vehicle or convoy. This type of attack can be conducted against civilian targets as well vehicles such as a bus.
- Attacking an outpost of the security forces by approaching the roadblock in an innocent guise and detonating the car nearby.
- A car bomb in the form of a "roadside" charge; the attacker parks the car at the side of the road or pretends that his car has broken down, and detonates the car bomb when the target passes by.

Motorcycle and Bicycle Bombs

The use of a motorcycle or a bicycle as a vehicle bomb for a suicide attack is identical to the characteristic use of a car bomb. The motorcycle and bicycle have an advantage from the aspect of their ability to maneuver on dirt paths and in open areas, thus circumventing roadblocks and control points. For the most part, an explosive charge on a motorcycle or a bicycle can be placed in the saddlebags or in external baskets. However, explosives can be concealed in other parts of a motorcycle as well. This way (which requires a relatively prolonged preparation period) the motorcycle can carry scores of kilograms of explosives, with the motorcycle's body serving as an explosive outer shell. In some cases the bicycle or motorcycle has served solely as a mode of transportation, while the explosive charge was planted on the suicide terrorist's body either in a belt or a backpack.

The first suicide attack using a motorcycle was perpetrated in the Middle East in Egypt, during the assassination attempt on the Egyptian Minister of the Interior in August 1993. In the Gaza Strip, several suicide attacks were discharged via terrorists riding bicycles. The interrogation of an Islamic terror cell that was exposed in Singapore in 2002 and linked with Bin-Laden's terror organization, indicates that the terrorists intended to perpetrate the attack through the use of bicycle bombs against American soldiers near the Singapore subway.

Animal and Cart Bombs

In Lebanon and in the Gaza Strip, several suicide attacks were carried out through the use of donkeys, mules, horses, and animal-drawn carts. Saddlebags can contain explosive charges ranging anywhere between a dozen and 100 kilograms, according to the type of animal. The explosive charge can also be placed in an animal-drawn cart.

During the war in Afghanistan, the mujahidin used camels loaded with explosives in order to perpetrate attacks against the Soviet forces. The use of an animal enables the terrorist to carry a relatively large device, while taking advantage of the opportunity to move in an open area or on the sides of the roads, thus evading roadblocks and checkpoints. The "innocent" look enables the suicide terrorist to draw close to his target without arousing suspicion, thus causing multiple casualties.

Boat Bombs/Boat Devices

Suicide attacks using a boat bomb are familiar to various places in the world as well as in the Israel-Arab arena. A boat bomb can contain a large amount of explosives, up to several hundred kilograms (according to the vessel's size). Motorboats, fishing boats, and even larger vessels may serve as possible platforms for attacks. The suicide bomber will detonate the explosive device when he approaches the target ship, whether under an innocent guise (in a fishing boat), or by frontal storming. The most prominent example of a maritime suicide attack is the detonation of a boat bomb near the American destroyer (*USS Cole*) in Yemen. A large vessel loaded with explosives or flammable materials may be utilized for a "mega terror" attack against large facilities such as ports, or against strategic targets along the coasts.

Airplanes and Other Types of Aircraft

The use of an aircraft as a platform for the perpetration of a suicide attack was first effected in World War II by Japanese "kamikaze" pilots against American vessels in the Pacific Ocean. The September 11 attacks in the United States illustrated the possibility of using hijacked planes for the perpetration of suicide attacks. In this type of attack, suicide terrorists take over an aircraft and crash it into a chosen target, thus causing the deaths of the passengers and the people occupying the attack premises. These types of attacks can also be executed in smaller kinds of aircraft (private planes and helicopters, ultra-lights and windsurfers). The scope of the attack will obviously depend on the size of the aircraft.

In the September 11, 2001 attacks the airplane itself served as the "attack weapon," but in other scenarios it is possible to load the aircraft with large amounts of explosives and fuel. An attack using an aircraft is relatively complex, because the attacker must be trained to fly the aircraft, and it is also necessary to overcome existing security systems at airports and on flight routes (air control, etc.)

A different model of an aeronautical attack is indicated by Richard Reed's attempted attack (the man with the shoe bomb). In this case, the hijacker intended to blow himself up inside the plane, thus causing it to crash with its full load of passengers.

The Stages Involved in Suicide Attacks

The terrorists involved in suicide attacks do not usually act independently, but rather are sent by or represent terror organizations. These organizations include political leadership, which defines the organization's policy, and the military arm, which realizes the violent aspects of this policy. Suicide attacks are one modus operandi of many that terror organizations use. During the Al-Aksa Intifada this method has become central and is considered a strategic tool to be used in the framework of the struggle against Israel. The perpetration of a suicide attack involves a complex system of preparations in which various circles of terror activists are involved. Although the suicide attack is perceived as the action of an individual who is sacrificing his own life, it is actually an intricate activity necessitating organizational and operational infrastructure, which enables the suicide attacker to realize his objective. The suicide terrorist is generally the final link in a long organizational chain.[31] The execution of a suicide attack necessitates the organization carrying out the mission to conduct a series of preparations in which organizational activists and collaborators are involved, with the purpose of translating the decision into reality.

Recruitment of the Suicide Attacker

When the motivation to execute suicide attacks is especially high there exists a phenomenon of volunteerism on the part of potential suicide terrorists to perpetrate attacks, with the suicide attacker actively initiating his recruitment for the mission. This phenomenon has been particularly prominent in the Palestinian public in the course of the Al-Aksa Intifada. However, as a rule, several modi operandi for recruitment can be identified as characteristic of terror organizations.

1. Recruitment via "spotters" at mosques and religious seminaries. In these cases the basis for recruitment is religious.
2. Recruitment of volunteers from among the ranks of the organization's activists. This applies to both Islamic organizations and secular terror organizations such as the Popular Front, the Palestinian Fatah, or the Kurdish PKK that recruit their own activists for the execution of attacks.
3. Recruitment via a relative. This modus operandi exists in both Islamic and secular organizations.
4. Forced recruitment. There have been cases in which a Palestinian suspected of collaboration with Israel, an individual with a criminal record serving a prison sentence, or someone persecuted by adversaries has perpetrated a terror attack in order to clear his name.
5. Volunteers who regard a suicide attack as a way to avenge a personal tragedy.
6. Women who regard the suicide attack as a way to improve their status and enhance society's respect for them.

Table 1.1
Stages in the Perpetration of a Suicide Attack

Recruitment of the suicide attacker

Physical & emotional training of the attacker for the mission

Preparations for the attack
  Gathering Intelligence
  Formulation of the operational plan
  Preparation of combat means
  Preparation of the collaborators' infrastructure

Farewell ceremony for the suicide attacker and his sendoff to execute the mission

Perpetration of the suicide attack

Tapping the media potential of the attack

After the suicide attacker's recruitment there follows a process of examining the candidate's suitability for the mission. Once he is found to be suitable, he must undergo emotional and physical training. Among the Palestinians during the 1990s, the preparation and training stages sometimes took several months; this is also true of suicide terrorists who acted as Al-Qaida emissaries. During the course of the Al-Aksa Intifada, the schedules became tighter and often only days or several weeks elapsed between the candidate's recruitment and the perpetration of his mission.

The Suicide Attackers' Training

The suicide attacker's training is conducted on three main levels:

1. Religious and ideological training.
2. Coping with a fear of death.
3. Technical-operational training.

The religious training is mainly characteristic of Islamic terror organizations and is conducted by clerics who grant religious authorization to conduct a suicide mission and provide explanations regarding the shahid's reward in the world to come. In secular organizations, the national/patriotic aspect is given greater emphasis, though even in this respect religious facets are not completely absent. The religious training provides the candidate with emotional support and alleviates his fear of death. Candidates have sometimes undergone additional training including lying inside an open grave in a cemetery for several hours. Clerics play a decisive role not only in the emotional training of the potential suicide attackers, but also in the creation of a social atmosphere that encourages martyrdom and contributes to the motivation to recruit suicide terrorists.

Another training component includes technical and operational aspects such as becoming familiar with the means to be activated by the suicide attacker (belt bombs or explosive charges), briefs regarding ways to conceal the bomb and reach the target in an innocent guise, and guidelines pertaining to the mission's details such as the type of chosen target, the mode of transportation, or arrival at the target and the attack's timing.

At the end of the suicide attacker's training stage, he is isolated from his family and friends until the time of the attack. The attacker sometimes joins a cell of three or four suicide attackers, each waiting for his "turn" to execute an attack.

Preparations for the Attack

At the same time that the suicide attacker is being trained for the mission, preparations are being made by the operating organization and the network of collaborators who work for it. Primarily, intelligence regarding the target is gathered. The intelligence facilitates the planning of the attack, and the operational details are formulated on this basis, such as timing, the mode of transportation, the modus operandi, etc. After the formulation of the operational plan, the roles of the collaborators are allocated prior to the execution of the mission, such as the transfer of the belt bomb, the explosive device or the booby-trapped car for the suicide attacker, his transfer to the target while circumventing roadblocks and control points, etc. Organizations dealing with the perpetration of suicide attacks must develop technological capabilities in the fields of devising explosive charges, the development of operating mechanisms, and their preparation for transfer by the attacker, either on his body or in a vehicle.

Each organization has its "engineers" (like the "engineer" Yihya Ayash of the Hamas) who specialize in the development and manufacture of explosive devices. For this purpose, the organizations operate bomb-making workshops where the explosive devices are developed and prepared along with the means of concealment. Sometimes preparations for the attack also necessitate the transfer of funds to the activists involved in the activity, in order to pay for their transport, their concealment in a safe house until the attack, and additional needs. The system of preparations for the attack necessitates advanced operational capabilities designated to ensure that following the attacker's training and dispatch all of the prerequisites necessary for the attack's success are in place.

The Suicide Terrorist's Farewell Ceremony

As part of the terrorist's preparation for the attack a ritual setup exists that generates deep commitment to the group and to the execution of the mission. The suicide attacker undergoes a ceremony documented on videotape, where he generally states his name, his mission, and the background for his act. In Islamic organizations, the suicide attacker holds the Koran in one hand and a weapon in the other, and in secular organizations he grasps his weapon against the background of the organization's banner or symbol. In some of cases, the suicide attacker is filmed in the clothes he will wear during the attack or, alternatively, he may appear in military uniform. Most suicide attackers also leave a written will that is presented to their relatives after their death. After the ceremony, the suicide attacker turns into a "living martyr" or into the "walking dead." In this state he regards himself as dead and thus psychologically crosses the point of "no return," as any reconsideration would cause considerable loss of pride. Professor Ariel Merari describes the suicide attacker's status at this point as "a coiled spring waiting to be released."

Tapping the Attack's Potential in the Media

The goal of suicide attacks, much like other terror activities, is to plant fear in the adversary's heart and weaken his determination. Therefore, the terror organizations attribute considerable significance to the media fanfare accompanying the attack.

After the perpetration of the attack, there comes the stage when the organization attempts to tap the media potential pertaining to the bombing. In this framework, the following steps are indicated:

- The organization claims responsibility accompanied by an explanation regarding the reason for the attack.
- The tape is aired of the suicide bomber's "will."
- Threats are made over the media to execute more attacks if the victim reacts to the attack.

Today, suicide attacks afford the organization prestige and glory among its supporters and radical Islam, and constitute the basis for its capability to recruit suicide attackers for subsequent attacks. In this connection, one of the leaders of the Hamas, Salah Shekhada, stated that the Hamas is careful to carry out the type of suicide attacks that will serve as a source of inspiration for additional attacks in the future. Since the beginning of 2002 a "competitive" process vis-à-vis suicide attacks has developed among the Palestinian organizations, with the media component serving as the main consideration.

Circles of Influence Surrounding the Suicide Terrorist

There are several circles surrounding the suicide terrorist that affect his willingness and ability to perpetrate the attack.

The closest circle is the suicide terrorist's family. The family's support for his act (see greater elaboration in the chapter about Palestinian mothers), and the social and financial rewards heaped on the family constitute an important source of encouragement for the suicide attacker's deed. On the other hand, the knowledge that his deed will cause his family harm (exile, demolition of the family home, and a life of suffering) may diminish the terrorist's motivation to be recruited and commit a suicide attack.

The second circle is the operational entity that recruits the candidate for the attack and trains him for the mission. Often this entity isolates the terrorist from his family and friends, to ensure that he will not reconsider his intention to execute the suicide mission.

The third circle, the logistical element, acts in close coordination with the operational entity. Its role is to deal with the suicide terrorist's needs until he sets out for the attack and to transport him to the target. Although the influence wielded by the organization activists who play a role in this circle is weaker than that of his family or of his operators, the success of the "logistic circle" is crucial to the ability of the organization and the attacker to make the attack happen.

The widest circle is the Palestinian society. The degree of that society's solidarity and support for suicide attacks, the attackers and their families, is pivotal to the recruitment of new volunteers to carry out suicide attacks.

As coordination and support offered by the above-mentioned circles vis-à-vis suicide attacks rise, so the scope of volunteers for suicide attacks will grow within Palestinian society.

The relatively extensive circles of influence surrounding the suicide terrorist constitute an arena of action in which it is possible to act with the purpose of diminishing the phenomenon and its damages, because aside from the suicide terrorist himself, all other entities involved in the activity are not interested in sacrificing their lives. They regard the suicide terrorist's martyrdom as a means to further their personal or organizational goals.

Figure 1.1
Circles of Influence Surrounding the Suicide Terrorist

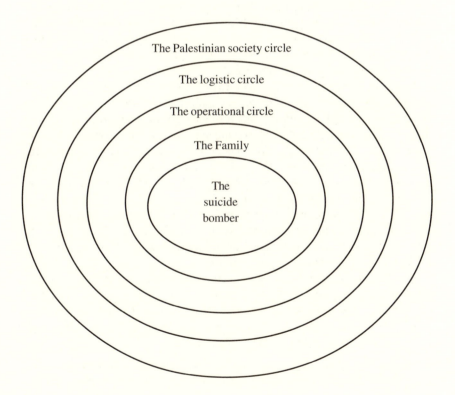

The Palestinian society circle

The logistic circle

The operational circle

The Family

The
suicide
bomber

Historical Examples of Suicide Attacks in the Name of Islam

The Hashashin (The Assassins)[32]

The Hashashin Order within the Shiite stream of the new Ismailia (*Dawa Jadida*) was founded in the tenth century AD. The Ismailia was the offshoot of a secret order that gained enough power to establish a monarchy (the Fatimites) in the tenth century. However, despite the growth of its scope of influence, the Ismailia was an esoteric religion, which remained a minority among the Shia, not to mention the Sunni majority. Many of the Ismailia "missionaries" in Egypt were of Iranian descent, and naturally returned to Iran in order to recruit converts to their religion. The Ismailia missionaries were persecuted by the Seljuk rulers who were in power in Persia at that time and regarded the dissemination of the Ismailian ideas a threat to their regime.

Hassan al-Sabah, founder of the Hashashin sect, was born in the city of Kum in Iran and was recruited to join the Ismailia by one of the missionaries active in Iran, Abu Malek of Isfahan. Hassan al-Sabah went to Cairo to complete his studies of the religious principles and in 1080 returned to Persia. His charismatic personality enabled him to enlist a large group of followers, which caused the Persian rulers, who regarded his activities as a threat, to persecute him and his group. In 1090, through the use of stealth, he succeeded in taking over an isolated fortress in the Albruz Mountains called Alamuth, from which he expanded his control to other areas throughout Persia and, subsequently, in Syria as well.

Hassan al-Sabah remained in his fortress, from which historians believe he emerged only twice in his lifetime. He dedicated his time to contemplation, writing, and struggling with his enemies. He rigorously enforced the laws of the Sharia and did not hesitate to execute even his own sons (one for drinking wine and the other for murder, which later was found to be a false accusation).

The Hashashin (Assassin) Order acted out of a worldview calling for the development of one's individual spiritual skills through profound study and comprehension of religion, as well as willingness for self-sacrifice at its request. The Order's members undertook an oath of fidelity and were bound by blind obedience to its laws and mainly to its leader. Details about the Order appear in the writings of historians from that period as well as in the chronicles of the well-known explorer Marco Polo.

The Hashashins were embroiled in constant conflict with the rulers of the Muslim world as well as with the Crusaders. Thus, they were involved in an existential struggle against adversaries stronger than themselves. They developed a unique system for recruiting and training their men for suicide attacks against their political foes as follows:

The potential suicide attacker was drugged with hashish (from which the name of the Order "Hashashin" stemmed) and was taken to a palace encircled by gardens, where he was entertained by beautiful women and surrounded with a plentitude of pleasures and delicacies as promised to a Muslim who falls in battle (the Shahid) in the Garden of Eden. After spending several days in the "Garden of Eden" he was drugged again and returned to his previous location in order to prepare him for his mission. The suicide believed that when he completed his mission and gave his life for its success, he would reach the Garden of Eden, whose fruits he had already savored.

In some writings, an incident is recorded whereby during the visit of one of Hassan al-Sabah's important visitors, in an effort to impress his guest, Hassan called over one of the suicides and instructed him to jump into the abyss from the palace's parapet. The suicide did so immediately, without any hesitation.

The targets of the Assassins' (Hashashin) suicide attacks were chosen carefully. The assassin carried out his mission with a dagger dipped in poison, thus ensuring the victim's death. The Assassins deemed death in the course of the mission a great honor for the assassin and his family.

There are many stories about the Assassins, including the legend about the mother of one of them who put on her best clothes and expressed her joy when she learned that her son had been killed in a suicide mission. But when she was told that he had survived and returned home, she was deeply saddened because he had not brought himself and his family honor. The Assassins often carried out their assassinations in public and crowded places. Frequent sites were mosques where their victims came to pray on Fridays. Assassinations were perpetrated while entering or leaving the mosque, thus achieving the murder's "media effect" because rumors about the deed would be circulated immediately by the masses present at the event.

Between the years 1090 and 1256, the Assassins enforced a reign of fear, terrorizing their Persian, Crusader, and Muslim enemies.

In 1118, when the Turks surrounded the Alamuth citadel, Hassan encouraged his men to fight and not surrender despite their inferior numbers and isolation. Alamuth was miraculously saved from falling into Turkish hands because the forces surrounding the citadel learned of the death of the sultan and left. Hassan al-Sabah died of an illness in 1124 and was replaced by his deputy.

The Crusades were a series of wars launched by Europeans between the eleventh and fourteenth centuries to recapture the Holy Land from the Muslims. Tensions between Christian Europe and Muslim rulers had grown steadily following the capture of Jerusalem by Muslims in the seventh century. The First Crusade was sparked by rumors of the desecration of the Holy Sepulcher. Despite the holy pretext for war, the criminal nature of the affair also became evident. Many of the pilgrims engaged in acts of pillaging and violence on their way to the Holy Land (such as massacring Jews in the Rhenish cities), and much of the fighting was directed against the Byzantine Empire (which was Christian) because Europe's Christian monarchs coveted its oriental riches.

The First Crusade accomplished its mission in July 1099 by capturing Jerusalem. The city's Muslim and Jewish inhabitants were massacred, which triggered a series of vendetta killings and set the tone for the rest of the Crusades.

The conquest of the Land of Israel and Jerusalem by the crusaders, and the spreading of the crusader kingdom towards Syria and north Lebanon generated a fresh threat against the Assassins' stronghold by a new enemy. The weakened Muslim world was forced to face the greater strength of the crusaders. Some Muslim rulers even expressed their willingness to sign alliances with Christian princes.

Only some 100 years later did the Jihad begin to garner strength in the campaign against the Crusaders under the leadership of Saladin. The Jihad against the Crusaders gathered momentum due to intentional acts of provocation by the Crusader commander who in 1182 violated the agreement between the King of Jerusalem and Saladin, and attacked and robbed Muslim caravans, including caravans of Muslim pilgrims on their way to Mecca (Haj). He even dispatched a naval force to the Red Sea in order to raid the African Coast and the Arab Peninsula. In the course of their naval expedition, the Crusader sailors burned boats at al-Hura and Yenba, Medina's ports, and in 1183 they even reached Ravig, one of Mecca's ports.

The location of the Crusaders opposite the gates of Mecca, one of Islam's holiest sites, posed a challenge that no self-respecting Muslim leader could possibly ignore. Therefore, a Muslim navy was dispatched immediately from Egypt that succeeded in almost totally decimating the Crusader navy. From this point onward, the Jihad under Saladin's leadership commenced, which eventually led to the vanquishing of the Crusader kingdom based in Jerusalem.

Harsh conflicts also erupted between the Assassins and the Crusader orders of the Hospitalers and the Templars.

The Assassins found themselves under heavy pressure both from their enemies in the Muslim world on the one hand, and the Crusaders, on the other. Thus, the Assassins were fighting for their very survival in the face of stronger adversaries and they utilized the most effective weapon at their disposal—suicide attacks. One of their most famous victims was Conrad of Montferrat, King of Jerusalem, who was murdered in 1192 by Assassins disguised as Christian monks.

In the thirteenth century, the Mongolians conquered Persia and Syria, thus bringing an end to the reign of the Assassins (Hashashin) in various areas in this region.

Suicide Attacks of Islamic Terrorists in Asia

An historical example of the use of Islamic terrorists in suicide attacks can be found in three Muslim societies in Asia during the era of Colonialism, between the eighteenth and the twentieth centuries. Stephan F. Dale described three Muslim societies in India, Indonesia, and the Philippines that were embroiled in conflict against the European colonialism and produced extremist groups that acted against the colonial forces through the instigation of terror attacks, mainly suicide missions.[33] The most prominent example in the three groups described by Dale relates to the struggle and suicide attacks of Muslims in the Philippines (the Moro) who fought both the Spanish and American colonialism.

Islamic Suicide Attacks of the Moro in the Southern Philippines (the Jihad against the Spanish and American Colonialism)

The land of "Moro," which is currently known as the Southern Philippines, contains the Mindanao Island, the Julu Archipelago, the Palawan and Basilian Islands, and several additional islands. The country of Moro includes islands covering an overall area of 117,000 square kilometers, with a population of approximately 20 million people, including about 12 million Muslims. Islam reached the land of the Moro in 1210 through Muslim clerics and merchants. A short time after the arrival of Islam in the "Moro," the first Muslim Sultanates were established.

The Spanish, headed by Ferdinand Magellan, arrived in the Philippines in 1521 and began to spread Christianity in the region. For three hundred years the Spaniards attempted unsuccessfully to enforce their reign and convert the Moro inhabitants to Christianity. The inhabitants declared a Holy War (Jihad) against the Spanish conquerors. The failure of the Muslim Sultanates to withstand the Spaniards pushed Muslim groups and communities throughout the Southern Islands, like Solo and Mindanao, to organize a struggle in which individual members of the group were required to carry out a personal Jihad against the Spaniards and the Christian Philippines who cooperated with them.[34]

The personal Jihad expressed itself in an attack instigated by the Muslim (Mujahid) against his Spanish and Christian Philippine enemies, with the aim of murdering as many infidels as possible until the assailant himself was killed. Most of these attacks were perpetrated with swords and daggers because of the lack of guns and rifles in the possession of the Moros at that time.[35] There are also accounts of women who carried out this religious mission, and religious clerics had no trouble finding volunteers for these acts of suicide/martyrdom. Sometimes these volunteers were people who had sinned during their lifetime and who believed that only self-sacrifice could atone for their behavior and enable them to enter the Garden of Eden. The Spanish called this type of suicide/martyrdom action *juramentado*. In Spanish this term means "he who takes an oath" (rooted in the Spanish verb *juramentar*, meaning to swear or investigate under oath). The Muslims named the execution of this religious commandment *perang sabil*. In Malaysian, *perang* means war, while in Arabic the word *sabil* means a way, and serves as an abbreviation of the full term *fi sabil Allah*—"in the way of God." Whoever set out on these suicide and martyrdom missions was prepared by religious clerics, an imam or pandita, with the help of prayers and purification rites that trained him to kill and be killed for the liberation of Muslim land. His head and eyelashes were shaved, he put on white clothing, took an oath on the Koran, and then set out on his mission. The juramentado missions were subsequently conducted against American forces as well.[36]

Despite the striking Spanish military superiority and their victories in battles, the Moro opposition persevered and the Spaniards did not succeed in achieving anything beyond formal rule over their territories until the end of their control in the Philippines. The Moros' social and political structure, their religion, legal system and norms were unaffected by the Spanish presence in the south, and the Moro did not regard themselves as occupied or part of the Spanish empire that ruled in Manila.

In 1898, Spain was defeated by the United States and the Paris Accord signed that year obligated Spain to hand over the Philippines (among other areas) to the United States, including the Muslim areas of Mindanao and Solo. In the years 1899-1901, the Americans were busy fighting the Philippine independence movement that was active in the northern islands of Luzon and Visava, and adopted a policy of noninvolvement in developments among the Muslims in the south. The Muslims were pleased with this situation, but once the fighting ended in the north, the American military commanders opted for implementing a policy of direct rule over the Muslim territories in Moro land. Moro attempts to confront the American forces resulted in heavy losses for the Moro and few American losses. Consequently, the Moros' standard attacks lessened and they adopted guerrilla warfare and suicide attacks from out of the jungles as they had done previously against the Spanish conquerors.

We can learn more about the American policy from a letter that one of the volunteers sent home:[37] "No more prisoners. The [Filipinos] take none...we will kill the wounded and all of them."

That this practice became widespread, if not universal, is attested to by the ratio of killed to wounded Filipinos in the insurrection—forty dead to one wounded. (The usual battle figure is three wounded for each killed.)

David S. Woolman categorizes two types of suicide attacks:[38]

- An amok attack—A Moro who for various personal reasons carries out an "amok attack" and tries to assail as many of his enemies as possible before they neutralize him.
- A juramentado attack—A Moro who perpetrates a suicide attack for religious reasons, undergoes preparation and religious training prior to the attack, and tries to attack as many Islamic enemies as possible before they neutralize him.

The suicide attacks always contained an element of surprise and took place in various locations such as city centers and villages, as well as attacks against American strongholds and forces in the form of forays from within the jungles. In most of the suicide attacks the Moro used a weapon called the "Malay Kris," a type of short sword that could be concealed in the suicide attacker's clothing until the launching of the attack. Nevertheless, in some suicide attacks firearms (either a handgun or a rifle) were used, or alternatively bayonets and poisoned arrows. Woolman notes that most suicide attacks ended with the injury and death of at least one victim (sometimes the suicide attacker was able to attack a larger number of victims before his termination).[39]

The conflict between the American soldiers and the Moro became even more intense after the appointment of John Pershing as commander of the U.S. forces in the Philippines. Pershing believed that the only language the Moro understood was force and thus adopted an aggressive policy. In skirmishes between the Moro and the Americans, the latter always prevailed due to their superior weaponry (guns and canons), and the Moro suffered heavy casualties compared to the small number of casualties among the American forces. (In a battle near Lake Lamno, 120 Moro were slain compared to one American soldier. In another battle near the same lake, 200 Moro were killed compared to two American soldiers wounded, etc.). Despite their inferiority, the Moro continued to conduct defensive battles vis-à-vis the Americans, but gradually suicide attacks became a more effective and significant means, from their point of view, to inflict casualties among the American forces.

Due to Pershing's success in fighting the Moro, he was promoted to the rank of brigadier general by President Theodore Roosevelt.

Pershing's successor as commander of the U.S. forces in the Philippines was major general Leonard Wood, who, like his predecessor, believed in taking a tough stand against the Moro. Thus, he continued the relentless and ruthless battle against the Moro.

In March 1906, Wood attacked a stronghold of Moro fighters who had entrenched themselves near the mouth of a volcano called Bad Dago. This battle was called the "Cloud Battle" because it took place at an altitude of some 2,000 feet. In the bloody battle about 600 Moros, fighting to the bitter end, were killed (the ranks included women dressed as men who also fought the Americans). The Americans counted a toll of twenty-one fatalities and seventy-three casualties. Wood was criticized severely in the United States. Many maintained that the battle and fatalities were superfluous. As a result, Wood was reposted in the United States and Pershing returned to command the forces in the Philippines.

Pershing succeeded in gaining control over most of the Moro areas, but the rebellion still continued, and until the end of American control in the Philippines no solution was found for the problem of suicide assaults. As a result of American inability to quell the Moro opposition, it adopted a policy of no direct involvement in the Muslim areas and in reality enabled the existence of an almost complete autonomy of the Muslim population in the south (Moro land).

When the United States granted the Philippines independence, the residents of Moro objected to their annexation to the Philippine state and demanded independence for the Muslim areas. In the first years of independence, the Moro Muslims enjoyed a large degree of autonomy, but from the early 1950s the government began a campaign to impose its rule in the southern islands and formulated a policy of settlement and transfer of Christian populations, mainly from the Island of Luzon, to the Muslim territories in Moro. The massive settlement of Christians in the Muslim south and the transfer of the governmental and economic focus of power into the hands of the new settlers triggered widespread dissension among the Muslims and caused increasing violence. During the 1960s and mainly in the early 1970s the situation in the southern islands deteriorated into a civil war, forcing the government in Manila to dispatch large-scale military forces in order to suppress the Muslim terror and subversion. The government's tough methods of suppression instigated the unification of armed groups and organizations in order to fight the central government, and in 1972 the Moro National Liberation Front (MNLF) was established. The organization was headed by Nur Misouari, Hashem Salamaat, and others.

The refusal of the Philippine government to grant independence or autonomy to Moro triggered the declaration of the Moro Jihad against the Manila government. Since the 1970s the struggle has continued between the Moro and the authorities. During these years, the MNLF split ranks several times and organizations of a radical Islamic character were established (the Moro Islamic Liberation Front and the Abu Sayyaf Organization) which demanded independence for Moro, while in 1996 the MNLF agreed to accept the solution of autonomy for the Muslim regions in the Southern Philippines.

The ethos of the Muslims in the Philippines (the "Moro") thus points to the Jihad as a formative concept in their history:

- The first Jihad against the Spanish conquest (1521-1898).
- The second Jihad against the American conquest (1898- 1946).
- The third Jihad against the Philippines' Christian government (from 1946 to date).
- A sum total of almost 480 years of struggle—Jihad.

As stated above, the struggle against the central government in Manila continues to this day. It is led by Muslim terror organizations, the most prominent of which are the Moro Islamic Liberation Front (MILF) and the Abu Sayyaf Organization, which are affiliated with Bin-Laden's Jihad Front and

Al-Qaida. The United States assists the Philippine government in its struggle against the Islamic isolationists and the terror organizations in the country's southern region.

Stephan Dale, who studied suicide attacks in Asia, claims that the suicide attacks took place during periods when the groups felt that other opposition methods had failed, and were perpetrated out of a sense of frustration and desperation. The suicide attacks were directed against European targets or the local Christian population.[40] The suicide terrorists considered their activities a "personal Jihad" aimed at liberating the Muslim community from foreign conquest, in addition to reaping the reward that a Muslim earns when sacrificing himself during a Jihad.[41] The "shahids" in Asia enjoyed wide popular support and their courageous deeds became part of the ethos and narrative of the Muslim communities as expressed in songs, folklore, and various texts in which their memory is extolled.[42]

Dale states that the suicide terror, to which his study pertains, developed as a last resort only after the failure of the violent struggle against colonialism, and that the phenomenon ceased when a new political reality was created that aroused hopes of a better future for the Muslim community.[43] According to Dale, when nationalist political movements were established in these countries, the terror groups and suicide attacks became anachronistic and irrelevant, and gradually expired. And further, "terrorism was as much instrumental as emotional."[44] Dale adds that when terror becomes a cultural norm, the correlation between later terror attacks and the original reason for their use becomes indistinct.[45] The historical case of the Philippines indicates that the Spaniards and the Americans did not succeed in finding a military solution to the suicide attacks, and the latter, claims Dale, ended as the result of a change in the political reality.

Today, Islamic terror organizations in the Philippines no longer use suicide attacks in the framework of their struggle against the Manila administration. There is no unequivocal explanation for their abstention from the use of suicide attacks except for the deduction that at the present time they have found sufficiently effective modes of operation without resorting to suicide attacks, which, according to historical precedent, constituted a last resort.

Notes

1. The historical review is based on the book by Yoram Shweitzer and Shaul Shay, *The Globalization of Terror: The Challenge of Al-Qaida and the Response of the International Community*, Transaction Publishers, New Brunswick, NJ, 2003.
2. Yoram Schweitzer, *Suicide Terrorism*, ICT, Herzliya, 2000, p. 76.
3. These data refer to the period between September 29, 2000 and December 2003.
4. Thomas Friedman, as quoted in *Ha'aretz*, April 18, 2002.
5. Dr. Yoram Yovel, *An Emotional Storm*, Keshet Publishing, Tel Aviv, 2001, p. 215.
6. Ibid., p. 202

7.   Boaz Ganor, *Suicide Attacks in Israel*, ICT, Herzliya, 2000, p. 134.
8.   Ibid., p. 135.
9.   Ibid.
10. Nahman Tal, *Israel and Suicide Terror, Strategic Update*, Vol. 5, Issue 1 (June 2002), the Jaffe Center for Strategic Studies, Tel Aviv University.
11. Ehud Sprinzak, "Rational Fanatics," *Foreign Policy*, (September/October 2000).
12. Nahman Tal, *Israel and Suicide Terror, Strategic Update*, vol. 5, issue 1 (June 2002), the Jaffe Center for Strategic Studies, Tel Aviv University.
13. Ibid.
14. *Al-Raya* (Qatar), April 25, 2001.
15. *Al-Ahram Al-Arabi* (Egypt), February 3, 2001.
16. *Al-Istiqlal,* August 20, 1999.
17. *Al-Hayat,* (London-Beirut), April 25, 2001.
18. Ibid.
19. *Al-Hayat Al-Jadida* (Palestine), April 27, 2001
20. Ibid.
21. *Sout Al-Ama* (Egypt), April 26, 2001. Quoted in *Al-Hayat* (London-Beirut), April 27, 2001.
22. *Al-Quds* (Palestine), August 17, 1988.
23. *Yediot Aharonot*, June 21, 2001. (Shekhada was killed by the IDF in 2002.)
24. Ibid.
25. *Daily Star*, May 11, 2001.
26. Ibid., June 8, 2002.
27. Quoted in a document by Amnesty International: "Israel, the occupied areas and the Palestinian Authority: With no distinction—Attacks against citizens by armed Palestinian organizations," July 2002.
28. Walla News, quoting discussions held at the Islamic Conference in Malaysia, May 6, 2002 (news.walla.co.il).
29. Ibid.
30. An exception is the attack on the number 405 bus on its route between Tel Aviv and Jerusalem in which the terrorist made the bus roll down into a chasm. The terrorist was not killed in the attack, but was apprehended and sentenced to life imprisonment.
31. Ehud Sprinzak, "Rational Fanatics," *Foreign Policy* (September-October 2000).
32. This section is based on the following sources: Bernard Lewis, *The Assassins: A Radical Sect in Islam*, New York, Basic Books Publisher, 2002.
33. Martha Crenshaw, "'Suicide' Terrorism in Comparative Perspective," in *Countering Suicide Terrorism*, The International Policy Institute for Counter-Terrorism at the Interdisciplinary Center, Herzliya, 2001, pp. 28-29.
34. Moshe Jaeger, *Muslim Rebellions in the Philippines, Thailand and in Burma-Myanmar*, Posner and Sons Ltd., Jerusalem, 2000, pp. 42-43.
35. Ibid., p. 43.
36. Ibid.
37. Michael D. Haydock, "Marine Scapegoat in the Philippine Insurrection," *Military History* (February 2002), p. 48.
38. David S. Woolman, "Fighting Islam's Fierce," *Military History* (April 2002).
39. Ibid.
40. Stephan P. Dale, "Religious Suicide in Islamic Asia: Anti-Colonial Terrorism in India, Indonesia and the Philippines," *Journal of Conflict Resolution* 32, 1 (March 1988), pp. 37-59.
41. Ibid., p. 52.

42. Ibid., pp. 52-53.
43. Ibid., pp. 52-53.
44. Ibid., pp. 56-57.
45. Ibid., p. 39.

2

Suicide Attacks in the Modern Era— The Arab-Israeli Conflict

The Shia and Suicide Attacks

Following the Islamic revolution in Iran, and since the beginning of the 1980s, suicide attacks perpetrated by Shiite and Iranian entities have become a prominent characteristic of Shiite terror. These attacks took a high toll and proved to have an impressive psychological impact, particularly vis-à-vis Western countries and Israel, which served as central targets for these attacks.

The outlook of the leader of the Iranian Islamic revolution, the Ayatollah Khomeini, was structured on his interpretation of several key issues in Shiite Islam and on adapting the solutions to the reality of the twentieth century. In the center of his theory there stands the necessity for an activist approach to promote the goals of Islam and achieve redemption. Khomeini's theory grew and spread against the background of the Shiites' historical frustration, a difficult socioeconomic situation, and the escalation of fundamentalist thinking in the Muslim world.

Khomeini regarded "revolutionary violence" as a central tool for the solution of the problems in Islamic society, as well as the resolution of the individual's problems. The struggle is first and foremost directed at the purification of Islamic society from within, starting with the Shiite community and subsequently expanding to the wider Islamic circle. The struggle does not cease in the Islamic arena; it is designated to crush the "evil root"—the superpowers that cause world destruction. Thus, the revolutionary message transmitted by Khomeini is universal, with the Shiites representing the downtrodden of the entire world.[1]

Khomeini provided the religious/ideological and rational justifications for the use of violence to promote the goals of Islam, and placed the Jihad and "self-sacrifice" at the forefront of his philosophy. This fact gave the Shia a worldwide reputation of a fanatic religion that demands martyrdom of its believers in the name of its goals. One of the prominent innovations in

Khomeini's theory was the permission to sacrifice an individual's life for the realization of the goals of Islamic society, in contrast to the accepted Islamic ruling that prohibits suicide.[2]

Khomeini used several arguments to justify his stance: First, as he believed that the individual lives in a corrupt society whose main role is to meet material needs, therefore when the individual sacrifices himself he is sacrificing something material for an elevated spiritual goal (sacrifice of the "materialistic I" for the "spiritual I"). Khomeini regarded the story of the death of the Imam Hussein as the main argument justifying martyrdom in the name of Islam.[3] When Hussein set out on his long journey from Hejaz to Karbala, according to this interpretation, he knew that he would not return from his travels and that he would die a cruel death. But his martyrdom was important to the Shiite community because it enabled the latter to endeavor to claim the Islamic throne of leadership. Hussein's death is reconstructed every year at the Ashura ceremonies, but Khomeini claimed that this could not suffice, and stated that Hussein's martyrdom must be relived through its practical implementation via daily self-sacrifice in the name of Islam.[4]

The issue of martyrdom is also closely linked with the concept of Jihad. According to Islamic religious rulings, there are two types of Jihad: defensive and offensive. The defensive Jihad refers to the defense of Muslim territory conquered by infidels. The goal of offensive Jihad is the enforcement of Islamic rule in parts of the world that have not yet submitted to its reign. Falling in battle during the Jihad, including martyrdom in the battlefield, is a lofty commandment that entitles the martyr to the parting of the gates of the Garden of Eden in welcome.[5]

According to the time-honored concept of the Shia, only the "vanished Imam" may declare a Jihad, and thus until his return the duty of Jihad does not fall on the Shiite believers. Khomeini objected to this approach and claimed that until the return of the "vanished Imam," the responsibility for the leadership of the flock of believers falls upon the *mujtahad*, which is also permitted to declare a Jihad. During the 1980s, the encouragement of martyrdom became a central theme in Shiite combat, both in the framework of the war against Iraq and in the framework of the struggle of extremist Shiite organizations against Israel and Western targets in Lebanon.

In 1983, Khomeini gauged the tremendous attraction that war presented for Iranian youth and passed a religious ruling permitting boys over the age of twelve to volunteer to fight at the front even without their parents' permission. The young volunteers turned into the Imam's protégés and they were promised entry to the Garden of Eden if they fell in battle.[6] Tens of thousands of youthful volunteers received the "key to the Garden of Eden" (a plastic key made in Taiwan) and purple headbands bearing the slogan "long live Khomeini," after which they were thrust into the battlefield. The willingness to "die a 'martyr's' death" motivated the Iranians to use special tactics during the Iran-Iraq war such as dispatching human waves to face the enemy, clearing minefields by having young boys run across them, and suicide attacks against fortified targets and Iraqi tanks.[7]

Most of the "volunteers" wrote wills prior to their departure to battle through special messengers who were sent to the front for this purpose. The wills were worded as letters addressed to the Imam or the mothers of the soldiers. "How miserable, how unfortunate, how ignorant was I during all of my fourteen regrettable years, which passed by without my knowing Allah. The Imam opened my eyes.... How sweet, sweet, sweet is death, it is like a blessing that Allah has bestowed upon his beloved."[8]

The Iranian press published the wills of the shaids daily, in which they expressed their aspirations—before leaving for action from which they never returned—to be at peace and reach the shaded shelter of Allah's wings. In most of these wills there was idealization of death as a lofty value. Many of them ended with the verse from the Koran: "Do not think that the shahids are dead; they live and flourish in the shaded shelter of Allah's wings." Some closed with quotations from Islamic sources and Khomeini's letters, which describe the delightful eternal life of the shahids in the Garden of Eden, and promise that this is the destiny of anyone who lays down his life in a holy war. As to the injured, in one of his speeches Ali Khamenai promised that they would not feel their amputated limbs when they reach the Garden of Eden.[9]

A similar tone is to be gleaned in the obituaries published in the newspapers. Instead of expressing the accepted condolences (*taslit*) for the families of the fallen, "greetings" (*tavrich*) were sent to the families "because the family had the privilege of its son becoming a shahid." In other cases there were combined "greetings and condolences" for the families. The Iranian press was full of stories about Iranian mothers who had sacrificed four or five sons, and expressed joy because their sons had been privileged to reach the Garden of Eden.[10]

The Shiites in Lebanon and Suicide Attacks

The link between Iran and the Shiites in Lebanon was expressed in the adoption of Khomeini's ideology and rulings by religious clerics and Hizballah activists in Lebanon. The operational link between the Shiites in Lebanon and Iran lies in the connection of a spiritual authority and obedience to the Imam by his "soldiers in Lebanon," which is perpetuated through religious clerics of the Hizballah. The latter were responsible for interpreting Khomeini's rulings, which were perceived as operational orders, and provided inspiration and permission for violent actions perpetrated by Shiites against foreigners.[11]

The issue of suicide attacks was also given due consideration by Shiite philosophical circles in Lebanon. Sheikh Fadallah, the spiritual leader of

Hizballah, claimed that in the absence of the "Vanished Imam," the mujtahid is permitted to declare only a defensive Jihad. But he maintained that the struggle underway in Lebanon and Palestine was a defensive Jihad whose goal was to liberate conquered Muslim territory, and therefore martyrdom as part of the struggle against the invaders is allowed according to Islamic ruling. The Sheikh Hassan Trad, one of Hizballah's clerics, also clarified this matter:

> Lebanon would not have been liberated if not for the Jihad of Iran. Lebanon was only liberated thanks to the "istashad" (martyrdom) actions, and the only one who gave them his blessing was the Imam Khomeini. Bilal Pahatz, who became a symbol of the opposition, wrote me a letter as follows: "I am a *mukalid* (follower) of the Imam Khomeini who instructed to carry out *istashad* and strike out at the enemy and I answered him (positively) based on the rulings of his *marjha taklid* (source of authority), the Imam Khomeini."[12]

Another Hizballah cleric, Sheikh Yosef Damush, added another dimension to the link between Khomeini and the Shiite martyrs in Lebanon:

> The actions of the istashad carried out by our youth were due to our inspiration. Some of them came to consult with me regarding the perpetration of istashad. I explained to them that this matter requires a fatwa (a religious ruling) from the supreme authority, meaning the Imam Khowi or Khomeini, as no believer would carry out any act without taking the principles of religious rulings into account. The martyrs Ahmad Kutzir (a Shiite suicide terrorist who bombed the IDF headquarters in Tyre) and Hassan Kutzir (a Shiite suicide terrorist who detonated a car bomb near an IDF patrol) perpetrated istashad on the basis of a fatwa and there are acts of bravery that are still undisclosed and no one knows of their perpetrators.[13]

It is evident from the above statements that in the Lebanese arena the leaders of the Hizballah encouraged the perpetration of suicide attacks. Sheikh Subhi Tufeilli, one of the leaders of the Hizballah in Lebanon, defined the suicide attackers as the heroes of the Holy War," acting in the name of Islam. In August 1985, in a memorial ceremony commemorating three members of the Revolutionary Guards killed in Lebanon, Subhi Tufeilli said:

> The names of many of the heroes of the mujahidin who acted against foreign targets, including the American Embassy, are still unknown, but their actions were on behalf of Islam. We must remain loyal to their blood and imbue in the consciousness of the world and history that it is Islam that will destroy Israel and America.[14]

He explained that the non-exposure of the names "of many of the heroes and fighters who detonated the American Embassy and bombed American, French, and Israeli (targets), was meant to glorify the name of Islam rather than provide personal publicity for anonymous soldiers."[15] And indeed the Hizballah did not publish the names of the terrorists who perpetrated mega attacks against the American, French, and Israeli targets. The reason for this could stem from the desire to maintain confidentiality regarding the perpetrators in order to prevent any possibility of reaching their dispatchers.[16]

Two and a half years after the bombing of the IDF headquarters in Tyre, the Hizballah published details regarding the identity of the Shiite suicide terrorist who they claimed had carried out the attack, naming him as Ahmad Kutzir.[17] The Hizballah did not provide any explanation for the exposure of the identity of the fifteen-year-old Shiite.

Ahmad Kutzir disappeared about a month before being dispatched on his final mission. He was declared missing and his family published his photograph in the Lebanese newspapers, appealing to the public to assist in finding him.[18] It is possible that the exceptional exposure of his identity stemmed from the Kutzir family's repeated questions regarding their son's fate. Ahmad Kutzir became a hero in Lebanon and Iran. The *Alahad* newspaper published blowups of the Shiite teenager's picture, with his image rising from the ruins of the Israeli headquarters. The Kutzir family living in Dir Kanun Alnahar, a remote village in Southern Lebanon, received a certificate of esteem from "Ka'ad Al Uma Al Islamiya" (The commander of the Islamic nation—Khomeini).

Hizballah's religious clerics also had followers in the rival organization, Amal. Bilal Fahatz, who in his short life also served as the bodyguard of Amal leader Nabia Beri, was a member of the latter organization.[19] When Fahatz came to the decision to carry out a mission from which there was no return, he knew exactly to whom to turn in order to obtain Khomeini's approval. "The letter written by Bilal Fahatz, which was signed by one of the well-known clerics (Sheikh Hassan Trad), and in which it was stated that the Imam Khomeini had given the plan his blessing, was transferred to Abu Ali (Mustafa Dirani, who served as the director of Amal's operational apparatus), who then issued the appropriate instructions to assist Bilal Fahatz in realizing his wishes."[20]

In the framework of the ruling in principle allowing suicide attacks, the Hizballah leaders established guidelines regarding the conditions under which this activity was allowed. The Shiite setting out on a suicide mission for a just cause (in the service of Islam) is no different than someone who falls in the battlefield during Jihad, and martyrdom in this case is the main weapon of the weaker party in his war against the invaders who have the advantage when it comes to strength and numbers. Khomeini also believed that Shiite martyrdom was a vital and central tool in the struggle of the downtrodden against their oppressors with their superior strength, and that the human advantage could compensate for the quantitative and technological superiority of the enemy.[21]

Suicide attacks are meant to achieve exceptional results, which can be applied as leverage for political or military changes, and to strike out significantly at the enemy. In addition, the suicide terrorist must carry out his deed out of a sense of complete understanding and recognition regarding the value of his deed and his personal martyrdom. The use of suicide attacks against Israeli and

Western targets began in Lebanon in April of 1983, and subsequently spread to Kuwait where several attacks were perpetrated against Western targets.

As a result of the withdrawal of the American and French forces from Lebanon and the deployment of the IDF in the security zone, the scope of suicide attacks decreased, although subsequent suicide attacks were occasionally perpetrated against IDF forces in the security zone of Southern Lebanon. The major suicide attacks perpetrated by Shiite terror entities against Western targets in Lebanon were as follows:[22]

- April 18, 1983—A truck loaded with about four hundred kilograms of explosives detonated near the American Embassy in Beirut, killing sixty and injuring 120 (most of whom were U.S. staff members).
- October 23, 1983—Two car bombs exploded simultaneously in Beirut: one near the U.S. Marines Headquarters, causing 260 deaths, and the second near the headquarters of the French forces resulting in fifty-eight fatalities.

The "Islamic Jihad" organization (a cover name for Pro-Iranian radical Shiite entities—the Hizballah) claimed responsibility for all three attacks.[23] The attacks were carried out by suicide terrorists who perished in the attacks. The missions were characterized by the gathering of precise intelligence that enabled the penetration of the car bombs near their targets. In addition to these attacks, a Shiite suicide attack was also carried out in 1983 against an Israeli target in Lebanon:

- November 4, 1983—A car bomb exploded at the headquarters of IDF forces in Tyre, causing the deaths of sixty-one people (twenty-eight IDF soldiers and thirty-three Lebanese and Palestinian detainees).

From November 1983 to March 1985 the arena for Shiite terrorist attacks was expanded from Lebanon to Kuwait:

- December 12, 1983—A truck bomb meant to attack the American Embassy in Kuwait exploded near the building. The suicide bomber was killed as well as four Kuwaiti citizens. The attack was perpetrated by the Shiite al-Dawa Organization.
- September 20, 1984—A truck bomb rammed its way into the courtyard of the U.S. Embassy in Kuwait. The driver was shot and killed by the guards but the truck exploded, killing fifteen people. The Islamic Jihad claimed responsibility for this series of attacks.

From 1985 onwards Shiite suicide attacks were perpetrated against IDF troops in South Lebanon, but there were no additional cases of suicide attacks against Western targets, for the most part because of the lack of military forces or "attractive targets" of Western countries in Lebanon, and also due to the improved security measures at foreign facilities situated in Lebanon and in other countries.

Examples of Suicide Attacks against "Western" Targets in Lebanon and Kuwait

The suicide attack against the U.S. Embassy in Lebanon. On April 18, 1983, the Hizballah perpetrated its first suicide attack. A van loaded with about 400 kilograms of explosives and driven by a suicide terrorist exploded near the structure of the U.S. Embassy in Beirut. As a result of the explosion, part of the building collapsed, leaving sixty-three dead and 120 wounded, including most of the employees at the Embassy and at the branch of the CIA in Lebanon. The Islamic Jihad organization claimed responsibility for the attack (subsequently, the Hizballah continued to use this name in order to claim responsibility for attacks). As a result of the blast, the American Embassy was moved to Achar, north of Beirut.

On September 20, 1984, another suicide attack was carried out against the U.S. Embassy in Achar. A truck bomb driven by a suicide attacker exploded near the Embassy. In this attack eleven people were killed and fifty-eight were wounded. Here, too, the Islamic Jihad claimed responsibility for the attack.

The suicide attack against the headquarters of the U.S. Marines in Beirut.[24] On the morning of October 23, 1983 (at 06:22), a Mercedes truck loaded with explosives and driven by a suicide terrorist exploded near the building that housed the Marines Headquarters at the Beirut airport. The truck rammed through the gate and exploded in the courtyard near the headquarters. The four-story building, which served as both headquarters and barracks for the Marines, collapsed as the result of the explosion. Two hundred and forty-one people were killed and eighty were injured, most of whom were U.S. Marines serving in the multinational force in Lebanon.[25]

This was the terror attack to take the heaviest toll on the United States until the attacks of September 11, 2001. To quote the commander of the U.S. Marines Corp General Kelly:

> It was the largest terrorist act in United States history.... When 220 Marines died on October 23, 1983, the day became the Corps' bloodiest since February 1945, when Marines fought to secure Iwo Jima. October 23, 1983 surpasses even the Corps' bloodiest days during the Vietnam and Korean Wars."[26]

Suicide Attacks Perpetrated by the Hizballah against Israeli Targets

The first suicide attack perpetrated by the Hizballah against an Israeli target was on November 4, 1983 when a car bomb driven by a suicide terrorist exploded near the IDF headquarters in Tyre. The Islamic Jihad (a cover name for the Hizballah) claimed responsibility for the attack, which shared the same characteristics as suicide attacks perpetrated by the Hizballah against "foreign" targets in Lebanon in the months of April and October 1983.

Following the IDF's tightening of security means surrounding its head-quarters in Lebanon, the Hizballah moved its suicide attacks to the roads. On June 16, 1984, a car bomb driven by a suicide terrorist exploded near an IDF convoy south of the Zaharani. Five soldiers were injured in the attack. In the first months of 1985 the Hizballah carried out three similar attacks using the same method:

- February 5, 1985—The explosion of a car bomb near an IDF convoy at Al-Burge al-Shimali caused injuries to ten soldiers.
- March 10, 1985—The explosion of a car bomb at the "Egel Gate"[27] near Metullah caused the deaths of twelve soldiers. An additional fifteen were injured.
- March 12, 1985—The explosion of a car bomb near Ras al-Ayin—there were no casualties.

At the inspiration of the Hizballah, secular terror organizations in Lebanon began to carry out suicide attacks against the IDF in March 1985. They displaced the Hizballah as "leaders" in this area through the perpetration of their own attacks during the years 1985-1987 (see following specification).

Starting from 1985 there was a reduction in the scope of suicide attacks perpetrated by the Hizballah, with an average of one to two attacks per year (in the years 1986-1987 the Hizballah did not make any claims regarding suicide attacks although there were several attacks and attempted attacks which may have been carried out by the organization).

Between 1983 and 2000 the Hizballah definitely perpetrated thirteen suicide attacks. However, it seems that the number of attacks that it carried out in reality was greater because during that period fourteen unclaimed attacks took place, and it would appear that the majority of them were perpetrated by this organization.

The Hizballah focused its suicide attacks against IDF targets, while the secular terror organizations in Lebanon concentrated on the South Lebanon Army. It appears that this preference stemmed from the need for a religious ruling regarding the perpetration of suicide attacks. This ruling was granted for attacks against IDF targets, but it is doubtful if this were also valid vis-à-vis the South Lebanon Army. Moreover, the organization viewed the IDF as the main enemy, and for skirmishes with this entity it was justified to carry out the kind of attacks involving suicide.

Most of the Hizballah's suicide attacks were perpetrated via a suicide attacker driving a car bomb. As far as we know, there were only two incidents in which the organization attempted to carry out suicide attacks using belt bombs, on August 22, 1987, and on August 3, 1992.

With the exception of the 1983 attack against the IDF headquarters in Tyre, all of the attacks were directed against IDF convoys. The two attacks that took the highest toll of victims took place deep in the security zone near the "Egel" and "Fatma" gates (on March 10, 1985 there was an attack near the "Egel" gate that caused twelve fatalities and fifteen casualties, and on October 19, 1988, there was an attack near the "Fatma" gate which resulted in eight fatalities and seven casualties).

During the time that the IDF was positioned in Lebanon, Israeli forces formed action methods and drills that significantly reduced the damage caused by the suicide attacks in the form of car bombs driven by suicide terrorists. As a result, the Hizballah preferred to adopt different modi operandi, which it found to be sufficiently effective, without resorting to intensive activity in the framework of suicide attacks.

The Hizballah organization acted against Israeli targets, using suicide attacks outside of the Lebanese arena as well. In February 1992, the organization carried out a suicide attack using a car bomb that exploded near the Israeli Embassy in Buenos Aires. Twenty-nine people were killed and 250 were injured. The attack was carried out to avenge the termination of the organization's general secretary, Abas Musawi, in a raid carried out by IDF helicopters. Two years later, the organization carried out another suicide attack in Argentina, this time against the Jewish community's building (AMIA) in Buenos Aires. This attack came in response to a raid by the IDF Air Force against the Hizballah camp in Ein Dardara, which resulted in multiple casualties for the organization.

As stated earlier, Hizballah has served as a source of inspiration and instruction for the perpetration of suicide attacks by secular Lebanese organizations, as well as for Palestinian organizations such as the Palestinian Islamic Jihad and the Hamas or the Dawa organization in Kuwait. Although the Hizballah has carried out a relatively small number of suicide attacks since the 1990s, suicide attacks still remain its "business card," and an integral part of the organization's myth as well as a source of fear regarding additional attacks.

Iran and the Hizballah supported the Palestinians during the years of the Intifada (1973-1987). However, after the signing of the Oslo Agreements, Iran and the Hizballah positioned themselves at the head of the camp opposing peace and focused their support on Islamic terror organizations—the Hamas and the Palestinian Islamic Jihad—which began to perpetrate suicide attacks (through the adoption of the Hizballah's model) with the aim of torpedoing the peace process between the Palestinians and Israel.

Following are several examples of Iranian and Hizballah stances in this connection:

The Iranian Ayatollah Osama Fadi Lankrani made the following statement in a newspaper interview:[28]

> The aggression and oppression of the Zionists express their worldview which seeks to expand the rule of Zionism on to Muslim lands from the Nile to the Euphrates. It is the duty of Muslims in the occupied territories in Palestine and Lebanon and of every Muslim to fight a Holy War (Jihad) in any way possible without any restriction on the means that they use.

In an interview for the Al-Manar[29] television station, Hassan Nasrallah, secretary general of the Hizballah, stated that if it was the desire of the Palestinians to promote awareness of their problem in world public opinion, the right way to do so was through suicide attacks that would make bodies of men and women in Israel roll in the streets of Tel Aviv and Jerusalem. When asked why the Hizballah refrained from carrying out more suicide attacks, he explained that these activities should be perpetrated only when the goal cannot be achieved in other ways.

On September 5, 1997, after a Palestinian suicide attack in Jerusalem, Hassan Nasrallah said on Radio Nur:[30]

> Greetings to the holy martyrs who carried out the suicide attack yesterday in the heart of conquered Jerusalem, a mission which shocked the enemy and awakened the "devils" in the world. The mission proved the power of our nation yet again, its determination and desire to continue in its struggle and cause the enemy repeated defeats.

Suicide Attacks Perpetrated by the Hizballah against Israeli Targets in Lebanon

Suicide Attack against the IDF Headquarters in Tyre

On November 4, 1983, a car bomb exploded at the IDF headquarters in Tyre. The car, a Chevrolet, which was driven by a suicide terrorist, was loaded with some 500 kilograms of explosives. The driver rammed through the barrier at the entrance and despite the shooting in his direction managed to come within 5 meters of the structure. At that point he detonated the bomb. The powerful blast completely demolished one of the buildings and another was partially destroyed. Twenty-eight members of the security forces were killed in this incident and thirty-one were injured. In addition, thirty-three local residents, who were being detained in the building, were also killed.

1985 Suicide Attack against an IDF Convoy in Lebanon

On March 10, 1985, a suicide attack was perpetrated through the use of a GMC van loaded with some 100 kilograms of explosives. The latter was activated against an IDF convoy only a few hundred meters away from the border pass north of Metullah (the "Egel" gate). Twelve IDF soldiers were killed and another fifteen were injured. This was the suicide attack to claim the highest toll of fatalities from among IDF soldiers in Lebanon. The Hizballah claimed responsibility for the attack under the alias of "the Islamic Opposition."

1988 Suicide Attack against an IDF Convoy in Lebanon

On October 19, 1988, a suicide attack was carried out using a Toyota pickup truck loaded with some 250 kilograms of explosives against an IDF convoy at the border pass in Metullah. Eight soldiers were killed and seven more were wounded. The Hizballah claimed responsibility for the attack under the alias of "the Islamic Opposition."

1999 Suicide Attack against an IDF Convoy in Lebanon

On December 30, 1999, a suicide attack was perpetrated through a car bomb carrying explosive devices against an IDF convoy making its way from the headquarters of the communications unit in Marj Ayoun (located in the eastern sector) to "Fatma" gate. As a result of the explosion one IDF soldier and eleven Lebanese citizens were injured, in addition to the driver of the car. Next to the car were a hunting rifle, a forged identity card, and a copy of the Koran. The Hizballah publicly claimed responsibility for the incident, stating that it was perpetrated in commemoration of "Iranian Jerusalem Day" (which fell on December 31 that year), marking the anniversary of the death of the Imam Ali, founder of the Shia (which falls on December 28), as well as "Al-Qader" eve (which falls on the night between January 2-3). This was the first suicide attack carried out by the Hizballah since April 1995 and the last suicide attack before the IDF withdrawal from Lebanon in May 2000.

Suicide Attacks Perpetrated by the Hizballah in Buenos Aires, Argentina

In the beginning of the 1990s, the Hizballah, with Iranian assistance, perpetrated two suicide attacks in Buenos Aires against Israeli and Jewish goals.

- On March 17, 1992, a suicide attack was perpetrated against the Israeli Embassy in Buenos Aires.
- On July 18, 1994, a suicide attack was perpetrated against the Jewish cultural center (AMIA) in Buenos Aires.

The Attack against the Israeli Embassy in Buenos Aires

On March 17, 1992, a powerful explosion shook the Norte Quarter of Buenos Aires; a car bomb had detonated in front of the Israeli Embassy, demolishing the six-floor building. Twenty-nine people were killed including four Israelis and five Jews, all embassy employees. Two hundred and twenty-four individuals were wounded, including eight Israelis.

The Argentinean government immediately launched an investigation of the incident and the Israeli government dispatched a special team in order to investigate how the attack had happened and who bore responsibility for it.

The Islamic Jihad Organization (Hizballah had used this name in the past to claim responsibility for attacks) claimed responsibility immediately after the attack. However, out of fear of Israeli and international reprisals, the organization retracted its original announcement (on March 19), subsequently reassuming responsibility for the attack (on March 23).[31] The attack, which was apparently carried out by the Hizballah with Iranian assistance, was launched in reprisal against the termination of the secretary general of the Hizballah, Abas Musawi, by Israeli attack helicopters.[32]

Syrian President Hafez al-Assad announced in response to the attack that his country had no connection to the incident. In contrast, the chairman of the Iranian Parliament announced at a reception in honor of the new leader of the Hizballah, Sheikh Hassan Nasrallah, that Israel would be dealt ongoing blows of revenge in various areas of the world.

The investigation of the Argentinean authorities indicated that Imad Muraniya, a member of the Hizballah's attack special operations apparatus, stood behind the attack. He had availed himself of the assistance of Iranian intelligence entities in Argentina in order to obtain the required weapons and explosives, as well as documents for the assailants.[33] The Argentinean authorities disclosed that they had succeeded in proving that the truck that served as the attack vehicle had been purchased by a Brazilian citizen named Ruberio de Luz, who was suspected of having links with the entities that perpetrated the attack in Argentina via the tri-border (Argentina, Brazil, and Paraguay).[34]

In September 1999 (seven years after the attack), the Argentinean courts issued a warrant for the arrest of Imad Muraniya who was suspected of involvement in the attack. In an announcement published in Beirut, Hizballah denied Argentina's accusations and stated, "the accusation lacks any legal basis; it merely reflects political incitement and is not based on independent judgment. The fact that the judgment is based on information provided by the CIA, whose goals are known in advance, constitutes additional proof regarding the accusation's political nature." Hizballah appealed to the Argentinean government "not to become a victim of the American-Zionist conspiracies."[35]

The Attack against the Jewish Cultural Center (AMIA) in Buenos Aires

On July 18, 1994, at about 7:00 a.m., a car bomb exploded near a seven-story building that served as the cultural center of the Jewish community in Buenos Aires. There were ninety-seven fatalities and 230 casualties, most of whom were Jewish Argentineans. The "Islamic Commando—Hizballah Argentina" claimed responsibility for the attack.[36]

Following the attack, on July 19, an IDF rescue and evacuation team left for Argentina in order to assist the local authorities in handling the consequences of the attack against the Jewish community structure. During their work at the site, delegation members extricated sixty bodies of people who had been trapped in the rubble and eighteen body parts. The delegation returned to Israel on July 27, 1994.

The investigation launched by Argentinean security revealed that the cultural attaché of the Iranian Embassy, Muhsein Rabani, had been involved in the attack. He had gathered intelligence for the operation and purchased the car that served as the attack vehicle.[37] The investigation also revealed that four retired Argentinean policemen were involved, and had helped the Shiite and Iranian attackers to realize their intent. A short time after the attack, the Argentinean attorney general issued warrants of arrest for four Iranian diplomats, including Rabani, who had already left the country and never returned. Against the background of Argentina's accusations that Iranian entities had been involved in the attack, both countries recalled their ambassadors and diplomatic ties between the two countries were reduced to the level of economic attachés. Argentinean justice authorities and its intelligence identified Iran and Hizballah as the parties responsible for the attack. This was announced on October 2, 2002, by the attorney representing the organization of Jewish communities and state media.[38] Argentinean newspapers reported that the country would submit an official request to the Interpol to issue arrest warrants for the secretary general of the Hizballah, Hassan Nasrallah, and its senior leader Imad Muraniya, as well as several Iranian diplomats, for their involvement in the bombing of the Jewish community center in Buenos Aires. Juan Hose Galiano, the federal judge in Argentina who was appointed to the case, was quoted in the Saudi international daily *Al-Sharq al-Awsat* as saying that Argentina was requesting the extradition of the Hizballah leaders. Argentinean security entities were quoted in the local press as saying that the investigation had been conducted in cooperation with the American intelligence agency, the CIA.

The Hizballah responded in Beirut to these announcements and a source in the organization stated that the Hizballah "does not have branches outside of Lebanon." In the course of 2002, the Shiite organization was forced to deny several times that its activity had a "global dimension."

Advocate Marta Narchales, who represents the Jewish communities, stated "for the first time there are legal cases which contain evidence regarding the links of senior officials in the Iranian government and in the Hizballah, and their involvement in the preparation of the assault." Official entities in Argentina refused to respond to this statement. According to the advocate and the state media, the federal judge investigating the matter, Juan Hose Galiano, has recently gathered information based on the ongoing trial in Buenos Aires against entities defined as being involved in the affair.

This information is based on reports gathered by the counter-terror units and security services of Argentina. Narchales claimed to have read these reports, and her statement was based upon the latter. She argued that the names of the Iranian and Hizballah entities involved in the affair would be revealed shortly, but that at present their identities are not clear. If her claims are confirmed, it will be the first time since the attack that legal evidence will become available and Argentina will be able to prove, clearly and unequivocally, the assessments of intelligence entities in Israel and the United States, as well as the leaders of the Jewish community in Argentina. To date no one has been arrested as a suspect in this affair despite the prolonged investigation.

Immediately following the attack, Menem's government accused the Hizballah and Muslim radicals acting under Iran's sponsorship of being responsible for the attack. This accusation lost steam because of the snail's pace of the investigation, which was impaired due to the disappearance of witnesses, unexplained delays and obstacles placed in its way. To this day the nature of the impediments is not clear, but Iran has always denied any involvement in the attack.

Suicide Attacks Perpetrated by Pro-Syrian Secular Organizations in Lebanon

Starting from March 1985, the circle of perpetrators of suicide attacks in Lebanon was expanded by pro-Syrian secular organizations. These organizations were impressed with the Hizballah's success in forcing foreign forces to withdraw from Lebanon through the perpetration of suicide attacks and adopted this modus operandi as their main weapon against the Israeli forces and the South Lebanon Army in Lebanon.

The secular Lebanese organizations acted with Syria's blessing; the latter encouraged these organizations' activities against Israel, regarding them as a way of balancing the increasing success and growing influence of the Hizballah that acted under Iran's inspiration and influence. In contrast to the Hizballah members, who set out on suicide missions out of religious inspiration, volunteers from the secular organizations were motivated by nationalist reasons. Prior to setting out on a suicide mission they would pose for videotapes, which served as documented wills and as part of a ceremony that increased the volunteer's determination to execute the attack.

During the years 1985-1987, twenty-two suicide attacks were perpetrated by the following pro-Syrian secular organizations:

The Syrian National Party—eleven attacks
The Syrian Ba'ath Party—six attacks
The Lebanese Communist Party—two attacks
The Arab Socialist Union—one attack
The Nasserist/Socialist Organization—two attacks

In some of the attacks more than one organization claimed responsibility. Sometimes an attack was indeed carried out through the cooperation of several organizations.

The year 1985, when the IDF withdrew to the security buffer zone in South Lebanon, constituted a record year vis-à-vis suicide attacks (a total of twenty-two attacks). Out of this number, nineteen were perpetrated by pro-Syrian organizations. Seventeen attacks out of the nineteen used the modus operandi of a car bomb driven by a suicide terrorist and only two made use of explosive devices (against the South Lebanon Army headquarters in Hatzbaya and Aishea).

November 26, 1985 was the date of the first suicide attack perpetrated by a woman. A car bomb, driven by a female suicide attacker who was a member of the Syrian Ba'ath Party, exploded near the SLA roadblock at the village of Falus, injuring three Lebanese citizens. Another attempted suicide attack by a female terrorist took place on June 5, 1987, when a car bomb driven by the woman exploded on the Tyre–Siddon road, apparently as a result of a malfunction. There were no casualties.

The series of suicide attacks of the pro-Syrian organizations was apparently geared to serve a Syrian attempt to oust the IDF from Lebanon and thwart the establishment of the security buffer zone and the SLA. Therefore, these organizations focused their main efforts on weakening the SLA, which was at the initial stages of its establishment.

Despite the large number of suicide attacks, they caused a relatively low number of casualties. For example, in the nineteen suicide attacks perpetrated by pro-Syrian organizations in 1985, nine SLA soldiers were killed and seven were injured, and twenty-three Lebanese citizens were killed (in these attacks two IDF soldiers were also killed and two were wounded). The IDF sustained additional injuries that year as a result of Hizballah attacks. In 1986-1987, the activities of the pro-Syrian organizations waned in all areas, including that of suicide attacks (during these years the organizations perpetrated two suicide attacks a year), apparently due to the stabilization of the security buffer zone and the organizations' difficulty in establishing effective infrastructures in that zone.

The last suicide attack of the Syrian National Party was perpetrated in June 1989 when it attempted to carry out a suicide attack through the use of a fishing boat, but the attack failed. Since 1989 there have been no additional attempts perpetrated by pro-Syrian organizations and Hizballah again took the lead in this area in the Lebanese arena.

The Policy of the Hizballah and Iran vis-à-vis the Issue of Suicide Attacks after the IDF's Withdrawal from Lebanon

In May 2000, the IDF withdrew from Lebanon and redeployed along the line of the international boundary with Lebanon according to UN resolution 425. The Hizballah claimed credit for the IDF's withdrawal from Lebanon, but declared that this did not signify the end of the struggle against the State of Israel, as it argued that the latter was still occupying Lebanese land at the "Shaba Farms." The organization also declared its commitment to assist the Palestinian struggle against the Israeli occupation. Since May 2000, the Hizballah has continued perpetrating attacks against Israel, mainly in the "Shaba Farms" sector (Mount Dov area), but to date no actions have taken the form of a suicide attack. Although as stated above, the Hizballah decreased the perpetration of suicide attacks even during the IDF deployment in Lebanon, it still serves as a source of inspiration for Palestinian suicide attacks and encourages them to continue employing this method in the framework of the Al-Aksa Intifada. Iran, the Hizballah's patron, also aligned itself alongside the Palestinian Intifada, and its leaders provide the Palestinians with military aid (such as the shipment of weaponry aboard the ship *Karin A*), as well as political and moral support. Iranian religious clerics, and Iran's leader Ali Khamenai, grant religious legitimization and encourage the Palestinians to continue carrying out suicide attacks against Israel. Following are several examples of speeches delivered by Hizballah and Iranian leaders encouraging the Palestinians to conduct suicide attacks.

Speech Delivered by the Secretary General of the Hizballah Hassan Nasrallah on Jerusalem Day (Al Manar Television—December 14, 2001)

> Brothers and sisters, children of our nation, in view of the reverberating declarations of the American administration you have no other choice. Do you still have any illusions that by appealing to this great devil you will be able to restore a piece of land or honor? It has been decreed upon us, and this is not only within the bounds of an option, to struggle, to stand firm and hold fast to our rights and weapons. In Palestine the opposition will continue with suicide attacks (in the original: *al-Amaliat al-Istashadia*, meaning sacrificing one's life in martyrdom for the name of Allah), and the qualitative actions, and despite the many martyrs it is the only way to defeat these Zionists. Our brothers in Palestine, know that your actions have shaken the enemy from within and it is embroiled in an existential crisis. If these actions were for nothing, without value or benefit then why is there all this anger directed against you by the United States and Europe, and why is there all this rage in the Zionist society against you? This rage, this anger, and the concentration of the forces of arrogance constitute proof that your actions are striking at the heart and are laying the foundations for the victory that will not fail to come. What is required is to stand firmly and persevere. We must not make a mistake. On the last Friday of the Ramadan month I say to you: Do not listen to all of these people who tell you that you must not perpetrate suicide attacks (in the original: *al-Amaliat al-Istashadia*). Do not listen to all of those who speak of "civilians and soldiers" in Israel.

The suicide attacks (*al-Amaliat al-Istashadia*) are the shortest way to Allah, may He be exalted and praised. They are the most lofty and wondrous expressions of martyrdom in the name of Allah (*al-Istashad*). It is the weapon that Allah placed in hands of this nation and which no one can take away from us. They can take away our cannon or a tank or an airplane, but they cannot take away from us the spirit that yearns for Allah or our determination to sacrifice life in the name of Allah. As to the Zionist society, and I know that the words I am going to say to you cost a high price, I tell you with all legitimate, moral and "Jihad" responsibility that there are no civilians there. They are all conquerors, all are land stealers, and all are accomplices to the crime and the butchery. Therefore, we must continue on this road without any hesitation or illusion. As for Israel, it is the will of Allah and His promise, and the will of the believers, the Jihad fighters and suicide attackers (in the original *Istashadine*), that it will not have any existence and there will be no memory of it among us and among yourselves. Allah will pass judgment between them and us. Peace be with you, as well as Allah's compassion and blessings.

Speech Delivered by the Spiritual Leader of Iran (May 1, 2002)[39]

In a speech delivered on May 1, 2002, the spiritual leader of Iran, the Ayatollah Ali Khamenai, addressed the Israeli-Palestinian conflict and defined the acts that Israel committed in the territories of the Palestinian Authority as occupation, oppression, and crimes against humanity, and justified the martyrdom of the Palestinians as the just and legitimate choice in their struggle against Israel.

In response to the terrible oppression currently afflicting the Palestinian people there are two solutions. These solutions must be acceptable to everyone. The first solution is to continue the Intifada The people in Palestine must continue their opposition, praise to Allah, just as they have persevered with it until now. The climax of this opposition can be seen in the martyrdom seeking operations. Martyrdom is the pinnacle and symbol of human dignity: The youth, the boy and girl, who are willing to sacrifice their lives while serving the interests of their country and religion. This is the supreme expression of bravery and courage, and it is this which casts fear upon the enemy.

Therefore, we see that everyone, starting with the President of the United States and down to the last of his officials, have been trying to put an end to the acts of martyrdom and condemn their perpetrators.

Are these not acts of martyrdom when an army demands of its soldiers to sacrifice everything dear to them for the protection of the homeland? Are these not deeds of martyrdom when an enemy invades another country and its inhabitants oppose the conquering army? In such cases, who can condemn acts of martyrdom? Who can criticize these deeds and these values that are being conducted from the depth of their consciousness and awareness as human beings? The martyrdom of the Palestinians is the crowning glory of their struggle. This is the truth, even if there are those who deny fifty years of Palestinian suffering and struggle, and today they are left with no other choice but to sacrifice their blood in order to achieve their rights. The Palestinian people lives and is marching forward and this is the first solution."

Palestinian Suicide Attacks

The First Palestinian Suicide Attacks

The Islamic Palestinian terror organizations learned the modus operandi of suicide attacks from the Hizballah in Lebanon. Terrorists from the Hamas and the Palestinian Islamic Jihad organizations underwent terrorist training under the tutelage of the Hizballah and implemented everything they had learned in their struggle against Israel.

The first Palestinian terror attack took place on April 16, 1993.[40] A car bomb driven by a suicide terrorist from the Hamas exploded between two buses that were parked near the Mehola inn. As a result, seven soldiers were injured and a Palestinian employee of the inn was killed. The improvised explosive charge placed in the VW Transporter was estimated at about 150 kilograms and was activated via an electrical operating system.

Against the background of the signing of an agreement in principle between Israel and the PLO (September 1993) several suicide attacks were perpetrated by Islamic terror organizations, in an attempt to torpedo the agreement between Israel and the Palestinians.

In September 1993, a Hamas activist was arrested and during his questioning it was ascertained that he had attempted to perpetrate a suicide attack on a bus (line no. 23) near the Mahaneh Yehuda open-air market in Jerusalem. The terrorist boarded the bus with the device concealed in a backpack that he was carrying but the device malfunctioned and the would-be attacker returned it to the cell commander.

During the month of September 1993, a series of suicide attacks were perpetrated in the Gaza Strip:

- On September 12, a Peugeot 504 which was booby-trapped as a car bomb rammed into a bus transporting members of the Israel Prison Service. The car did not explode but its driver was seriously injured and subsequently died. The device did not detonate as planned, apparently as the result of a malfunction. The Hamas organization, "the Brigades of Az a-Din al-Kassam," claimed responsibility for the attack.
- On September 14, a suicide attacker carrying an explosive device on his body stormed the gate of the Gaza district police, ran towards the headquarters building and detonated himself at the entrance. The terrorist was killed. There were no casualties among the IDF soldiers and no damage was caused.
- On September 26, a Peugeot 504 was found burnt near the mosque at Sheikh Ajlin. The body of a terrorist was discovered in the car as well as the remnants of an explosive device, which had apparently exploded due to a malfunction. The Hamas claimed responsibility for the attempted attack. According to the organization's statement, the terrorist's intention was to perpetrate a suicide attack at the Netsarim settlement.

Later in 1993 additional suicide attacks were carried out in Judea and Samaria and in the Gaza Strip:

- On October 4, a Peugeot 104 driven by a suicide attacker stopped along-side a bus (no. 178) while passengers were disembarking near the gate of the Judea and Samaria headquarters (Beit El base). The car exploded and as a result the driver and thirty soldiers were wounded. The Hamas organization, "the Brigades of Az a-din al-Kassam," claimed responsibility for the attack.
- On October 25, a car bomb (a Peugeot), driven by a suicide terrorist, rammed into a car traveling in a convoy of the Civil Administration in Gaza. The car bomb failed to explode and the driver was arrested after attempting to flee.
- On November 2, a car bomb (a Subaru pickup truck) exploded in the morning hours on the road leading to Shilo. The car's driver was killed, and it appears that the device exploded as the result of a malfunction.
- On December 13, a terrorist carjacked an ambulance of the Red Crescent in Gaza. The ambulance was rapidly prepared as a car bomb and in the afternoon hours it veered towards a military jeep at the Sejaya intersection and tried to ram into it. The IDF forces shot at the ambulance, which exploded, and the driver, a Palestinian Islamic Jihad activist, was killed.

As mentioned, during 1993 nine suicide attacks were perpetrated, including attempted suicide missions. The majority (with the exception of one) was carried out through the use of a car bomb driven by a suicide terrorist. In three of the incidents the attackers in Gaza attempted to perpetrate the attack by ramming into an Israeli vehicle and detonating the device. In all of these attacks improvised explosives were installed in car bombs; the explosive devices included a combination of gas balloons with improvised explosive materials. All of the operating mechanisms were electrical. Most of the attacks during this year failed, apparently due to the lack of experience of those preparing the devices and that of the attackers.

Palestinian Terror Attacks during the Years 1994-2000[41]

During the reviewed period one can discern two main waves of suicide attacks:

- According to the Palestinians, the first wave was perpetrated in response to the massacre executed by Baruch Goldstein at the Machpelah Cave in Hebron (February 1994).
- The second wave was perpetrated in response to the termination of the "engineer," Yihya Ayash (January 1996).

During the years 1994-2000, a sum total of twenty-six suicide attacks and attempted attacks (including "work accidents") took place. All of the attacks were perpetrated by Islamic Palestinian terror entities, the Hamas, and the Palestinian Islamic Jihad (with the exception of two "work accidents" during 1999 in Tiberias and Haifa, in which three terrorists—Arab-Israelis [members of the Islamic movement]—were killed).

In suicide attacks during this period 163 Israelis were killed and 1,015 were injured. Most of the casualties were civilians. The majority of the suicide attacks were carried out within the "Green Line" (10 attacks) and Jerusalem (8 attacks). Seven attacks were perpetrated in the Gaza Strip. It is noteworthy that during this period no suicide attacks were perpetrated in Judea and Samaria. (The number of attacks includes a "work accident" in Nablus—the target of this attack was unknown.) The Hamas perpetrated the majority of suicide attacks during this period: sixteen attacks, while the Islamic Jihad carried out eight attacks.

An analysis of the distribution of the attacks over this period indicates that the years 1994 (6 attacks) and 1995 (8 attacks) were record years from the aspect of the number of suicide attacks. In 1996, the number of suicide attacks (four) dropped, but they caused a record number of Israeli fatalities (seventy dead, as compared to thirty-nine killed in 1994-1995).

From the aspect of method, the following characteristics are indicative of that period:

1. Most of the attacks were perpetrated by a lone attacker.
2. In four of the attacks there were two attackers (including one "work accident") and in a single attack three terrorists took part.
3. The attacks were perpetrated according to two main characteristics:
   - A suicide attacker/s carrying belt bombs or an explosive device in a bag which they detonated themselves at a target of their choosing
   - A suicide attacker/s in a vehicle who detonated it at the target of their choosing. In most cases a private vehicle or a van was used, with the exception of two cases in the Gaza Strip, one of which was perpetrated by a terrorist riding a bicycle and the other by a donkey-drawn cart.
4. The main targets for the attacks were:
   - Commercial and crowded places
   - Bus stops and or transportation depots for soldiers
   - Buses constituted central targets, and the attacks were perpetrated through the use of several methods:
     i. A terrorist boarded the bus and detonated himself (these attacks caused massive damage because the explosion took place in a closed area).
     ii. A terrorist detonated himself at a bus stop while a bus was standing at the bus stop.

iii. A car bomb exploded near a bus.

From the aspect of the attacks' timing there are three occasions when two attacks took place on the same day, sometimes with a geographical link:

- On April 9, 1995, two attacks occurred one after the other in the Gaza Strip: an attack at Kfar Darom (Islamic Jihad) and another at the Netsarim intersection (Hamas).
- On November 2, 1995, two attacks took place in the Gaza Strip at the Kisufim roadblock and at the Geffen roadblock; both were perpetrated by the Islamic Jihad.
- On February 25, 1996, two attacks were perpetrated by the Hamas, on Jaffa Street in Jerusalem and at a transportation depot for soldiers at the Ashkelon intersection.

During this period, seven suicide attacks were perpetrated in the Gaza Strip. The Islamic Jihad perpetrated five attacks and the Hamas two attacks. In several cases, there appeared to be cooperation between the two organizations in the perpetration of an attack. The majority of the attacks were carried out on thoroughfares against civilian and military vehicles, as well as against IDF roadblocks. The gravest attack in the Gaza Strip occurred on April 9, 1995, when a car bomb driven by a suicide terrorist detonated near a bus in Kfar Darom. Eight Israelis perished in the attack and thirty-six were wounded.

During this period, Jerusalem became a central target for attacks. Eight suicide attacks were perpetrated in Jerusalem; half of them were directed against buses and the remainder occurred in commercial areas and places of entertainment: at the Mahaneh Yehuda open-air market (two attacks), at the pedestrian mall, and on Yaffo Street. Ten attacks were perpetrated within the Green Line, four of them in Tel Aviv and Ramat Gan (against bus lines nos. 5 and 20 in Ramat Gan, the Dizengoff Center, and the Apropos Café). The cities Hadera, Afula, and the Beit Lid intersection, all situated near the border, also served as targets for suicide attacks.

The wave of attacks that took place in February-March 1996, which included four attacks that occurred in the course of eight days (two in Jerusalem—bus line no. 18, one in Tel Aviv—Dizengoff Center, and one in Ashkelon—a hitchhiking stop for soldiers), had far-reaching impact on public opinion and the political system in Israel, as well as on the results of the election that year. In consequence of the murderous attacks, heavy pressure was placed on the chairman of the Palestinian Authority, as a result of which for the first time he made a decision to take significant action against the Hamas and the Palestinian Islamic Jihad. In consequence of this decision, the Palestinian security services arrested hundreds of Hamas and Islamic Jihad members, large amounts of weapons were confiscated, and the infrastructure of the *dawa*, the civil-educational-economic infrastructure of the Hamas, was impaired.[42]

From 1996 until the outbreak of "Ebb and Flow" (i.e., the Al-Aksa Intifada), there was a consistent decrease in the number of suicide attacks, which was accompanied by a drop in the number of Israeli casualties (1997—3 attacks, 1998—3 attacks, 1999—2 attacks; 2000—no attacks until the outbreak of the "Ebb and Flow" incidents).

It is also important to note that in the course of the reviewed period there were relatively prolonged "time windows" without suicide attacks:

- March 1996–March 1997
- September 1997– July 1998
- November 1998–October 2000 (with the exception of "work accidents" in 1998 that took place in Tiberias and Haifa).

As stated, during the years 1996-2000 there was a decrease in the scope of suicide attacks due to action taken by the Palestinian Authority against the Hamas and Islamic Jihad, an intensive thwarting of activities on the part of the Israeli security forces, and even occasional security cooperation between the two sides.

During these years, several studies were conducted in order to characterize the phenomenon of suicide attacks. Several points emphasized in these studies follow:

In an article published by Professor Ariel Merari at the Woodrow Wilson International Center for Scholars,[43] he stated that in the 1980s, after the initial suicide terror attacks in Lebanon, such as the attack against the U.S. Embassy and the Marines Headquarters in Beirut, there existed a widespread concept according to which the perpetrator of suicide terror was seen as an Islamic fanatic who acts out of a deep religious urge and the desire to turn into an Islamic martyr (shahid). An examination of data related to suicide attacks and the biographies of the attackers indicated that half of the attacks were perpetrated by secular organizations whose attackers were not motivated by religion. Moreover, even among the Hizballah suicide attackers some did not have a radical religious background before their recruitment and preparations for the attack.

Professor Merari examined thirty-six cases of suicide attacks and attempted suicide attacks that took place in the years 1993-1996, in an effort to outline the profile of the Palestinian suicide attacker. He found that there are few joint identification lines among the Palestinian suicide attackers. The shared characteristics that he identified are as follows:

- A relatively young age (the average age was 22)
- Most of them were single
- The majority was not extremely religious
- None of them suffered from emotional (psychiatric) illness.

In his study, Merari reached the conclusion that suicide attacks constitute a phenomenon onto themselves that is not comparable to other destructive behavior.

> Professor Ehud Sprinzak also addresses perceptions that were prevalent in the past, namely that the suicide terrorist is a radical and isolated individual who acts out of deep religious consciousness.[44] Sprinzak claims that the suicide terrorist acts within and out of a wide organizational framework that directs his activity. While the suicide terrorist is willing to sacrifice his life for a goal that he perceives as worthy, the leaders of the terror organizations lack the desire to make martyrs of themselves, and act out of rational and cold considerations. For them and for the organization, the suicide attack is a modus operandi that offers several prominent advantages vis-à-vis other action methods. These advantages include the following:[45]

- Suicide attacks are simple and inexpensive in comparison to other modi operandi.
- Suicide attacks ensure the infliction of heavy casualties and damage upon the enemy as the suicide terrorist can choose the timing and venue of the attack in order to achieve the maximum damaging effect.
- There is little chance of the terrorist falling into the enemy's hands and divulging information about the organization, because his objective is to perish in the attack.
- Suicide attacks have significant psychological impact on the enemy's public opinion and decision-makers.

The various terror organizations have used the suicide terror weapon in different ways. There are organizations that used this tool infrequently and not methodically, while other organizations turned the suicide attacks into a strategy. An organization's decision to utilize or cease utilizing suicide attacks usually stems from rational cost/benefit considerations affected by the adversary's response and changes in public opinion, both within the population in whose name the organization functions and in the adversary's population, as well as in the international system.[46] The suicide attack is usually carried out by a lone attacker; however, the execution of the attack involves many members of the terror organization, each of whom has designated tasks that ultimately enable the action of the lone attacker. Thus, the suicide attack must not be regarded as the act of an individual but rather as an action that is primarily organizational and social.

Examples of Palestinian Suicide Attacks during the Years 1994-2000

The attack at Kfar Darom. On April 9, 1995, at 12:00, a car bomb driven by a suicide terrorist detonated alongside a bus near the Kfar Darom settlement. Seven soldiers and one tourist were killed. Thirty-one soldiers and five civilians were injured, all passengers on the bus. The device used in the car bomb included dozens of kilograms of standard TNT explosives, "Satchi" Italian anti-tank mines (used by the Egyptian army), Egyptian-made anti-personnel landmines, improvised explosives (apparently the triacetone type), a regular detonator converted into an electrical one, and a quantity of lead shot consisting of nails which caused most of the fatalities. The explosive device, which was covered by a pile of straw and a sheet of canvas, did not detonate fully so in the attack arena there remained three anti-tank landmines and three anti-personnel landmines which were neutralized subsequently. The attack was perpetrated by Khaled al-Khatib, a twenty-four-year-old Palestinian Islamic Jihad activist, who was a resident of the Nuzirat refugee camp.

The attack at the Netsarim intersection. On April 9, 1996, at 13:45, a car bomb driven by a suicide terrorist exploded in a convoy of Israeli vehicles near the Netsarim intersection. Two soldiers were injured in the explosion in addition to ten civilians. As a result of the blast, there were no remains of the explosive device, but the police demolition department determined that the device contained scores of kilograms of TNT, and no lead shot was added. Imad Abu Amunah, a twenty-four-year-old Hamas activisit and a resident of the Shati refugee camp, perpetrated the attack. The Islamic Jihad and the Hamas publicly claimed responsibility for the attack, as well as for an additional attack that was carried out on the same day at Kfar Darom (also by a suicide terrorist), explaining that the attacks had been executed to avenge an explosion that had taken place on April 2 at a residence in the Sheikh Raduwan quarter in Gaza (which had been attributed to Israel), and in retaliation against the continued arrests of Hamas and Islamic Jihad activists by the Palestinian Authority. In their announcement the two organizations stated that they would perpetrate additional attacks against Israel, and warned the Palestinian Authority not to arrest their members.

Suicide attacks in Jerusalem and Ashkelon. On February 25, 1996, two suicide attacks occurred, one after the other, causing scores of deaths and casualties: Majdi Abu-Varda, a Hamas suicide terrorist from the Al-Fuar refugee camp in the Hebron area, detonated an explosive device on bus line no. 18 at the intersection of Yaffo and Sarei Israel streets in Jerusalem. Twenty-six people perished in the attack (one died later of his injuries on April 13, 1996), including nine soldiers and seventeen civilians. Forty-seven individuals were injured including thirteen soldiers and thirty-four civilians.

Ibrahim Tsarakhna, a Hamas suicide terrorist also from the Al-Fuar refugee camp, detonated an explosive device at the soldiers' transportation stop at the Ashkelon intersection. A woman soldier was killed and twenty-nine were injured, including seventeen soldiers and twelve civilians.

A Hamas cell activated by Hassan Salameh, a senior activist in the organization's military branch in Gaza, perpetrated these attacks. In declarations and anonymous calls to the media, in which the organization members claimed responsibility for the attacks under the name "cells of the martyr Yihya Ayash—the new pupils," they stated that the attacks were meant to avenge Ayash's death, and mark the second anniversary of the massacre in the Machpelah Cave in Hebron.

Salameh infiltrated the "Green Line" in June 1996 with the assistance of criminal elements in Gaza and among Israeli Arabs. He stayed in the Israeli city of Ramla for a period of time and then moved to the Ramallah area in the West Bank. Salameh smuggled in weapons, explosives, and additional sabotage materials, which he hid in the Yavne-Ashdod area. During his stay in the West Bank, via Muhammad Abu-Varda, a minor Hamas activist from the Al-Fuar refugee camp, Salameh recruited volunteers for three attacks (the three were Abu-Varda's relatives or friends)—Majdi Abu-Varda (bus line no. 18 on February 25), Ibrahim Altsrakhna (Ashkelon, February 25), both from the Al-Fuar refugee camp, and Rajib Sharnubi (attack on the no. 18 bus on March 3, 1996).

Salameh assembled the devices in a house belonging to the Hamas cell at Ras al Amud in Jerusalem (the members of this Jerusalem cell, headed by Iman Razem, helped gather intelligence for the mission, and aided with concealment, transporting and leading the suicide terrorists to their targets). The explosive devices detonated at each of the suicide attacks were similar. They were composed of TNT crushed into pellets to facilitate the explosion, metal ball bearings to increase the distribution effect, and an electrical operating apparatus. The devices were carried in khaki side bags. In the explosion detonated on the no. 18 bus in Jerusalem, they used about 10 kilograms of explosives, and in Ashkelon they used 5-8 kilograms of explosives. In both attacks, collaborators transported the suicide terrorists to a short distance from the target. The suicide terrorists wore khaki-colored clothing and military paraphernalia to emulate the appearance of soldiers.

After the attacks, the IDF enforced a closure on Judea, Samaria, and the Gaza Strip, and initiated widespread arrests in the area under its control in the West Bank. The Palestinian Authority (responding to U.S. and Israeli pressure) also initiated intensive activity against the Hamas and carried out arrests that led to the apprehension of Muhammad Abu-Varda, among others.

The Suicide Attack on the No. 18 Bus in Jerusalem. On March 3, 1996, at 6:45 a.m., a powerful explosive device carried by suicide terrorist and Hamas activist Rajib Sharnubi detonated on bus line no. 18 at the intersection of Heshin and Yaffo Streets in central Jerusalem. The device contained about 10 kilograms of

TNT and nails. This attack was perpetrated by the same cell that had carried out the attacks in Jerusalem and Ashkelon on February 25, 1996. The Hamas claimed responsibility for the attack. Three IDF soldiers and sixteen civilians were killed, and six Israeli civilians sustained medium to serious injuries.

The suicide attack at Dizengoff Center in Tel Aviv. On March 4, 1996, in a suicide attack perpetrated in Tel Aviv, Ramez Avid, an Islamic Jihad activist from Gaza, detonated a large explosive device at a zebra crossing near Dizengoff Center. Fourteen Israelis were killed and 125 were injured in the attack. After the attack, as a result of Israeli pressure, the Palestinian police carried out a series of arrests, during which some 800 Hamas and Islamic Jihad activists were rounded up.

Palestinian suicide attacks in the Al-Aksa Intifada—main characteristics. Since the beginning of the Al-Aksa Intifada approximately 123 attacks have been perpetrated.[47] The phenomenon of suicide attacks, which until 2001 was an operational tool exclusive to the Islamic terror organizations, that is, the Hamas and Islamic Jihad, currently serves all of the different types of organizations including secular organizations such as the Fatah (and its various factions) and the Popular Front for the Liberation of Palestine. Moreover, suicide attacks have become a norm in Palestinian society.

As stated in the Israeli daily newspaper *Maariv*: "Today suicide attacks are no longer perceived as an act of desperation, disappointment or revenge but rather as hopeful attacks. The goal of the attack is not killing for killing's sake but rather a means to break Israel's staying power—to destroy the society and crush its economy…"[48]

An interesting expression of these ideas can be gleaned from an article by Amira Hess entitled "The suicide attacker is a happy person who loves life."[49] The article contains an interview with Osama Mazini, a Ph.D. in psychology at the Islamic University in Gaza. Mazini claims that personal desperation is not what impels the suicide attackers, but rather a national objective. The feeling of general fury and the patriotic desire to facilitate the struggle for liberation and independence are the main motives for the suicide attacks. Mazini states: "Psychologically one must differentiate between someone who puts an end to his life because of emotional suffering and the istashad, who is a happy person that loves life, an individual with inner strength." Among other factors, Mazini bases this statement on his acquaintance with several Lebanese and a Palestinian with whom he served time in prison at the beginning of the 1990s; they had been caught prior to setting out on suicide attacks. Mazini was a Hamas activist sentenced to six years imprisonment (after six months under administrative arrest). He was released within eleven months (before completing his sentence) in the framework of the prisoners' release under the Oslo Agreements.

"Anyone going out to fight an Israeli soldier," explained Mazini "knows that chances are that he will never return, because the Israeli soldier is trained, skilled and has more weapons. Thus, psychologically, anyone who goes out to fight a soldier wearing a belt bomb—there is the similarity. They are similar in the tension that impels them to endanger themselves." Mazini claims, "The Israelis have a central role in impelling the young men to choose a martyr's death. The random deaths that we have experienced during the months of the Intifada have caused each young man to say 'if I am doomed to die arbitrarily, why shouldn't I go and die honorably?' This inner discussion has generated tension, and the tension awakens excitement to the point that thought is neutralized. Thus, the will to take risks grows."

Mazini adds that the religious promise of eternal life in the Garden of Eden plays a central role. "Life on earth is dear to every person, so it is not easy to relinquish it for happiness in the world to come. He who chooses to be a martyr is not ending his days but rather extending them, and therefore the martyrdom (perishing in the name of Allah) is really a love of life." According to Mazini, the promise of 72 virgins shows how far before Freud the Islamic religion understood sexual urges (for men far more than women, Mazini is convinced. Therefore, the woman-shahid must be satisfied with one man throughout eternal life.) "The promises in the Koran and in Islam correspond to human nature."

Dr. Iyad Saraj, a Palestinian psychiatrist who heads the "program for mental health in Gaza," states that "the potential pool of those willing to become shahidim has grown stronger," and correlates between the rise in the number of suicide terrorists and desperation among the Palestinians, which he claims has reached its peak. According to Dr. Saraj, the "typical suicide attacker" has several characteristics, the most prominent of which is "a traumatic experience linked to the Israeli presence in the territories." He states, "we must keep in mind that today's suicide attackers are the children who saw their parents humiliated and struck by IDF soldiers during the first Intifada and they are ashamed that they did nothing to stop it. So they are impelled by a strong sense of revenge motivated by those personal scars."

An examination of the targets of the suicide attacks indicates two main trends:

- Most of the suicide attacks were carried out within the "Green Line" and Jerusalem.
- The targets of the attacks were "civilian" oriented (modes of transportation, crowded places at shopping and entertainment centers).

This stands in contrast to the status at the boundaries of the "Green Line," in the areas of Judea, Samaria, and the Gaza Strip, where most of the suicide attacks were perpetrated against military targets, causing a relatively low number of casualties due to the preparedness and better protection of the IDF forces.

The Palestinian leadership views suicide attacks as a weapon and a means to provide the Palestinians with deterrence and strategic balance vis-à-vis Israel. The phenomenon of the suicide attackers is not a marginal one in Palestinian society but rather the reflection of a new social norm that has earned the encouragement and support of the general public. This is expressed in the manifestations of joy after each suicide attack, at the suicide attackers' funerals, in their pictures plastered on every street corner, in the glorification afforded to them in the Palestinian media, and in Palestinian public opinion polls. In Palestinian terminology, even the official kind, there is no mention of suicide operations but rather of acts of martyrdom.

During the events of "Ebb and Flow" (October 2000-December 2003) Palestinian terror entities perpetrated over 20,000 attacks. Of these, 123 attacks were characteristic suicide attacks. Thus it appears that quantitatively suicide attacks constitute less than 1 percent of all attacks carried out during the said period. An examination of the number of fatalities as a result of suicide attacks indicates that about 900 Israelis were killed in these attacks.[50] (50 percent of all Israeli victims killed during this period died in suicide attacks)

These data testify to the grave significance of the suicide attacks and the conversion of "suicide attacks" into a highly effective strategic weapon that is at the disposal of the Palestinians in the confrontation against Israel.

The Background and Reasons for the Increase in Suicide Attacks

The dramatic increase in the scope of suicide attacks since the beginning of the current confrontation stems from a combination of several motives and reasons.

1. The renewal of the armed struggle against Israel—Arafat's strategic decision to renew the armed struggle against Israel, and the view that the current struggle constitutes a momentous test prior to the establishment of a Palestinian state, has generated an atmosphere on the Palestinian streets calling for unity among the ranks and Palestinian martyrdom to achieve this goal. The mobilization of all of the organizations and mechanisms to further this struggle has enabled the Hamas and Islamic Jihad to initiate the recruitment of suicide attackers without disruption from the Palestinian Authority, and sometimes with its encouragement, and to perpetrate suicide attacks inside Israel and the territories.

   Since October 2001, the circle of perpetrators of suicide attacks has widened to include secular organizations such as the Popular Front and the Martyrs of the Al-Aksa Brigades—a branch of the Fatah which has even undertaken the lead in the area of perpetrating suicide and martyrdom attacks.

2. Reinforcement of the religious and ideological motive—The motivation in Islamic circles, which was also existent in the past, has been reinforced due to the recognition that during this time the Palestinians are involved

in a Jihad and existential struggle against Israel. The extensive popular solidarity, the incitement in the Palestinian media and the Palestinian Authority's support for suicide attacks, have significantly fortified the motivation of those dispatching the suicide attackers and the attackers themselves in the Palestinian streets. Alongside the religious motivation, in recent months motivation and recognition among secular circles have developed regarding the importance of carrying out suicide attacks for a secular ideological reason, based on the view that suicide attacks are the ultimate weapon the Palestinians possess in their struggle against Israel.

3. The increased deterioration within the Palestinian Authority—The grave economic and social conditions in the area of the Palestinian Authority due to the many months of combat, accompanied by closures and heavy restrictions imposed upon the lifestyles of the Palestinian general public, and the lack of hope or signs indicating any upcoming political solution have all increased the feelings of frustration, desperation, and hatred towards Israel. The deaths and injuries of many Palestinians, including prominent political and military activists, also contribute to the generation of an individual and communal thirst for revenge, which is often translated into the readiness of young Palestinian men and women to perpetrate suicide attacks.

In interviews with several "suicide attackers" apprehended prior to perpetrating their mission, the most prominent claim was that life in the current reality in the Authority's territory has little value in the eyes of the potential suicide. Therefore, he prefers to find the solutions to current day distress and the lack of hope in this world through a suicide attack that will ensure happiness in the next world, and which is also sometimes accompanied by various benefits for the "shahid's" families, thanks to various contributions and the enthusiasm of the Palestinian public for the families of its heroes.

Professor Khalil Shkaki[51] pointed out in an article the changes that have taken place in Palestinian public opinion as a result of the renewal of the violent struggle between the Palestinians and Israel at the end of September 2002. He claims that there has been a significant increase in the amount of support for violence against Israelis among the Palestinians; in December 2001 over 82.6 percent of the population supported violence against Israel and 16 percent opposed it; this compares to 52 percent that supported violence against Israel in July 2001 and 43 percent that opposed violence.

In July 2001, 71 percent of the Palestinians felt that violence pays off in comparison to 57 percent who believed this in July 2000. These findings and others reinforce the claim regarding an essential shift towards radicalism and escalation currently influencing the Palestinian people, which impacts on the degree of their support for suicide attacks and the willingness of young Palestinians to be recruited for suicide attacks.

An additional survey conducted by the Palestinian Policy and Public Opinion Research Center under Shkaki's direction on August 18-20, 2002, indicated that 70 percent of Palestinians believe that the armed struggle will facilitate the achievement of national rights more than negotiations. The survey also indicates that 52 percent of the Palestinian public support suicide attacks inside Israel.[52]

In mid-June 2002, a petition was published that called for the cessation of suicide attacks in Israel, because these acts are against Palestinian interests. The petition aroused considerable interest in Israel and public criticism among the Palestinians. An interesting aspect vis-à-vis this issue can be gleaned from the article written by Amira Hess where she states, "The petition published in mid-June which called for reexamination of the suicide attack method in Israel was signed by someone named Dr. Sa'adia Takhla. This is what was sent to a fax number in Jerusalem, with that name placed at the bottom of the petition, and published in a second round with the names of supporters. But Sa'adia Takhla is no longer among the living and was never a doctor; for years she was known as the lunatic of Gaza, and was the object of scorn and pity. Someone relying on Takhla's anonymity in Jerusalem found this way to express his true opinion of the petition, its content and signatories, which in Gaza as well as in the West Bank underwent a gamut of defamation until plummeting to the level of de-legitimization.[53]

The Attacks according to a Division to Periods

Suicide attacks in the year 2000—the first months of the Al-Aksa Intifada (October 1, 2000-January 1, 2001). In the first months of the Al-Aksa Intifada, four suicide attacks took place, all of them outside of the "Green Line" boundaries: Three occurred in the Gaza Strip and one at an inn at the Mehola settlement in the Jordan Valley. Four soldiers were injured in these attacks. Three of the four attacks were carried out by the Hamas and one by the Islamic Jihad. Two of the attacks in the Gaza Strip were perpetrated against an IDF outpost and roadblock. In two of the incidents a single terrorist carried out the attack, either by detonating an explosive device or a belt bomb that he carried on his body. In one of the cases, the terrorist approached the outpost on a bicycle.

On November 6, 2000, for the first time in the Palestinian arena a suicide attack took place in the form of a boat bomb that approached a "Dabur" of the IDF navy in the Rafiah region. There were no casualties. The Hamas claimed credit for the attack. Starting in January 1, 2001, a significant change took place in the scope of suicide attacks and their targets; most of the terror organizations reverted to attempts to perpetrate attacks that involved mass killing, mainly against the civilian population in Jerusalem and inside the "Green Line" (similar to their characteristic operations in the years 1994-2000).

Suicide attacks in March-September 2001.[54] From March 2001 there was a sharp increase in the scope of suicide attacks. This trend continued until September 11, 2001, a date that constituted a milestone with far-reaching repercussions on the issue of suicidterrorism. During these months (March 1, 2001-September 9, 2001) there were twenty-three suicide attacks.[55] Sixteen were perpetrated by the Hamas and seven by the Palestinian Islamic Jihad. Most of the attacks occurred within the "Green Line" (14 attacks) and took a high toll on human life. Among the most prominent attacks was the one at the Dolphinarium, two attacks in Netanya, the attack at the Sebarro restaurant in Jerusalem, and the attack at the train station in Nahariya.

The intensification of the attacks apparently stemmed from the "green light" given by the Palestinian Authority to the Hamas and Islamic Jihad organizations to step up their activities, as well as the "maturation" of the operational infrastructures of these organizations mainly in the Samaria region.

Sheikh Ahmad Yassin and other official representatives of the Hamas gave several reasons that they claimed justified the attacks against Israeli civilians.[56] Sheikh Ahmad Yassin told representatives of Amnesty International in July 2001 that according to international law, "We are entitled to protect ourselves against aggression using any means." He also stated that the Hamas opposes attacks against civilians, especially women and children, but if these occur by mistake or in order to implement the principle of an eye for an eye, then this must be considered a legitimate form of retaliation. In his opinion, when the Hamas killed Israeli children, the responsibility for this must be placed on Israel because Israel, by causing the deaths of Palestinian children, provoked a response.

Sheikh Yassin added that the Hamas is ready to stop attacking Israeli civilians if Israel ceases its attacks against Palestinian civilians. He also proposed an agreement under international sponsorship that would be similar to the agreement between Israel and the Hizballah, in which both sides undertook not to attack civilians.[57] Another senior representative of the Hamas, Abd al-Aziz al-Rantisi, described the attacks against civilians as retaliatory actions and stated in May 2002: "As long as Jews continue to massacre Palestinians, we will strike in Haifa, Tel Aviv, and Afula. If a Palestinian child is hurt, we will strike back. That is the formula."[58]

Position holders in the Hamas were quoted as saying that the "actions to sanctify the Lord" will continue because they are considered a legitimate and effective way of fighting the Israeli occupation.[59] For example, when the PA denounced a suicide attack by a terrorist which caused fatalities among Israeli civilians in March 2002, Hamas spokesman Mahmoud Zaher stated that the denunciation of the Palestinian Authority does not represent Palestinian or Arab public opinion, and it would not prevent the Hamas from perpetrating additional attacks. He also clarified that according to the Hamas sages the attack is "the highest level of sanctifying God," and that no one from the Palestinian side, or from the opposition movement or even from the Arab public can denounce these sanctifying acts "that are justified according to our sages."[60]

An expression of the feeling of success stemming from the suicide terror campaign is discernible in an interview granted by Sheikh Ahmad Yassin to the British newspaper, *The Observer*.[61] "The use of suicide terrorists is the democratic right of the Palestinians anywhere in the world. That is the only democracy that Israel recognizes: That is the price that we pay for liberty," stated Yassin, in response to the closure that Israel enforced on the territories and the high economic price that the Palestinians are paying for the Intifada. "The Israelis do not feel like mounting an offensive and they will drop to their knees. You can already feel the fear that exists in Israel; they are anxious all the time, when and where the next attack will take place. In the end, the Hamas will win."

The September 11, 2001 Attacks in the United States and Their Effect on Suicide Attacks in Israel

The attacks of September 11, 2001, which caused the deaths of over 3,000 people in the United States and instigated a tough response by the United States government, brought an immediate if temporary cessation of attacks in the Palestinian arena. On the very same day, the Palestinian Authority declared a ceasefire, denounced the attacks in the United States and rushed to prevent any parades of joy or expressions of solidarity with Bin-Laden, who was behind the attacks in the United States. A short time after the September 11 attacks, seventeen Palestinian groups declared their condemnation "of the attacks that were directed against the innocent."[62]

Among the signatories, who called themselves "Islamic and national Palestinian forces," were armed organizations that had claimed responsibility for attacks against civilians in Israel and the territories. They did not see any contradiction between the condemnation that they expressed against the massacre of innocent citizens in the United States and the situation in Israel and the occupied territories:

> When we repeat our unequivocal condemnation of terror, we will not tolerate the definition of our legitimate struggle against the invasion of our lands as such. Therefore, we call upon the entire world to distinguish between terror and a legitimate struggle against conquest, which is acceptable according to the principles of religion and international conventions.

The Palestinian Authority, and possibly Arab states (like Saudi Arabia), put heavy pressure on the Hamas and the Palestinian Islamic Jihad to refrain from carrying out suicide attacks, at least within the "Green Line," out of the fear that in the international atmosphere that had come about, these actions would be defined as acts of terror, and their perpetrators would be renounced as terror organizations and included on the U.S. "black list." Moreover, the PA feared that in the new circumstances the United States would grant Israel carte blanche and enable it to strike out at the Authority beyond the restrictions that had been set in the past. In order to improve his international standing and create a distinction between Palestinian activities and Bin-Laden's terror, Arafat rushed to make his declaration that the PA stands alongside the United States in its war against terror.

September 11, 2001, however, had a short-term "preventive effect" from the aspect of suicide attacks in the Palestinian arena; a short time after the American policy was clarified and the immediate targets of the war against terror were defined, the Hamas and Islamic Jihad renewed their activities and suicide attacks with vigor.

In the short term, the September 11 attacks caused a brief lull in the perpetration of suicide attacks, but in the long term the intensity and targets of these attacks became a source of inspiration for radical Islamic entities, along with the increased awareness that the suicide tool is the main strategic weapon at the disposal of radical Islam in its struggle against the superior strength of the United States and in the Middle East arena—Israel. The few voices that were heard among the Islamic religious clerics condemning the suicide attacks in the United States were gradually silenced, and a wave of religious rulings, siding with martyrdom in the name of Islam, became the dominant message (among which the most prominent were the rulings of Sheikh Kardawi, who is considered one of the most influential clerics in the radical Islamic circles).

The first suicide attacks after September 11 were already perpetrated in early October (on October 7 a suicide attack initiated by the Islamic Jihad took place near Kibbutz Shluchot in the Beit Shean valley). On October 17, a secular Palestinian organization joined the circle of perpetrators of suicide attacks for the first time. A terrorist from the Popular Front detonated himself with a belt bomb near the Karni Pass in the Gaza Strip, injuring two Israelis. Since the end of November 2001, there has been an intensive renewal of the series of suicide attacks, including within the "Green Line" and Jerusalem.

Suicide Attacks after September 11, 2001

As stated above, a short time after the events of September 11, 2001, the Palestinian terror attacks were renewed. By the end of 2001, eleven suicide attacks had been perpetrated. Thirty-three Israelis were killed and 257 were injured in these attacks. Five of the attacks were perpetrated by the Hamas. On December 15, a suicide attack was attempted for the first time by the Fatah, near an IDF outpost in the West Bank.

In the beginning of 2002, suicide attacks, and the multiple casualties caused by them, became the main characteristic of these attacks. The relative portion of casualties among the civilian population (in comparison to the security forces) rose dramatically, and feelings of uncertainty, insecurity, and frustration were widespread among the Israeli population. The climax of the series of suicide attacks was in March, in the course of which seventeen suicide attacks took place, causing eighty Israeli fatalities and 497 injuries.[63]

Against the background of the intolerable escalation in the number of suicide attacks, the State of Israel initiated the "Defense Shield" campaign (March 29-April 25, 2002), aimed at destroying the terror infrastructure in the areas of the Palestinian Authority and minimizing the number of attacks as much as possible. The Defense Shield campaign and the perpetual operational activity of the IDF in Judea and Samaria brought about a significant decrease in the scope of the attacks in general and a temporary reduction in the number of suicide attacks in particular.

However, even during the campaign several (10) suicide attacks took place and a short while after the campaign ended the number of attacks increased. Starting in January 2002, the Fatah and all its various factions became the dominant organization carrying out suicide attacks. If one adds to this number the attacks perpetrated by the Popular Front, it becomes clear that the secular organizations carried out a larger number of suicide attacks than the Hamas and Islamic Jihad. Most of the attacks were leveled against civilian targets in Jerusalem and within the "Green Line," and only a few were directed against the military. During the period following the end of the "Defense Shield," until December 2003, fifty-three suicide attacks were perpetrated while about 150 suicide attacks were thwarted during the same period.[64] Forty-three attacks were perpetrated within the Green Line and Jerusalem, three in the area of the Gaza Strip, and six attacks in the Judea and Samaria. During this period, the Fatah and the Hamas were the leading organizations in perpetrating suicide attacks.

Since the "Defense Shield" operation there has been a significant decrease in the scope of successful suicide attacks. The decrease in the number of attempts to perpetrate attacks attests not to the fact that there was a drop in the motivation of Palestinians to carry out attacks, but that there was considerable improvement in the thwarting capabilities of the Israeli security forces.

To summarize, it is possible to indicate several new trends in the area of suicide attacks since the beginning of the Al-Aksa Intifada in comparison to the previous suicide attacks (1999-2000):

- The scope of the attacks. Since the beginning of the Al-Aksa Intifada, 123 suicide attacks were perpetrated. Two hundred fifty-five attempted attacks were thwarted.

- The drastic increase in the scope of attacks stems from the fact that the secular organizations (mainly the Fatah and the Popular Front) joined the ranks of the suicide attack perpetrators. From 2002, the Fatah became the leading organization in the perpetration of suicide attacks.
- For the first time, suicide attacks were perpetrated by Palestinian women (6 suicide attacks). In addition, several women intending to carry out suicide attacks were arrested before setting out on the mission or after they had reconsidered.
- There is indication of a growing trend vis-à-vis the involvement of Israeli Arabs in collaboration and perpetrating attacks.

Suicide Attacks by Secular Palestinian Organizations

Throughout all the years of the Palestinian-Israeli struggle, suicide attacks were the exclusive expertise of the Islamic organizations, the Hamas and the Islamic Jihad. From October 2001, the ranks of suicide attack perpetrators were joined by secular organizations as well. The first was the Popular Front, which carried out a suicide attack in the area of the Karni Pass in the Gaza Strip on October 17, 2001.

On December 15, 2001, a suicide terrorist exploded near an IDF roadblock in the West Bank. It is not clear if this was a first suicide attack attempt by the Fatah or whether it was a "work accident," and the attacker had intended to detonate himself elsewhere. In any case, a suicide attack was perpetrated in January at the "Armon David" hall in Hadera, and the Martyrs of the Al-Aksa Brigades claimed responsibility.[65] The first discernible suicide attack of the Fatah was carried out on January 27 in Jerusalem. During this period, the Popular Front executed five suicide attacks. All together secular organizations perpetrated twenty suicide attacks during this time span.[66]

The addition of the secular organizations, mainly the Fatah and its factions, to the ranks of suicide attackers caused a significant increase in the scope of the attacks, and even created a kind of competition between the organizations regarding the execution of suicide attacks.

The first half of 2002 was a record period in the perpetration of suicide attacks. During this time span the number of suicide attacks (45 attacks) exceeded the number of attacks during the entire period from the beginning of the Al-Aksa Intifada (the end of September 2000) until January 2002 (about 40 attacks). The month of March 2002 constituted the climax of the series of suicide attacks; the Fatah was the organization to carry out the largest number of attacks.

The Al-Aksa Intifada created a completely different reality compared to the previous period (1994-2000) when suicide attacks were carried out by the Hamas and Islamic Jihad, and the policy of the PA fluctuated between different approaches: from encouraging the attacks, to joint activity with Israel to thwart the suicide attacks. In the framework of the Al-Aksa

Intifada, the PA encouraged the Hamas and the Islamic Jihad to carry out suicide attacks, and from December 2001 onwards it adopted suicide attacks as a strategic weapon against the State of Israel and began activating the Fatah and all its factions in the perpetration of these attacks. This strategic decision constitutes a substantial shift in the relationship pattern between the PA and the State of Israel, and forced Israel to plan a new action strategy, which expressed itself in the Defense Shield campaign, as stated above.

As long as there is no substantial change in the policy of the PA, the suicide attacks will continue to serve as a strategic weapon in the hands of the Palestinians, along with the moral legitimization and operational support for their perpetration. These attacks will continue to constitute a major threat against the security of the inhabitants of the State of Israel.

Suicide Attacks by Palestinian Women

In the course of the Al-Aksa Intifada, for the first time, suicide attacks were perpetrated by Palestinian women. Thirty-five women were involved in suicide attacks, five of whom exploded and the rest were apprehended. All of the women who executed suicide attacks were sent by the Fatah organization (with the exception of one, who was apparently activated by the Fatah and the Palestinian Islamic Jihad).

The Hamas's approach to the issue of suicide attacks perpetrated by women underwent several changes. In the mid-1990s, the leader of the Hamas, Sheikh Ahmad Yassin, claimed that Islam did not allow the participation of women in martyrdom missions (Istashad). And indeed, in the Hamas attacks during the years 1995-2000 Palestinian women did not take part.[67]

However, during the Al-Aksa Intifada, after two Palestinian women perpetrated suicide attacks (January 27, February 27, 2002) Sheikh Yassin stated in an interview for Abu-Dhabi television that in the current confrontation women may perpetrate suicide missions (Istashad).[68] It would appear that Sheikh Yassin adapted his ruling to the times. Nevertheless, despite this ruling, no suicide attack perpetrated by a woman representing the Hamas has been recorded to date.

The spiritual leader of the Hizballah also expressed his opinion about the issue of suicide attacks perpetrated by women and claimed, "it is permitted for women to perpetrate suicide attacks during the Jihad." He stated, "Islam does not ban the involvement of women in the struggle and in the battle for Allah. Women are not required to fight, because that is the role of men, but due to the special circumstances, combat also becomes the duty of women."[69]

An internal pamphlet of the Islamic Jihad movements published an interview with a group of young women who declared their willingness to perpetrate suicide attacks for the organization. The young women, ages 16-24, were interviewed at a training camp in the Gaza Strip. The pamphlet featuring the interview was recently distributed among universities and colleges throughout Judea and Samaria as part of the organization's propaganda, with the aim of achieving the following goals:[70]

- To recruit female suicide attackers among Palestinian women who support the Hamas and other organizations.
- To raise funds for the organization in the territories, in the Arab countries, and Western countries.

The propaganda mentions the first suicide attack perpetrated by a woman on behalf of the Islamic Jihad (see the attack at the Afula mall, May 19, 2003). As noted, the interview with this group of women is part of the organization's efforts to widen the circle of female perpetrators. One of the interviewees, Fatma, expressed pride at having been accepted as a member of the group of suicide attackers, but she also spoke of her dream to marry and have children. "Her intention to perpetrate a suicide attack does not diminish these dreams, as long as she understands that she is giving her life so that others may live in dignity and freedom," states the pamphlet.

Fatma claims that her mother has congratulated her for her undertaking and wishes her good luck with her training. In addition, she is proud of how she has succeeded in "taking advantage of her leaving the house in order to attend university so that she can spend an hour each day at the training." Among other things, Fatma talks about her training in assembling and disassembling a weapon, as well as how to transfer an explosive device from one place to another. "I can already shoot an RPG missile without shaking," she added.

"Asma'a," a 16-year-old girl, says in the interview: "When I was young, I always dreamed of being a fighter and I was bored with children's games. Later I wanted to be like Iyat al-Akhrat, the woman who perpetrated the suicide attack in Kiryat Hayovel in 2001, and I asked why I shouldn't be the next in line." "The affiliation with a party or organization is unimportant," says the person who is presented as the supervisor over the women's camp. "Any boy or girl who wants to perpetrate an attack can join. This is a great action." The supervisor even appeals directly to women and manifests solidarity with almost feminist contents. "Suicide has removed women from routine frameworks that society has created for her—the image of a tearful and demanding creature always crying for help. She is replaced by the women who hoist the banner, the true banner-carrying partner that emulates the women of Jenin who aided their husbands against the invasion."

"There is no difference between a man and a woman," claims one of the women in the camp. "The aspects that affect a male suicide attacker also affect a woman. Can anyone say that a man is a greater patriot than a woman?"

Umm Hassan, who serves as the girls' spiritual mentor, is also described in the interview. "The suicide culture is a new one, which astounded the Zionists because of the chances of succeeding—which are greater for a woman due to the relative ease in concealing the explosives and passing through the roadblocks," she maintains. "The fact that they have not found a solution for the problem causes them to feel desperation and frustration. They have no response for women."

A Palestinian security entity, who is knowledgeable about recruitment and operating methods of suicide attackers and is following the Jihad's propaganda campaign, states that its main motive is to awaken internal controversy among Palestinian women regarding the suicide issue. "The target audience is women who support the Hamas, which up until now has refrained from activating women in suicide attacks," states the source. "The Hamas presents a religious example mixed with social conservativeness that refrains from recruiting women with the exception of aiding male cells.

"The Jihad, on the other hand, bases itself on the Iranian revolutionary pattern and has adopted an almost Shiite approach to women. On the one hand, more attention is focused on external issues but they also demonstrate a more liberal approach towards women."

The source continues, "The interview emphasizes the viewpoint of the female suicide attackers and indicates that the action can be perpetrated easily. It exploits the difficulties of women in the Palestinian society—marital problems, divorces, etc., in order to recruit them."

The incorporation of Palestinian women in the perpetration of suicide attacks has several main ramifications:

• The martyrdom of women will become part of the Palestinian national ethos and part of the narrative related to the Palestinian war of liberation, much like the role of women in the Algerian struggle for liberation from French rule during the years 1954-1962.
• The involvement of women in suicide attacks presents a new and complex challenge to the Israeli security forces that have always been careful about the honor of Palestinian women.
• The incorporation of Palestinian women in suicide attacks expands the pool of suicide attackers, which has been growing since the beginning of the Al-Aksa Intifada.

A list of suicide attacks perpetrated by women includes:
January 27, 2002—The female suicide attacker Wafa'a Idris, from the al-Amari refugee camp near Ramallah, detonated herself on Yaffo Street in Jerusalem. One person was killed in the attack and 127 were wounded. The Fatah claimed responsibility for the attack.

February 27, 2002—A vehicle carrying the female terrorist Darin abu Aishara and two Israeli Arabs from Lod stopped at the Maccabim roadblock.

When the passengers were asked to step out of the car in order to identify themselves the woman detonated herself near the roadblock. Three border guard policemen were injured in the explosion.

March 29, 2002—The suicide attacker Iyat al-Akhras from the Dehaisha refugee camp detonated herself in a supermarket on Uruguay Street in Kiryat Yovel, Jerusalem. Two civilians were killed and twenty-two were injured. The Fatah claimed responsibility for the incident.

April 12, 2002—The female suicide terrorist Andaliv Taktaka of Bethlehem detonated herself near a bus standing at a bus stop at the entrance to the Mahaneh Yehuda open-air market in Jerusalem. Six civilians were killed and eighty were injured. The Fatah claimed responsibility for the attack.

May 19, 2003—The female suicide terrorist Hiba Azam Daramca from Tubas in northern Samaria detonated herself at the entrance to a mall in Afula. Three civilians were killed and fifty-two were injured. The Palestinian Islamic Jihad and the Fatah (the Brigades of the Al-Aksa Martyrs) claimed responsibility for the attack.

October 4, 2003—The female suicide terrorist Hamdi Jaradat from Jenin denotated herself at the entrance to a restaurant in Haifa. Twenty-one civilians were killed and sixty were injured. The Palestinian Islamic Jihad claimed responsibility for the attack.

A partial list of thwarted suicide attacks planned by women includes:

April 14, 2002—A Palestinian woman who was suspected of intending to carry out a suicide attack inside Israel was apprehended by a border policeman at a gas station near the town of Neveh Yemin.

May 20, 2002—A resident of the village of Jeba in northern Samaria was arrested in Tul Karem under the suspicion that she was on her way to perpetrating a suicide attack on behalf of the Fatah-Tanzim.

May 23, 2002—IDF forces arrested a potential female terrorist in Betunia.

May 25, 2002—A potential suicide terrorist was arrested in Bethlehem after she was supposed to participate in a suicide attack in Rishon Lezion on May 22, 2002 and reconsidered. The Fatah was responsible for the attack.

June 13, 2002—In the framework of IDF proactive action, six Palestinians, including two women (one from Hebron and the other from the al-Arub refugee camp), were arrested. Both confessed that they had been planning to perpetrate suicide attacks.

Palestinian mothers and suicide attacks. A relatively new phenomenon is the support and encouragement of Palestinian mothers for suicide attacks. Mothers not only express their support after the event, but they also encourage their sons to perpetrate suicide attacks. In this framework, more and more mothers have their pictures taken with their sons prior to the sons' leaving on the suicide mission in order to give them their blessings and encouragement.

Mahmoud Hassan al-Abed, one of the terrorists who perpetrated the attack near the Dugit settlement in the northern part of the Gaza Strip (June 22, 2002), in which two soldiers were killed and three others were wounded, had his picture taken with his mother prior to the attack. Twenty-four-year-old al-Abd was killed in a skirmish with IDF soldiers and his mother disclosed that she had given the mission her blessing even though she clearly knew that he would probably not return.

The mother of eighteen-year-old Muhammad Farkhat, the suicide terrorist who perpetrated the attack at the Israeli pre-military service preparatory program in Atzmona, in which five Israeli teenagers were killed, encouraged him to participate in the mission and later boasted about her son, the shahid. Um Farkhat published a letter several days later in which she appealed to Palestinian mothers to educate their sons to become shahids. The mother of twenty-year-old Muhammad Khilas, who carried out a shooting attack at the Netsarim settlement on March 11, 2002, admitted to urging her son to carry out the attack and added that she had prayed to Allah to turn her son into a shahid. The mother of Khamza Samudi from the village of Ya'abed in Samaria, who detonated the bus at the Megiddo intersection on June 5, 2002, was proud of her son: "Khamza wanted to get me into the garden of Eden…he took women, the beautiful girls in the Garden of Eden. He lived and died as a hero, a blessed hero."

In an attempt to encourage Palestinian mothers to send their sons on suicide missions, the Hamas recently published praise for "the bravery of Palestinian mothers." This message appeared in the April issue of the monthly magazine, *Palestine al-Muslimiya*, in which the mothers were called "Hansa" after Hansa bint Amru, who lived during the lifetime of the Prophet Muhammad and became a model for emulation.

Hansa participated in the Kadsiya battle, one of the more important battles for the Arabs, and encouraged her four sons to fight, even if it cost them their lives. According to tradition she said, "Remember that the eternal world (the Garden of Eden) is better than the transitory world."

In order to encourage mothers to turn their children into shahids, the Hamas is currently in the process of establishing a "religious cultural center" in Gaza with the aim of glorifying the contribution of Palestinian mothers to the struggle and to commemorate the memory of the shahids.

A'atdal al Jariri, a psychologist and member of the Palestinian Association for Working Women, explained in an interview how social pressure creates an environment that encourages suicide attacks:

Of course, society and the media play an important role as well in establishing these ceremonies. The jubilation and calling Shahids' funerals weddings is a kind of deception of emotions in order to adapt to the common social position. The world must understand that there are certain social criteria that force the Palestinian mother to express (her joy) in this manner…

There are commentators who believe that a link exists between this phenomenon and the growing economic distress within the PA, which enables families whose sons were killed while perpetrating attacks to receive generous aid from the terror organizations and various countries. However, there is no doubt that even beyond this aspect, the general atmosphere among the Palestinian public has significant influence in making the suicide phenomenon normative, without any connection to the economic benefits involved. The public and universal mobilization of the Palestinian mothers in favor of the perpetration of suicide attacks reflects the social-cultural norm and contributes to its reinforcement.

Suicide Attacks and Israeli Arabs[71]

Since the beginning of the Al-Aksa Intifada in September 2000, a sharp increase has been noted in the scope and severity of terror attacks involving Israeli Arabs. This phenomenon expresses itself not only in the aid given to the terrorists, whether proactively or passively, but also in the direct involvement in the attacks themselves, including their perpetration.

A suicide attack by an Israeli Arab was perpetrated for the first time during the Al-Aksa Intifada.[72] On September 9, 2001, an Israeli Arab from Abu-Snen named Shakher Khubeishi detonated himself near the train station in Nahariya, causing the deaths of three Israelis and injuries to another forty-six. The Hamas claimed responsibility for the attack. Shakher Khubeishi was older (about forty-eight) than all of the other suicide attackers; he was married and had children. He served in public roles, and even ran in the elections for the mayor of Abu Snan. To date, his motives for carrying out the attack are still unclear.

In 2001, twenty-five instances of terror involvement were exposed (at different levels, including forty-four activists who were arrested) among Israeli Arabs; this can be compared to eight such instances in 2000 and two in 1999. A segmentation of these involvements indicates that three were activated at the initiative of the Hizballah, two were independent, nine were activated by the Fatah-Tanzim, eight by the Hamas, and three by the Islamic Jihad. These activities include thirteen instances of attackers (i.e., individuals who perpetrated or intended to perpetrate attacks themselves), eight who were fully aware of the nature of the activity, and four who were duped (meaning that they were persuaded that they were merely driving workers to their jobs). Nine of these instances of terror activity were initiated solely by Israeli Arabs, while four other cases were joint efforts of Israelis Arab and Palestinians from the territories who were entitled to blue (Israeli) identity cards because they are related to Israeli Arabs (in the framework of family unification).

A deeper segmentation of the data indicates that five terrorists were under the age of 25, eighteen were aged 11-18, twenty-five were aged 26-35, and three were over the age of 36. It is also clear that twenty-one of the cells were activated from Samaria; as mentioned earlier, two were independent and only two were activated from the Gaza Strip.

As stated above, most of the links were between Israeli Arabs and residents of the West Bank, with an emphasis on Samaria. The geographical proximity played an important role, but no less important were the family and commercial ties, shared university studies, and, of course, ideological solidarity and nationality. It is important to note the increasing incitement in mosques and sermons delivered by radical Muslims, and alongside this, the growing sense of discrimination, mainly against the background of the tough economic and employment situation in Israel, which has hit the Arab sector several times harder than other areas.

The terror activity of Israeli Arabs can be divided into two main categories: involvement as the attackers or the practical planners of attacks, and involvement as collaborators. Shakher Khubeishi, who carried out the suicide attack in Nahariya, belongs to the first group. The son of the suicide attacker in Nahariya planned to kidnap and murder Israeli soldiers. A cell from Um el-Fahem was instructed by the Tanzim in Nablus to purchase a car with "yellow license plates" (an Israeli license), booby-trap it, and drive it into Afula or Hadera.

The second group, consisting of collaborators, focuses on gathering intelligence and transporting the terrorists, mainly residents of the territories. Their role is to gather information about the targets for attacks and about access roads unhindered by security roadblocks (as aptly described by an Israeli Arab residing in Daheisha, who transported three terrorists to attacks in Israel). Collaborators also deal in transferring weapons for the terror infrastructures in the territories, including into Israel, as well as the purchase and theft of Israeli cars, which will serve to transport the terrorists, or as a car bomb.

Among the members of these groups are four Bedouins from the town of Lakiya in the south, who provided Gaza terrorists intending to carry out suicide attacks in Israel with sleeping arrangements and refuge. Another Israeli Arab worked for the Tanzim terrorist cell in Nablus and opened a route for it so that an explosive device (which was ultimately discovered by the security forces) could be planted on Paulo Street in Nazareth. A resident of Bakah el-Garbia, transported the terrorist who was supposed to commit suicide at the "City Hall" club in Haifa. A taxi driver from Lod, was supposed to transport a Hamas cell designated to carry out attacks in Israel. A Taibe resident married to a Jewish woman who lives in Hadera, transported the Hamas terrorists who, on May 18, 2001, perpetrated the suicide attack at the Hasharon Mall in Netanya, killing five Israelis and injuring seventy-four.

These are only examples from 2001. The year 2002 proved to be even more turbulent, and it witnessed the continually rising trend vis-à-vis the involvement of Israeli Arabs in terror: Two Taibe residents planted a bomb under the Taibe Bridge. An unaffiliated man from Nazareth established a military cell to carry out attacks during the Defense Shield campaign, but was injured while preparing an explosive device. Four Druze from Ein-Kinya in the Golan Heights, intended to perpetrate attacks against civilian and military targets, as well as commit arson and theft of weaponry.

At the same time the phenomenon of collaboration also expanded: A resident of Taibe, a private bus driver with a criminal record, was arrested before transporting a suicide terrorist affiliated with the Tanzim from Kalkilya to Israel. A resident of Tira, who dealt in the illegal transport of illegal workers, transported (unknowingly, according to his version) the terrorists who perpetrated the suicide attack in January 2002 at Tel Aviv's old central bus station. A Sakhnin resident was supposed to enable the infiltration of a female Tanzim suicide attacker from the Hebron vicinity into Haifa (worthy of notice is the fact that the connection between her and the terror organizations in the territories was obtained through the Internet.) A female resident of Arabeh in the Misgav region, who turned out to be a collaborator for the Islamic Jihad, transferred blue Israeli ID cards to a terror cell in Jenin and agreed to gain access for suicide attackers into Israel. A resident of Kfar Kassem was to have led Tanzim suicide attackers into Israel under the guise of car thieves.

In several cases, Israeli Arabs from Nazareth and Taibe who dealt in the transfer of weaponry to terror cells in the territories were arrested during 2002. The Taibe cell also hoarded weapons for a possible confrontation with the Israeli authorities. Along with these occurrences there was a rise in the scope of terror activities carried out by individuals possessing the blue Israeli identity card: A resident of Wadi Burkin near Jenin (who possessed Israeli citizenship, thanks to his mother, a resident of Kalkilya), carried out the suicide attack at the "Matsa" restaurant in Haifa on March 31, in which fifteen Israelis were killed. A resident of Jiyus near Kalkilya (married to an Israeli from Jaljuliya) was supposed to arrange access for a female suicide attacker from the Tanzim to carry out her mission in Israel. A resident of Tulkarem (married to a female resident of Jasser-a-Zarka) was recruited by the Hamas and gathered intelligence prior to perpetrating attacks against Israel. Mahmud Nadi transported the terrorist who detonated himself outside the Dolphinarium in Tel Aviv. A resident of Kalanswa helped the Tanzim to transport suicide attackers to Israel. A resident of Ilut, intended to carry out an attack in the Haifa area together with an activist of the Islamic Jihad from the Jenin area.

Israeli Arabs constitute an attractive target for recruitment to the terrorist organizations for the following reasons: the freedom of movement that they enjoy, their familiarity with Israeli roads, cities and customs, their fluency in Hebrew, and the fact that they possess Israeli ID cards and license plates.

Recruitment is based on familial, commercial, or study ties, while exploiting the geographical proximity of some of the Arab towns to the territories.

This is how the route leading through Samaria—the triangle towns—the Galilee towns was created; this road serves as the main travel route for the terrorists from the territories to Israel, usually to perpetrate attacks in nearby cities—Afula, Hadera, and Netanya. It is clear to the terror organizations that chances that the driver or Israeli vehicle will be checked are minimal. In order to ensure success they started dressing the suicide attackers in women's clothing or in soldiers' uniforms, sometimes with the aid of the collaborators themselves, believing that this will add to the passengers' authenticity.

There is an additional link between terror organizations and criminal entities among the Israeli Arabs. The latter do not fear confrontation with law enforcement agencies, and are willing to serve as terrorists or collaborators for monetary compensation. Their intimate familiarity with the field (including houses and private vehicles) turns them into a "power multiplier" from the point of view of the terror organizations, which avail themselves of their assistance in order to ensure the success of the attacks and increase their destructiveness.

The mobilization of Israeli Arabs in aiding and perpetrating attacks in general and suicide attacks in particular constitutes a new phenomenon that can perhaps be explained against the background of the following facts:

- The influence of the Al-Aksa Intifada and the solidarity of the Israeli Arabs with the Palestinians in the territories, particularly with the unprecedented Palestinian willingness to commit martyrdom (it is possible that the events of September 11 also contributed to the increased motivation to perpetrate terror attacks).
- Recruitment and persuasion attempts by the Palestinian terror organizations, led by the Fatah and the Hamas, a phenomenon that was nonexistent in earlier periods.
- Deepening frustration and alienation in the Israeli Arab society and the events of October 2000 in which Israeli Arabs were killed.

Examples of Suicide Attacks during the Al-Aksa Intifada (October 2000-July 2002)

The suicide attack at the Dolphinarium in Tel Aviv—June 1, 2001

On the night of June 1, 2001 a suicide terrorist detonated himself near the entrance to the Dolphinarium club in Tel Aviv. The suicide attacker, twenty-four-year-old Sayyid Khuteri, was a Jordanian-born Palestinian who had arrived in the territories two years earlier and worked as a construction electrician in Kalkilya. Twenty individuals were killed and scores sustained injuries. Most of the victims were teenagers. The Hamas's Az-a-Din el Kassam Brigades claimed responsibility for the attack.

The Suicide Attack at the Sebarro Restaurant in Jerusalem—August 9, 2001

At lunchtime on August 9, 2001, a suicide terrorist detonated himself in the Sbarro restaurant. The twenty-two-year-old suicide terrorist was a Hamas member named Az a-Din Shahil Ahmed Al-Matsri from Jenin. The device carried by the terrorist in a bag contained 5-10 kilograms of explosives along with nails and nuts to increase the spray effect. Fourteen individuals died in the attack and over 130 were injured. The military branch of the Hamas, the Az-a-Din el Kassam Brigades, published a declaration in Jenin in which it claimed responsibility for the attack.

A Suicide Attack and Detonation of a Car Bomb in Jerusalem—December 1, 2001

On December 1, 2001, at around midnight a complex suicide attack was perpetrated that included:

- An attack by two suicide terrorists with belt bombs who acted simultaneously.
- The detonation of a car bomb about twenty minutes after the terrorists' attack.

As mentioned, the first part of the attack was perpetrated at around midnight, when two suicide attackers wearing belt bombs, Nabil Mahmud Khalbia and Osama Muhammad Ayid of the town of Abu Dis, perpetrated a suicide attack. The first suicide terrorist detonated himself near Zion Square (at the corner of Ben Yehuda and Yaffo Streets), while the second attacker detonated himself about forty meters away at the top of Ben Yehuda Street (on the corner of Luntz Street). Eleven individuals were killed and 254 were wounded as a result of the blasts. Some twenty minutes later, a car bomb installed in an Opel detonated on Rabbi Kook Street. The Hamas organization claimed responsibility for the attacks.

The Suicide Attack at the Park Hotel in Netanya ("the Seder night massacre")

On Seder night, (March 28, 2002) a twenty-three-year-old suicide terrorist Abd el-Bassat Udda of Tulkarem, infiltrated the Park Hotel during the Seder, and detonated himself in the center of the dining room with 250 people in attendance. Twenty people were killed and 140 were injured. The suicide terrorist carried a 10 kg. device in a belt bomb. The military branch of the Hamas, the Az-a-Din el Kassam, claimed responsibility for the attack in Netanya.

The Suicide Attack at the Megiddo Intersection—June 5, 2002

On June 5, 2002, a booby-trapped car driven by a suicide terrorist detonated near a bus at the Meggido intersection. The attack took place at 7:15

a.m. when the car bomb drew alongside the bus and exploded. Seventeen people were killed in the attack and forty-five were injured. The Islamic Jihad claimed responsibility for the attack. From his headquarters in Damascus, Sheikh Abdallah Shalakh announced, "the attack was perpetrated to commemorate the thirty-fifth anniversary of the occupation of the West Bank and Gaza."[73]

The Attempt to Hijack an El-Al Plane and Crash into a Skyscraper in Tel Aviv[74]

On November 18, 2002, a twenty-three-year-old Israeli Arab, attempted to hijack an El-Al aircraft, flight 581 from Israel to Istanbul, Turkey. During the flight, he made repeated attempts to enter the Business Class although the flight attendants clarified each time that he was not allowed to enter that area and asked him to return to his seat. Immediately prior to the landing in Istanbul, when all of passengers were asked to take their seats and fasten their seatbelts, he attacked a female flight attendant and attempted to break into the cockpit. The aircraft's sky marshals, who noticed his actions, overtook him quickly and handcuffed him. A body search conducted by the sky marshals revealed a small pocketknife. It is not yet clear if he attempted to make use of the knife during the attempted attack.

After the landing, he was handed over to the Turkish authorities. Initial findings of the incident's investigation indicate that his actions were premeditated and not spontaneous. He told the sky marshals that today was his day to die and that he decided to hijack the aircraft because the Israelis had killed his brothers. In his interrogation by the Turkish authorities, he confessed to attempting to hijack the aircraft with the intention of forcing the pilots to return to Israel and crash into a skyscraper in Tel Aviv. He claimed to have acted on his own and to be unaffiliated with any terror organization. In his home at the village of Bueina, police found photos of shahids and a sheet of paper on which he had written (among other things): "I take my leave from you, beg forgiveness, and I hope you will have a good future..."

Maritime Suicide Attacks in the Arab-Israeli Conflict

Maritime Suicide Attacks in the Lebanese Arena

The first maritime suicide attacks occurred opposite the Lebanese shores in 1988. Shiite Palestinian terror organizations as well as secular Lebanese organizations took part in the attempted attacks. The maritime arena constituted a secondary arena in the terror organizations' struggle against Israel. All of the attacks and attempted attacks at sea were carried out against Israeli boats patrolling the Lebanese coast.

- On April 25, 1988, a fishing boat loaded with explosives detonated near an Israeli patrol boat west of the city of Tyre. There were no casualties or damage. Ahmad Jibril's organization (Popular Front for the Liberation of Palestine—the General Command [PFLP-GC]) claimed responsibility for the attack.
- In June 1989, a failed attempt was made by the Syrian National Party to carry out a maritime suicide attack by using a fishing boat loaded with explosives.
- On October 30, 1989, a fishing boat loaded with explosives detonated near an Israeli patrol boat west of Rashidia. An Israeli sailor was injured in the attack. The Popular Front for the Liberation of Palestine, led by George Habash, claimed responsibility for the incident.
- On March 27, 1991, an Israeli patrol boat opened fire at an empty fishing boat about a kilometer south of Rashidiya. The boat, which was loaded with explosives, detonated without causing any damage. The Fatah announced that the boat was theirs. It was apparently designated for a maritime boat bomb that was thwarted.
- On May 19, 1997, a fishing boat loaded with explosives detonated near an Israeli patrol boat near the Tyre coast. No one was hurt in the attack, nor was there any damage. The Shiite Amal organization claimed responsibility for the attack.

Maritime Suicide Attacks in the Palestinian Arena[75]

The night of November 6, 2000. During the night between November 6 and 7, a Palestinian suicide terrorist detonated himself on a fishing boat loaded with explosives north of Rafiah, not far from the Egyptian border and near an Israeli patrol boat. This was the first suicide attack in the Palestinian maritime arena.

On the coast opposite the Gaza Strip there is extensive fishing activity involving hundreds of fishing boats that set out for sea from jetties throughout the Gaza Strip. Israeli patrol boats are active in this arena to identify Palestinian boats that deal in the smuggling of merchandise and weapons to the Gaza Strip.

On the night of November 6, an Israeli patrol boat identified a suspicious-looking fishing boat coming from the West (from the direction of Egypt) and moving towards the northeast (in the direction of Rafiah). When the patrol boat signaled the fishing boat to stop, the latter changed its direction and moved towards the Israeli patrol boat. At a distance of 100 meters it exploded. The explosion caused no casualties or damage to the patrol boat. The Hamas claimed responsibility for the attack.

The thwarting of a suicide attack plan on a cruise ship in Eilat.[76] Az-a-Din el Kassam Brigades planned on infiltrating a suicide attacker into Eilat. According to the plan, the terrorist was to be disguised as a tourist and would blow up a passenger boat carrying tourists and vacationers on cruises that set out from the marina in Eilat. The plan was exposed due to the apprehension of a senior leader of the Az-a-Din el Kassam Brigades. A resident of Sawakhra al-Sharkia was arrested under suspicion of being responsible for a series of attacks. In the course of his interrogation, he revealed the plan to detonate a cruise ship in Eilat. He disclosed that he and his brother had planned to perpetrate a suicide attack by attempting to infiltrate explosives into a video camera. He also told the interrogators that he asked his brother to perpetrate the attack in Eilat in order to cause the deaths of as many civilians as possible. He claimed that he had told his brother that the attack in Eilat was important because no attacks had been perpetrated in that city up to that date. The two brothers agreed that the planned attack on an Eilat cruise ship would be perpetrated by a suicide terrorist with an Israeli identity card. For this purpose, it was agreed that the brother would arrive in Eilat, locate a boat at the marina to be used in the attack, and purchase a ticket for the suicide terrorist. The Hamas' intensions were thwarted following the arrest of the two brothers and the exposure of their plans.

A maritime suicide attack in the Palestinian arena—the night of November 23, 2002).[77] On November 23, 2002, two suicide attackers of the Palestinian Islamic Jihad detonated a boat bomb off the coast of Gaza. The incident occurred at 22:30 that night when a suspicious boat was identified and the Israeli Navy's patrol boat *Dabur* was sent out to investigate. Crewmembers identified a Palestinian boat attempting to leave the Gaza Strip's territorial waters and moving towards the Israeli coast. The *Dabur* signaled to the Palestinian boat to stop, and when its signals were ignored, warning shots were fired in the air. When the *Dabur* was within a few dozen meters of the boat, the Palestinian vessel exploded, causing injury to four soldiers and damaging the ship.

Does a Profile Exist for a Palestinian Suicide Terrorist?

Suicide terrorism in general is a dynamic, broad phenomenon, which is on the rise. It involves various nationalities, and it occurs on different continents and in a wide range of cultural, social, and religious contexts. It is particularly difficult to evaluate if a common denominator exists among all those individuals who chose to respond to "the organization's call" and sacrifice their lives for an idea, whether it is religious, national, or social, as the vast majority of them does not survive to talk about their motives, and the wills that they leave behind, with the help of the organization, are to be suspected of intentional distortion. However, in the Palestinian connection it is possible to point out several central characteristics.

The Sex of the Suicide Attackers

Most of the suicide attackers were masculine. To date only six suicide attacks (out of 123 attacks) were perpetrated by Palestinian women.

Nevertheless, during the years 2002-2003 several Palestinian women were arrested who had planned to perpetrate suicide attacks or reconsidered at the last minute and did not carry out the attack.

The Age of the Suicide Attackers

The youthful age of the attackers is evident (ages 17–23), although there have also been suicide attackers aged 16–17, on the one hand, and aged 40 and up, on the other. The large gap in the age span of the suicide attack perpetrators, which ranges from adolescents to attackers in their late forties, indicates significant disparity in the personal maturity of the various suicide attackers. The Hamas generally dispatches relatively older suicide attackers, assuming that they will give balanced operational and ideological deliberation that will contribute to the success of the mission, while the Islamic Jihad and the Fatah pay less attention to the ages of the suicide attackers and are willing to send 16 and 17 year olds.

Religion

All of the Palestinian suicide attackers (since 1993) have been Sunni Muslims. The suicide attackers dispatched by the Hamas and Palestinian Islamic Jihad all acted out of religious motivation, although even in the case of suicide attackers from secular organizations, like the Fatah, the religious connection (the promise of the Garden of Eden for the shahid) also carried some weight in the motivation of the suicide attacker.

Education

The number of high school and college graduates is prominent particularly among the suicide attackers during the Al-Aksa Intifada. Part of this phenomenon can be explained due to the relatively high number of suicide attackers from the ranks of the Al-Najah University in Nablus and the Islamic University in Gaza, who were recruited by the Hamas. However, among the perpetrators there are also those lacking any education.

Family Status

Most of the suicide attackers were bachelors. As a rule, the Palestinian organizations prefer to dispatch single suicide attackers, in order to minimize the damage to Palestinian families. Nevertheless, among the suicide attackers there were also married men with families. Suicide attacks are perpetrated by both sexes: Men only in the Islamic organizations and both men and women in the secular organizations.

The Economic Status

The economic status of the suicide attackers did not constitute a decisive factor in their decision to undertake a suicide mission. The economic background of the suicide attackers is not different than that of the rest of the population. Some of them came from poor refugee families and others from families with a reasonable economic status in relative terms vis-à-vis the lifestyles in the territories of the PA. Some of the suicide terrorists were unemployed, while others worked or studied, and some even served in the Palestinian security forces.

Living Accommodations

Most of the attackers were from Judea and Samaria, although some were from the Gaza Strip, Jerusalem, and places within the "Green Line." The suicide terrorists' activity is explained by a wide range of motives: in the name of religion, nationality, the group, the idea, and sometimes in the name of revenge and deterring the enemy. Suicide attackers are often influenced by peer pressure or the public environment supporting the national struggle.

Health Status

A few of the suicide attackers, and among those apprehended during the preparatory stages prior to the attack, were people suffering from a terminal illness, or individuals with a proven background of mental disorders.[78]

Motivation for Suicide

The main motives for the decision made by healthy suicide attackers to set out on suicidal missions were a combination of religious belief, faith in the contribution of the attacker's death to the realization of the vision of Palestinian independence, and investment in the social and economical upward mobility of the attacker's family, which is to win prestige and monetary grants after the son's passing.[79]

Duration of the Preparatory Stage Prior to the Attack

During the years 1993-2000, the recruitment process of a suicide attacker and his preparation took several months, and sometimes even longer. During this time he was diligently prepared for the mission, his religious consciousness was developed, and he received tutoring from the clerics of the Islamic organizations. In the course of the Al-Aksa Intifada, the tremendous willingness to perpetrate suicide attacks caused the preparation span to shrink to weeks, and even to several days.

In the religious groups there exists the backing of the clerics who provide religious rulings justifying the suicide attacks. The religious-traditional-cultural component that promises the Garden of Eden to the shahids also affects the suicide attackers who act on behalf of the secular organizations.

In summary, it can be stated that the range of characteristics of suicide attackers is too wide and diversified to be able to sketch "the profile" of "the typical suicide attacker." We can and must be satisfied with the statement that there exists a series of profiles or joint characteristics shared by some of the suicide terrorists in some of the groups. A comprehensive effort made during the years 2002-2003 to build a "profile" of the suicide terrorist did not bring about a major breakthrough in the study of this issue (beyond the characteristics already mentioned above). At the end of 2002, the security network set up a team of terror experts including intelligence representatives and psychologists, who were to thoroughly question suicide attackers who were caught alive. The aim was to try and discover what would deter them from participating in a suicide mission. This was not an academic mission, but rather work that was meant to provide the GSS and the military forces in the field with operational tools, in order to attempt to disrupt the suicide attacker's activities already at the organizational stage.[80]

Thus, twenty surviving suicide attackers were "studied" meticulously. In an effort to sketch their personal psychological profile, their motives were analyzed and the question regarding what might influence them to change their minds was studied. Among other discoveries, it became clear that the leading motive for setting out on a suicide mission was ideological-religious: hatred for the Jews and Israel. Another motive: personal, emotional or economic distress, or revenge. Another reason: emulating the heroes of the Palestinian society, the shahids. Much like in other studies, here, too, one of the explanations for the perpetual increase in the number of shahids is that this phenomenon is perceived in Palestinian society as the absolute epitome of the Jihad, thus it is not only a positive phenomenon but also a model for emulation.

Ultimately, the study was frozen because it became clear that its conclusions were very similar to those drawn in previous studies carried out over the years regarding the suicide issue. For example, the religious influence on the motivation to commit suicide is decisive. Conclusion: Attempt to recruit respected Muslim religious leaders to issue a fatwa against the suicide attacks. It goes without saying that attempts made over the years to implement this conclusion did not meet with any success. Similarly, the handling of the imams dealing in incitement in the mosques did not succeed. Another conclusion drawn from the study that is already well known: Inflicting damage upon the terrorist's close family—demolishing homes, deportation, etc.—is effective.

Comparative Aspects of Suicide Attacks in the Arab-Israeli Confrontation Arena

A comparative study of the perpetration of suicide attacks in the years 1983-2003 indicates the following phenomena:

1. The number of suicide attacks throughout the entire period, in comparison to the sum total of attacks, always constituted less than 1 percent. This figure is also true from the aspect of the number of suicide attacks occurring in interim periods.
2. Suicide attacks perpetrated against military targets in Lebanon and the territories in Judea, Samaria, and the Gaza Strip caused a relatively low number of casualties, due to effective protection and suitable action taken by the security forces.
3. Suicide attacks are granted religious and public legitimization in the Lebanese and Palestinian arenas when they are effective (for the martyrdom of a suicide attacker the enemy must be made to suffer a high level of losses and damage). A drop in the effectiveness of the suicide attacks results in decreased use of this tool within the struggle.
4. In the Lebanese arena, the Hizballah and Lebanese organizations could only implement suicide attacks against Israeli military targets. Thus, the benefit derived from these attacks decreased and the organizations chose alternative methods that proved to be more effective (shootings, planting of devices, etc.). The Hizballah, albeit its radical image, is sensitive to the lives of its members, and therefore despite the religious ruling enabling suicide missions, this organization avoids the perpetration of these attacks if at any time it believes it can realize its goals in other ways, or that the benefit to be gained from the attack does not justify the sacrifice.
5. In the conflict with the Palestinians, the majority of suicide attacks are directed against Israel's civilian population, mainly within the "Green Line." In the eyes of the terror organizations Israel's population is perceived as a preferred target for the following reasons:

   • The home front in Israel is vulnerable and it cannot be protected everywhere and at all times.
   • Attacks against the civilian population take a heavy toll because it is highly vulnerable and exposed.
   • Attacks against the civilian population are granted maximum media exposure, thus serving the goals of the terror organization to spread frustration and anxiety.
   • Attacks against the civilian population render Israeli's military and security forces irrelevant because of their inability to protect the public, and generate demoralization within the population and in the security forces.
   • The repeated attacks against Israel's civilian population weaken the fortitude of Israeli society, stir up political controversy, and are meant

to lead to the capitulation of the Israeli government to Palestinian dictates.

6. The first Islamic entities to use suicide attacks as a way to confront Israel came from Lebanon and the Palestinian arena. Subsequently, the secular terror organizations joined the ranks of suicide attackers and even "took the lead" (in Lebanon, the pro-Syrian organizations in 1985; in the Palestinian arena the secular organizations, mainly the Fatah, since the end of 2001).

7. The Islamic groups, the Hamas and the Islamic Jihad, regard suicide attacks as a central tool in their struggle against Israel as well as a means to torpedo agreements and arrangements between the PA and Israel. These organizations abstained from carrying out suicide attacks only when the PA exerted heavy pressure on them. "The commitment" of the secular Palestinian organizations to the use of violence in general and suicide attacks in particular is less than that of the Islamic organizations, and, therefore, the key to ending the suicide attacks lies in the hands of the political and military leadership of the Fatah—PLO—the PA. It is impossible to detect a systematic rationale in the choice of suicide attack targets (from the geographical, political or military aspect), and in the timing.

8. It appears that the attacks are perpetrated out of a general ambition to cause maximum casualties and damage to property, while the definition of the attack's target is attributed secondary importance.

9. The attacks are generally perpetrated in cities that are easily accessible to the attacker, and, thus, most of the attacks have been carried out in cities near the border and Jerusalem. However, when it is possible, attacks are perpetrated at locations "deeper" in the heart of the State of Israel, such as Haifa and its satellite cities in the north, or in the Tel Aviv area—Rishon Lezion and the central region.

Notes

1. Martin Kramer (ed.), *Protest and Revolution in Shiite Islam*, Hakibbutz Hameuhad, Tel Aviv, 1985, pp. 11-15.
2. Ibid.
3. Ibid.
4. Gustav Thasis, "Religious Symbolism Social Change: The Drama of Hussein," in Nikkie R. Keddie (ed.), *Religion and Politics in Iran: Shiism from Quietism to Revolution,* Pale University Press, New Haven, 1983, pp. 364-366.
5. Emanuel Sivan, *Islamic Fanatics*, Am Oved, Tel Aviv, 1986, pp. 196-197.
6. *Kihan*, Teheran, October 26, 1983.
7. Amir Taheri, *The Holy Terror—Inside Story of the Islamic Terrorism*, Shere Books, London, 1987, pp. 85-86.
8. David Menshari, *Iran in Revolution*, Hakibbutz Hameuhad, Tel Aviv, 1988, pp. 237-238.
9. Ibid.
10. Ibid.
11. Shimon Shapira, *Hizballah between Iran and Lebanon*, Hakkibutz Hameuhad, Tel Aviv, 2000, pp. 167-169.

12. Ibid.
13. An interview with Sheikh Yosef Damush, *Alsapir*, Beirut, August 14, 1986.
14. *Alsapir*, Beirut, August 25, 1985.
15. *Alahad*, Beirut, August 15, 1985; *Alnahar*, Beirut, August 15, 1985.
16. Shimon Shapira, *Hizballah between Iran and Lebanon*, Hakibbutz Hameuhad, Tel Aviv, 2000, pp. 197-169.
17. *Alahad*, Beirut, May 24, 1985.
18. *Alsapir*, Beirut, November 10, 1982.
19. Mark Juergensmeyer (ed.), *Violence and the Sacred in the Modern World*, Frank Cass, London, 1992, pp. 30-47.
20. "The Life Story of Nabil Hajaz, the Commander of Amal," *Alsapir*, Beirut, June 10, 1986.
21. Shaul Shay, *Terror in the Name of the Iman*, The International Policy Institute for Counter-Terror, The Interdisciplinary Center in Herzliya, Mifalot, 2001, pp. 70-71.
22. Ibid., p. 72.
23. Ibid.
24. http://www.Beirut-Memorial.org.history.
25. The multinational force was composed of forces sent by the United States, Italy, and France.
26. Part of a eulogy delivered by General Kelly on the eighteenth anniversary of the attack on the Marine Headquarters.
27. Egel and Fatma Gates—these were gates on the Israeli-Lebanese border.
28. *Jumhury al Islam*, Iran, April 20, 1996.
29. Al-Manar television station, August 29, 1997.
30. Radio Nur, September 5, 1997.
31. Reuters, March 19, 1992; Reuters, March 23, 1992.
32. Shaul Shay, *Terror in the Service of the Imam*, p. 86.
33. *Maariv*, Tel Aviv, September 5, 1999.
34. Ibid.
35. *Ha'aretz*, Tel Aviv, September 7, 1999.
36. AP news agency, Buenos Aires, July 18, 1994.
37. The Argentinean attorney general in an interview for a local radio station, as quoted by Reuters, May 5, 1999.
38. *Ha'aretz*, Tel Aviv, October 2, 2002.
39. Muslimedia International, Islamic Movement, May 16-31, 2002: http://www.muslimedia.com/archives.
40. There were several attempts to perpetrate terror attacks beforehand, but for various reasons they did not transpire and are therefore not specified here.
41. The data refer to suicide attacks between 1994 and October 1, 2000. Starting from that date, the suicide attacks were perpetrated as part of the Al-Aksa Intifada.
42. Nahman Tal, *Israel and Suicide Terror*, strategic update, Vol. 5, issue 1 (June 2002), the Jaffe Center for Strategic Studies, Tel Aviv University.
43. Robert Litwak, *Who is the Suicidal Terrorist?* Woodrow Wilson International Center for Scholars, WWICS News, who is the suicidal terrorist.htm.
44. Ehud Sprinzak, "Rational Fanatics," *Foreign Policy* (September-October 2001).
45. Ibid.
46. Ibid.
47. This figure applies to June 2003.
48. *Maariv*, Tel Aviv, June 21, 2002.
49. Amira Hess, *Ha'aretz*, Tel Aviv, July 16, 2001.

50. These figures are accurate up to May 2003.
51. Professor Khalil Shkaki is a lecturer at the Bir Zeit University and director of the Palestinian Policy and Public Opinion Research Center in Ramallah. The article "Palestinian Public Opinion and the Al-Aksa Intifada" was published in a strategic update, vol. 5, issue 1, June 2002.
52. Roni Shaked, *Yediot Aharonot*, Tel Aviv, August 2, 2002.
53. Amira Hess, *Ha'aretz*, Tel Aviv, July 16, 2002.
54. In January-February 2001 a single suicide attack took place (on January 1, 2001 in Netanya).
55. The number of attacks does not include an attack perpetrated by the Hamas on May 14, 2001, against the Orhan outpost in Gush Katif, which is categorized as an attack involving sacrifice.
56. An Amnesty International document, Israel, "The Territories and the Palestinian Authority, the Indiscriminate Attack against Civilians by Armed Palestinian Organizations."
57. An interview with the Palestinian Communication Center, reported by *Al-Sharq al-Awsat*, May 28, 2002. The text of the "understandings" regarding a ceasefire between Israel and the Hizballah is to be found on the Internet site of the Israel Foreign Ministry: www.israel-mfa.gov.il.
58. Nidal al-Mugrabi, "Palestinian fighters say that the suicide missions must continue," Reuters, May 13, 2002.
59. For example, declarations made by Sheikh Ahmad Yassin and Mussa abu Marzuk as reported in *Al-Zman*, London, May 29, 2002; reported by the BBC.
60. AFP, "The Hamas: The Authority does not speak in the name of the Palestinians in the matter of the attacks," May 8, 2002.
61. An interview with Sheikh Ahmad Yassin, *Observer*, August 1, 2001.
62. "A declaration published by the Palestinian and Islamic National Forces," September 14, 2001. The armed organizations included the National Front for the Liberation of Palestine, the Islamic Opposition Movement-Hamas, and the Islamic Jihad. Among the other organizations were the General Union of Palestinian Women and a Palestinian chain of nongovernmental organizations.
63. It is to be noted that during the month of March a total of ninety-one Israelis were killed in attacks; this figure includes fatalities from other types of attacks, not only suicide attacks.
64. Data refer to the period between April 25, 2002 and December 2003.
65. The figures relate to the period between December 15, 2001 and July 2002. This number does not include "joint" attacks of the Fatah and Islamic organizations and independent suicide attacks.
66. Although the characteristic process of this incident is more similar to an attack involving martyrdom than a suicide attack.
67. Nahman Tal, *Israel and Suicide Terror*.
68. Ibid.
69. *Daily Star*, June 8, 2002.
70. Arnon Regular, "The Islamic Jihad Operates a Propaganda Campaign to Recruit Suicide Attacker," *Ha'aretz*, Tel Aviv, May 26, 2003.
71. This section is based mainly on an article by Yoav Limor, *Maariv*, June 21, 2002.
72. The first attempted suicide attack was apparently in 1999, but it ended in a "work accident."
73. *Yediot Aharonot*, Tel Aviv, June 6, 2002.

74. This paragraph is based on the following sources: *Maariv*, November 19, 2002; *Yediot Aharonot*, November 19, 2002; *Ha'aretz*, November 19, 2002.
75. *Yediot Aharonot*, November 8, 2000; *Maariv*, November 8, 2000; *Ha'aretz*, November 8, 2000.
76. *Maariv*, October 16, 2002.
77. *Yediot Aharonot*, November 24, 2002; *Maariv*, November 24, 2002; *Ha'aretz*, November 24, 2002.
78. Amir Oren, *Ha'aretz*, Tel Aviv, July 14, 2002.
79. Ibid.
80. Alex Fishman, "The IDF In the Wake of the Sleeping Cells," *Yediot Aharonot*, Tel Aviv, May 2002.

3

Suicide Attacks in the Modern Era— Throughout the World

Suicide Attacks by Egyptian Terror Organizations

The two main Islamic terror organizations in Egypt, Al-Jama'a al-Islamiya and the Egyptian Islamic Jihad, have carried out suicide attacks in Egypt and beyond its boundaries. Al-Jama'a al-Islamiya perpetrated a suicide attack in Egypt against the minister of the interior, and an additional attack using a car bomb against a police station in Croatia (October 1995), to avenge the arrest and extradition of an organization activist to the Egyptian authorities. The Egyptian Islamic Jihad perpetrated an attack using a vehicle driven by a suicide attacker to the Egyptian Embassy in Pakistan. The Embassy was demolished in the attack, seventeen people were killed, and scores were injured. This attack was also meant to avenge the extradition of an organization activist into the hands of the Egyptian authorities. As a rule, since 1993 both organizations have abstained from carrying out suicide attacks on Egyptian soil, apparently out of a desire to prevent harm to innocent Egyptian civilians, and also because of the difficulty in carrying out these types of attacks in Egypt as a result of the rigid supervision of the Egyptian authorities vis-à-vis the organizations' activities.

It is important to note that since 1995, the Egyptian Islamic Jihad has been an integral part of Bin-Laden's Global Islamic Jihad, and has therefore been a partner to the suicide attacks perpetrated by Al-Qaida.

The Assassination Attempt against the Egyptian Minister of the Interior[1]

The first suicide attack perpetrated by an Egyptian organization occurred on August 8, 1993, with the attempted assassination of the Egyptian Minister of the Interior Hassan al-Alfi in the heart of Cairo. General al-Alfi, who was in charge of the country's internal security, was injured in the attack, sustaining gunshot wounds in the arm and the chest. The attack took place in the morning as the minister's convoy was passing in front of the American University near Cairo's Liberation Square, the city's busiest location. The assassins activated an explosive device near the minister's car and then opened fire in its direction. Some of his bodyguards and passersby were killed and injured.

The minister of the interior had taken some precautions: he altered his travel route daily and, in addition, a car identical to his own drove in front of him in order to cause doubt and confusion. However, the assassins took advantage of the vulnerable aspect of the plan--the arrival at the entrance to the Ministry. Previous ministers of the interior had always instructed that the street be closed off at least a quarter of an hour prior to their arrival, but al-Alfi was aware that this step was a cause for grievance and therefore opposed the closure. The radicals noticed the breach and took advantage of it, and also succeeded in overcoming other security means.[2] It is important to note that this assassination attempt was different than its predecessors because explosives were used; in previous attacks, automatic weapons were fired only at close range. The investigation revealed that the mission planners had apparently intended for the assassins to be killed, in order to prevent any possible identity of their operators. In Egypt, the minister of interior constitutes a central target for assassination attempts by Islamic terror organizations because he is in charge of the struggle against terror organizations.[3]

The Suicide Attack at the Police Station in Rica, Croatia

On October 16, 1995, a suicide driver detonated himself in front of a police station in Rica, Croatia. Twenty-seven people were injured and serious damage was caused to the police station, as well as surrounding buildings. The Egyptian terror organization Al-Jama'a al-Islamiya claimed responsibility for the attack.[4]

The attack was meant to serve as a warning to the Croatian authorities that were apparently involved in the apprehension of one of the organization's senior military commanders, Tala'at Fuad Kassem and to exert pressure on the Croatian government, which was suspected of collaborating with the Egyptian authorities, to release the arrested terrorist.

On May 16, 1996, in the year after the attack in Rica, an activist of Al-Jama'a al-Islamiya named Salim al-Khursani threatened the Croatian authorities that the organization's campaign of vengeance would continue as long as Tala'at Fuad Kassem (called Abu-Talala) remained behind bars.[5] Khursani claimed that an organization called "The Bosnian Islamic Jihad" had been established and that it was cooperating with the Al-Jama'a al-Islamiya. Its members had undergone training in terror activity, including the perpetration of terror attacks, and they would act as had their brethren in Lebanon and Palestine. Khursani completed his message by issuing a warning to release Abu Talala or inform the organization of his fate.[6] Despite this warning, since

October 1995 there have been no further attacks by Islamic terror organizations.

The Attack at the Egyptian Embassy in Islamabad, Pakistan

On November 19, 1995, the Egyptian Jihad perpetrated a suicide attack at the Egyptian Embassy in Pakistan. The attack was perpetrated in two stages: In the initial stage, an explosive device was detonated which blasted through the entrance gates, and in the second stage a car bomb carrying about a half a ton of explosives and driven by a suicide terrorist exploded in the center of the embassy compound. As a result of the blast, seventeen people were killed and fifty-eight were injured. The attack was carried out at 10:45 a.m., a peak hour when the embassy is open to the public.[7]

Three Islamic organizations claimed responsibility for the attack—Al-Jama'a al-Islamiya, Al-Jihad, and "The Group for International Justice."[8] The second secretary and three Egyptian security guards were killed, but the Egyptian ambassador was not hurt. The remaining victims were Pakistani security guards, local embassy employees, and passersby. This attack had the gravest consequences of any attacks to be perpetrated against an Egyptian target outside of Egyptian territory.[9]

The cell included two Egyptian attackers who were members of the Egyptian Jihad, youths in their twenties (one was 21, the other was 25). One had resided in Pakistan for several years. Pakistan was chosen as the venue for the attack in order to deter the Pakistani government from further cooperation with the Egyptian authorities against the Egyptian organizations. The presence of collaborators and supporters of the Egyptian organizations in this country enabled the smuggling of weaponry and the perpetrators, as well as the escape of the mission commanders back to Afghanistan at the end of the mission. In this attack, the Egyptian Jihad, which was behind it, proved to have impressive capabilities vis-à-vis the recruitment of weaponry and suicide attackers to perpetrate a mega attack outside of Egyptian territory.[10]

Another attack occurred on December 21, 1995, when a car bomb was detonated on a busy street in the city of Peshawar in northeast Pakistan. At least thirty people were killed and about one hundred were injured. The blast occurred in a market, near a department store, while the area was teeming with people. The Al-Jihad organization claimed responsibility for the attack. It had warned the Pakistani government a week earlier not to extradite Islamic radicals to Egypt. A declaration of Al-Jihad, published in Cairo, stated that the organization was willing to act against the Pakistani government as well. In this connection, it is important to note that Egypt and Pakistan had signed an extradition treaty in July 1994, which had enraged the Islamic groups in Egypt.[11]

Suicide Attacks by the Armed Islamic Front (GIA) in Algeria

During the 1980s, a large group of volunteers (whose number was estimated anywhere between several hundred and three thousand) left Algeria for
Afghanistan to fight alongside the Afghan mujahidin. Some fought in the
framework of the "Algerian Legion," under the command of Sheikh Ahmad
Masoud. It was Sheikh Abdullah Azzam who forged the links between the
commanders of the Algerian fighters headed by Haj Bunua and Sheikh
Masoud.[12]

At the end of the 1980s, and particularly after the victory of the mujahidin
in Afghanistan, these volunteers began to return to Algeria taking with them
their rich experience in fighting and guerrilla combat, and fired with Islamic
revolutionism. These volunteers, who upon return to their homeland were
called "the Afghans," were incorporated in radical Islamic organizations
such as The Armed Islamic Movement and the Al-Hijra Al Takfir Organization.[13]

The first violent act of the "Afghans" was recorded in November 1991 in
the town of Gumar on the Algerian-Tunisian border, when a group of fighters
attacked a police station, causing multiple fatalities and injuries.[14] From that
point onward, as the struggle between the Algerian government and the Islamic opposition intensified, there were repeated reports regarding the involvement of the Afghans in terror activities throughout the country.

The terror activity of the Islamic organizations, which began with sporadic attacks against military targets and governmental institutions, gradually intensified into an overall civil war which, to date. has claimed tens
of thousands of victims. During this period, Islamic terror entities succeeded in taking over large portions of rural areas and even some sections
of large cities.

In 1994, and mainly in the years 1995-1996, the GIA began perpetrating
terror attacks abroad. All of these attacks took place in France or were carried
out against French citizens outside of their country, and were supposedly
justified by the fact that the French government supported the current regime
in Algeria. The intensity of the confrontation between the GIA and France was
also explained by its spokesmen in the context of the historical conflict
between Algeria and France during the Algerian war of liberation in the 1950s
and early 1960s. The GIA's terror campaign abroad included the hijacking of
an Air France airplane in December 1994 and two waves of attacks in France
(July-October 1995 and December 1996), in which some twenty people were
killed and scores were wounded.

As an Islamic terror organization, the GIA, like other fundamentalist organizations in Arab countries, believed in the establishment of a religious Islamic state and viewed the United States and Israel, and Jews, as enemies of
Islam. The GIA carried out three terror attacks against Jews in France as part of

the overall terror campaign against that country. These attacks included the positioning of two car bombs, one near a synagogue in Lyons on December 25, 1995 (which was defused), and the other near a Jewish school in Villeurbanne near Lyon (September 1995), as well as the dispatch of a letter bomb to the editor of a Jewish newspaper (December 1996).[15]

The GIA terror attacks abroad (all of which took place in France) resulted in the exposure of its infrastructure, which included deployment in several European countries, mainly France, Belgium, Britain, Germany, Italy, Sweden, and Spain. Terror cells that were active in these countries included a small number of members, which were mutually linked and cooperated in the sharing of logistic, financial, and operational roles. The main role of the European network was to raise funds and combat means and to smuggle them over to their fighting comrades in Algeria. Enforcement and thwarting efforts of security, which were initiated by France with international cooperation, impaired the Algerian terror network's infrastructure and put an end to the terror attacks initiated by the GIA in the international arena.

In 1998, additional terror cells connected to the GIA were exposed in Europe. The involvement of emigrants and emigrants' children from the countries of the Magreb in the terror attacks in France, and their membership in Algerian terror cells in various European countries, indicates a wide infrastructure for the enlistment of potential volunteers in Islamic terror organizations from among the emigrant population of the lower socioeconomic levels, who feel discriminated against and alienated by their countries of residence. These populations constitute a reservoir for the recruitment of new members: some of whom were sent to undergo terror training in Afghanistan in the early 1990s, and others who volunteered to fight in Bosnia.[16]

Examples of GIA Suicide Attacks in Algeria

During the years 1995-2002, the GIA organization carried out scores of attacks through car bombs, some of which followed the suicide attack pattern. Several examples follow.

A suicide attack against the power station in Algeria. In 1995, the GIA organization declared that its members were trained to perpetrate suicide attacks.[17] On August 7, 1995, three organization activists carried out a suicide attack through the use of a car bomb loaded with explosives near the power station at Boufarik. Eight people were killed and twenty-five were injured in this attack.[18]

A suicide attack at a market in the city of Algiers. In 1995, the organization perpetrated a suicide attack through the use of a truck loaded with explosives driven by a suicide terrorist into a market in Algiers. Forty-two people were killed. The GIA claimed responsibility for the attack.

Another suicide attack in a market in Algiers. On August 31, 1998, a car bomb driven by a suicide terrorist exploded in the heart of a crowded market at Bab al Qued. Twenty-five people were killed and sixty-one were injured. No organization claimed responsibility, but the Algerian authorities believe that, apparently, the GIA was responsible for the attack.

Hijacking of the Air France airliner to Marseille by the GIA (December 24, 1994). On December 24, 1994, an Air France airplane was hijacked in Algeria by a GIA terror unit. The unit, which consisted of four members, had disguised themselves as maintenance employees, and with the use of fake badges boarded the plane at the Algerian airport prior to its takeoff for Paris. The hijacked plane had 239 passengers and crewmembers on board. The hijackers' demands included the release of several organizational leaders incarcerated in Algerian prisons. They threatened to kill hostages if their demands were not met. At the very beginning of the incident, the hijackers killed two hostages, a local policeman and a Vietnamese diplomat. Their bodies remained on board the aircraft throughout the hijacking. Subsequently, the hijackers shot another hostage when their demands were not met. Following negotiations that went on for two days, the plane took off for Marseilles. After a short period of time, a special French counter-terror unit overtook the plane and killed the hijackers. In the course of the incident, there were five casualties and twenty-five were injured. On December 26, 1996, the GIA claimed responsibility for the hijacking via a manifesto faxed to the French news agency in Paris. An investigation of the incident by the French authorities (with the aid of information divulged by Britain) indicated that the original intention of the hijackers had been to perpetrate a suicide attack by ramming the aircraft along with all its passengers into the Eiffel Tower.[19] This attack would have caused a very high number of fatalities among the passengers of the aircraft and the many tourists who regularly visit the Eiffel Tower as one of France's central tourist attractions. Fortunately, the pilot succeeded in persuading the hijackers to enable the plane's landing in Marseille, thus preventing a terrible disaster.

Suicide Attacks in the Indian-Pakistani Conflict
Regarding the Kashmir Region

The "Lashkar e-Toiba" Organization (the Army of the Pure)[20]

The LET[21] is one of the largest terror organizations active in the Jammu-Kashmir (J&K) region. This organization, together with the "Army of Muhammad" organization, is responsible for the attack on the Parliament building in New Delhi on December 13, 2001, which brought India and Pakistan to the brink of war. The organization was founded at the end of the 1980s in the Kunar district of Afghanistan as the military arm of the Fundamentalist

Pakistani Islamic movement with Wahibian leanings (Markaz-ul-Dawa-wal-Irshid). At the end of the 1980s and in the beginning of the 1990s, the Lashkar e-Toiba organization was involved in the Jihad against the Soviets in Afghanistan. Parallel to its involvement on the Afghani front, the organization also started to become active at Jammu-Kashmir, with the aid and under the sponsorship of the Pakistani intelligence. The organization is headed by Professor Hafez Muhammad Sa'id, who also serves as the Emir (leader) of LET.

The Lashkar e-Toiba supports not only the establishment of Islamic rule in Jammu and Kashmir, but also in all of India, and it has joined the ranks of Moslems fighting throughout the world, in Chechnya and Moslem republics in Central Asia, among others. The LET's first attack was carried out in 1993 when a terror cell numbering twelve terrorists of Pakistani and Afghani origins infiltrated the Jammu-Kashmir area, which was under Indian rule.

From 1997 onwards, during the second term of Pakistani Prime Minister Nawaz Sharif, the organization steadily gained strength. At that time the Pakistani intelligence (ISI) sponsored the organization's activities, providing it with funding, training, and weapons.

The increased importance afforded to the organization was linked to a revision in the policy of the Pakistani intelligence, which had decided to shift the center of gravity for subversive activity from the Kashmir valley to the Jammu region, as part of an overall plan to carry out ethnic cleansing of minorities in the area by escalating terror activities. LET was an ideal means for this task due to its radical Islamic ideology and its willingness to carry out attacks and massacres against minorities in that area. The fact that most of the members of Lashkar e-Toiba originated from the Pakistani Penjab area helped them to blend in easily with the population of the Jammu region, which speaks the same dialect. The organization's fighters became famous for their willingness to sacrifice themselves and in most cases chose to die in battle rather than surrender when surrounded by Indian forces.

Lashkar e-Toiba carried out a series of suicide attacks against bases of Indian forces:

- An attack against an Indian border guard base in Bandipore, near Srinagar.
- An attack against a border police base at Handwara on September 4, 1999.
- An attack against the headquarters of the Special Forces on December 27, 1999.

Despite the fact that the head of the organization's suicide unit, Abu Muain, was killed on December 30, 1999, in a clash with Indian forces, the suicide attacks continued and during the year 2000 another three suicide attacks took place:

- On January 1, 2000, a military base in Surankote was attacked.
- On January 12, 2000, a military base in Anantang was attacked.
- On January 21, 2000, a border guard base was attacked in Srinagar.

The organization's suicide attacks contributed to its consolidation and intensified the level of fear and terror among Indian security forces and civilians. The LET raises funds from Pakistani populations in the Persian Gulf states through charitable organizations, as well as from Pakistani businessmen and the Pakistani government. The organization is closely affiliated with Bin-Laden and Al-Qaida, and it maintains military and religious groups throughout the world from the Philippines, via Chechnya to Bosnia. The organization also offered refuge to Ramzi Yusuf and Mir Imal Kenzi, two terrorists who were apprehended and extradited to the United States.

The Jeish Muhammad (Army of Muhammad) Organization[22]

This is a relatively new terror organization founded in February 2000. It has been in the limelight mainly thanks to its commander Maulana Masoud Azhar, who has a long record in the area of terror and was released from an Indian prison in December 1999. Masoud Azhar, a radical Islamic cleric from Karachi, was chosen by the Pakistani intelligence (ISI) to play a central role in the struggle at Jammu-Kashmir when he served as the secretary-general of the "Harkhat al-Antsar," a dominant terror organization until the mid-1990s. Masoud Azhar was arrested in Srinagar in February 1999, and over the years attempts were made to achieve his release, but they ended in failure.

In December 1999, members of the organization hijacked an Indian Airlines passenger plane in Kandahar, Afghanistan. In exchange for the release of the passengers, the Indian authorities agreed to release Masoud and two other terrorists from the organization who were incarcerated in an Indian prison. After Masoud's release, many of his supporters expected him to resume his position as head of the organization and lead it to play a central role in the struggle over Kashmir, but the Harkhat al-Antsar organization had already been weakened after two of its senior leaders had been killed by India's security forces.

Masoud's declarations about the need to persevere in the Jihad in Jammu-Kashmir caused the Pakistani authorities some embarrassment, as India already suspected them of being involved in the hijacking of the airliner and the subsequent release of Masoud. Therefore, the Pakistani authorities chose to play down their ties with Masoud and prevented his return to a senior position in the Harkhat al-Antsar, which was largely identified with the Pakistani regime. In light of these developments, Masoud decided to establish the "Army of Muhammad" organization, vowing to escalate the terror in Jammu-Kashmir.

The organization's first attack took place on April 23, 2000, when an organization member detonated himself along with a truck loaded with explosives near the gate of the Indian military headquarters in Srinagar. On May 18, 2000, rumors spread about the possibility that the Army of Muhammad and Harkhat al-Antsar had consolidated, but this information was not verified. On June 28, 2000, the organization claimed credit for an attack that included shooting and lobbing hand grenades at a government office building in Srinagar. In December 2001, members of the Army of Muhammad and Lashkar e-Toiba attacked the Indian Parliament building in New Delhi. The loud Indian and international outcry, and the escalation in the violence at the India-Pakistani border prompted the Pakistani government to take action against the organization by outlawing it and arresting some of its members.

The attack against the Indian Parliament building in New Delhi.[23] On December 12, 2001, five terrorists attacked the Indian Parliament building in New Delhi. They arrived in a vehicle that appeared to be a government car (according to its color and license plates), and passed through the ring of gates and outer barriers surrounding the building.

Four terrorists, who were armed with Kalachnikov assault rifles, stormed the VIP entrance of the Parliament while shooting and throwing grenades at the policemen guarding the building. A fifth terrorist detonated an explosive belt he was wearing at the entrance to the building. Policemen and the parliament guard returned fire and a forty-minute gun battle ensued between the two sides. At its conclusion, the five terrorists lay dead. Four policemen were also killed and eighteen were wounded. During the attack several government ministers and 300 members of Parliament were present in the building, but none of them was hurt.

The government of India accused Pakistan of supporting the terror organizations that had perpetrated the attack. An investigation indicated that the Army of Muhammad and Lashkar e-Toiba were responsible for the attack. The Pakistani government denied any involvement in the attack, expressed its sympathy, and proposed a joint investigation to discover the responsible parties, but the government of India rejected the Pakistani position and demanded vociferously that it take immediate steps to put a stop to the terror.

As a result of the attack, heavy tension prevailed all along the border between the two countries. Both countries reinforced their troops, and shooting incidents flared up along the boundaries.

Suicide Attacks against Foreign Targets in Pakistan

A suicide attack against a bus transporting foreign citizens in Karachi, Pakistan. On May 9, 2002, a car bomb driven by a suicide terrorist detonated alongside a busload of foreign French citizens near the Sheraton Hotel in Karachi, Pakistan. Fifteen people were killed and thirty-three were injured.

The Pakistani authorities suspect that Al-Qaida or affiliated entities are responsible for the attack, and that it was meant to further the following goals:[24]

- To strike out at the counter-terror coalition, which enjoys the cooperation of the Pakistani and French governments.
- To issue a warning to the Pakistani government regarding its war against terror.
- To impair Pakistan's international and economical status.
- To embarrass the administration of Pervaiz Mushraf.

The attack was directed against French citizens working in a submarine construction project for the Pakistani navy at the Karachi shipyards.[25] The attack apparently was perpetrated after the gathering of precise intelligence, which included surveillance of the French citizens' daily schedule. The suicide attacker arrived in a stolen 1994 Toyota Corolla, loaded with explosives, and pulled up at the front of the hotel just as the French workers were boarding a minibus that regularly drove them to work.[26] The terrorist detonated the car alongside the minibus when most of the passengers where already on board, thus increasing the number of casualties. The Pakistani authorities launched an extensive investigation, with the cooperation of French security agencies, in order to identify and arrest the entities behind the incident.[27]

The Pakistani government used the attack to cast accusations intimating the possible involvement of the Indian intelligence services in the attack, the probability of which is very low.[28]

The suicide attack against the U.S. Consulate in Karachi, Pakistan. On June 14, 2002, a suicide attack was perpetrated against the U.S. Consulate in Karachi, Pakistan, through the use of a car bomb driven by a suicide terrorist. Eleven people were killed in the attack and scores were injured.[29] In a written declaration delivered to the news agency, an unknown organization named Al-Kanun claimed responsibility for the attack. The organization also issued a warning to the United States, its allies and "their lackeys who govern Pakistan" regarding additional attacks that would be perpetrated in the framework of Jihad campaigns in Pakistan.[30] There may be a link between the attack and the arrest of several American citizens suspected of membership in Al-Qaida due to cooperation between the American forces and Pakistani security agencies in the border area between Pakistan and Afghanistan, where Al-Qaida activists sought refuge after fleeing the American onslaught in Afghanistan.

Suicide attack on Shi'ite mosque in Quetta, Pakistan.[31] On July 4, 2003, a blast tore through a Shi'ite mosque in Quetta, the capital of Baluchistan province, killing forty-one people and injuring as many as 100. Police say that at least four attackers were involved. Three were killed—one blew himself up and two others were killed by mosque security guards. A fourth assailant was captured. Police found two other bombs near the main wall of the mosque two hours after the blast. Rioting in the streets by angry Shi'ites who overturned cars and burned tires followed the attack. Authorities declared a curfew, asking people to remain indoors, while paramilitary troops and riot police were stationed around the city to quell disturbances. Shi'ites form about 20 percent of Pakistan's Sunni-dominated 145 million population. The minority Shi'ite ethnic Hazara community in Quetta has been targeted in the past by radical Sunni groups.

Suicide Attacks in Afghanistan

In Afghanistan, there has been a "tradition" of implementing suicide attacks since the days of the Jihad against the Soviets and the Marxist government in Kabul (1979-1992). The phenomenon of the suicide attacks continued during the period of the struggle between the Taliban government and the opposition of the Northern Alliance during the years 1994-2001, although on a smaller scale. The most prominent suicide attack during this period was the assassination of the Northern Alliance's military leader, Sheikh Massoud Sh'ah, just prior to Bin-Laden's attack in the United States on September 11.

The Assassination of the Military Commander of the Northern Alliance

On September 9, 2001, the assassination of Sheikh Massoud Sh'ah, the military leader of the Northern Alliance (which constituted the main opposition to the Taliban regime in Afghanistan) took place. Massoud Sh'ah was assassinated two days prior to the terror attack in the United States by a cell that was apparently linked with the Algerian GSPC (the Sulufi Group for Propaganda and Struggle) and acted according to instructions issued by the Al-Qaida headquarters in Afghanistan.[32] The attack was meant to neutralize the main rival of Al-Qaida and the Taliban in anticipation of the terror attack in the United States. It was carried out by two suicide terrorists who masqueraded as press photographers interested in interviewing Massoud Sh'ah. One of the two detonated himself, killing Massoud, and the other was killed by Massoud's bodyguards. An explosive device was apparently concealed in the TV camera carried by the reporters.

During the years 1994-2001, Afghanistan served as a key activity and training center serving Islamic terror organizations from all over the world. Within its boundaries, attacks were prepared that were subsequently carried out in various countries worldwide, the most prominent of which were the attacks planned and perpetrated by Al-Qaida. Osama Bin-Laden, who headed the organization, and his followers were based in Afghanistan and enjoyed the sponsorship of the Taliban regime (see details about the Al-Qaida attacks in a separate section). During the war against terror declared by the United States and the American operation in Afghanistan, several suicide attacks were carried out by the Taliban and Al-Qaida activists that refused to surrender to the U.S. forces and members of the Northern Alliance.

A Suicide Attack Carried Out by a Taliban Fighter

A typical example of this type of suicide attack is an incident that occurred on November 25, 2001. A Taliban fighter apprehended by the Northern Alliance forces in the city Mazar a-Sharif detonated himself and his captors through the use of a hand grenade concealed under his clothing. Three members of the Northern Alliance were killed in the attack.[33]

A Suicide Attack against the German Forces in Afghanistan[34]

Four German soldiers, members of the international peace force in Afghanistan, were killed on June 7, 2003, in a suicide attack perpetrated in the capital, Kabul. Twenty-nine soldiers were injured, seven seriously. Several Afghan bystanders were also hurt. Although no organization claimed responsibility, the Afghan government blamed what they called "remnants of Al-Qaida or the Taliban" for the attack. According to American reports, a lone suicide attacker detonated a taxi loaded with explosives next to a bus in which soldiers from the international force (ISAF) were traveling. The attack took place about five kilometers away from the town center, near the base of the German and Dutch units serving in the force, which includes 4,600 soldiers from twenty-nine countries. This was the gravest attack against the ISAF since its establishment a year earlier to assist the regime of President Khamid Kharzai to restore law and order to the capital and its vicinity. Germany currently leads the force. A special team, together with the Afghan government, will investigate the attack.

Suicide Attacks Perpetrated by the PKK (The Workers' Party of Kurdistan) in Turkey[35]

The Kurdish terror organization first used the modus operandi of suicide attacks on June 30, 1995, and ceased its suicide attack missions on July 5, 1999, after the capture of Abdallah Ocalan by Turkish authorities. During this period, the organization carried out fifteen suicide attacks, with an additional seven being thwarted by the Turkish security forces. In this campaign of attacks, the number of fatalities was relatively low; nineteen dead and 138 injured.

The organization began perpetrating suicide attacks when it sustained heavy blows afflicted by the Turkish army in the Kurdish areas of the country (southeast Turkey), and sought effective ways to revive its combat capabilities and improve the morale of its ranks. Suicide attacks became the organization's most effective tool to demonstrate its ability to continue the struggle against the more powerful Turkish forces. Some of the suicide attacks were carried out in response to or to avenge activities by the Turkish security forces against the organization.

In Turkey, the term "suicide" is controversial, because it is forbidden according to Islamic religious law. Therefore, the justification of suicide attacks necessitates the obtainment of a religious ruling or national substantiation. Both the Turks and the PKK people are willing to sacrifice their lives for lofty national or religious ideals. But a suicide attack is considered an exceptional act that necessitates legitimization. In its drive to achieve independence from a Muslim regime, the PKK Kurdish underground found it difficult to justify suicide attacks based on the argument of Jihad, which constitutes the main source of legitimacy for Islamic terror organizations worldwide. Therefore, the organization claimed that the Turkish government was a colonial regime, and that its struggle was in the name of national liberation, which is comparable to Jihad. The main motive of the PKK suicide attackers was nationalist and was founded on blind loyalty to the organization's leadership.

The source for most information regarding the PKK's suicide operations lies in attacks that were thwarted and in the information gleaned from potential suicide attackers and their operators, who were arrested and interrogated. Targets of the organization's suicide attacks were generally senior members of the Turkish administration, Turkish police, and army commanders, as well as security and government facilities. In many of the attacks directed against government targets, innocent bystanders were hurt because these targets are located in public places. Nonetheless, it is noteworthy that the PKK's suicide attacks were focused on targets that were chosen with great care, and the organization refrained from indiscriminate attacks against civilian Turkish targets (in contrast to Palestinian or Pakistani suicide terror).

The role of women is particularly conspicuous in the PKK suicide attacks: eleven of the attacks (out of a total of fifteen) were carried out by women. Professor Dogu Ergil explains this phenomenon from the social aspect. He argues that Kurdish society is basically conservative and women have an inferior status, which expresses itself in their being viewed as a man's chattel. The PKK, therefore, constituted the opening of a channel to bring about the emancipation and improved status of women in Kurdish society, which drew a large number of women to fight in its ranks. The women underwent the same training and indoctrination as the men in the organization. But due to their desire to prove their capabilities, they adopted patterns of unswerving loyalty to the organization and its leaders, thus generating outstanding motivation to perpetrate suicide attacks.

Professor Ergil offers several additional reasons for the prominent involvement of women in the PKK's suicide attacks:

- It was easier to persuade women to take part in suicide attacks while emphasizing their "choice" and importance in the eyes of the organization. The female suicide attackers were generally escorted to the target by men, thus expressing the honor and admiration accorded to them by the organization.
- Women had difficulty fighting in the battlefield like men. Therefore, they sought alternative action channels where they could make an equal and even preferable contribution to the organization.
- Most of the women who joined the PKK could not return to their families, which they had abandoned in contrast to family tradition. Therefore, their future and fate were unclear in any case.
- Women were less likely than men to arouse suspicion in the eyes of the Turkish security forces and they could conceal explosives under their clothing. As a rule, the Turkish authorities were very respectful of women, and thus there was less risk of body searches.
- Many of the women were motivated by personal revenge, and sought to avenge the deaths of relatives and friends who had perished in the struggle against the Turks.

The ages of the women ranged between 17 and 27. Most were uneducated and had no profession, and they came from poor families. Investigations by Turkish authorities indicated that in some of the cases suicide terrorists volunteered for the mission, but in other cases organizational peer pressure was placed on the suicide attackers impelling them to set out on the mission. The basic motive for a member to undertake a suicide mission was his or her organizational solidarity and indoctrination to obey the organization, its goals, and its leader. Candidates for perpetrating suicide attacks were isolated and distanced from the organization's ongoing activities for periods of three to six months prior to the attack. During this time, they underwent emotional and operational preparations, and an irreversible commitment of the candidate to carry out his or her mission was created. Regrets or second thoughts regarding the suicide mission would cause isolation and condemnation of the candidate, and sometimes even a threat to execute him or her.

Due to its secular outlook, the PKK did not promise its suicide attackers the "Garden of Eden," and instead anchored the need to carry out the mission in ideological and nationalist motives. Nevertheless, the religious theme existed on a personal level, though not as a central or established motive from the organization's point of view. The ages of Kurdish men who carried out suicide attacks ranged between 18 and 40. Two suicide terrorists were aged 18-22 and another two were aged 35-40. Most of the PKK suicide attacks were perpetrated in Turkey's southern regions, where the organization was struggling to achieve independence for its Kurdish residents. This preference stemmed from the organization's desire to demonstrate to the population for which it was fighting its determination and sacrifice to promote the establishment of a Kurdish state.

The PKK suicide attacks were stopped at the command of the organization's leadership when the top leader was arrested and a Turkish court sentenced him to death. The organization's leadership decided to cease the suicide attacks in order to prevent the Turkish government from carrying out the sentence, in the hope that the execution sentence would be commuted to life imprisonment.

Examples of Suicide Attacks Perpetrated by the PKK

1. On November 17, 1998, a female Kurdish terrorist detonated herself near a police station in the city of Yuksekova in southern Turkey. Six people were injured in the attack. The attack was carried out in retaliation for the arrest of the organization's leader Abdallah Ocalan.
2. On December 1, 1998, a female Kurdish terrorist detonated herself at a supermarket in the city of Lice where Turkish soldiers often shopped. Fourteen people were killed in the attack.[36]
3. On December 24, 1998, a female suicide terrorist detonated herself near a Turkish army base in the city of Van in east Turkey. Twenty-two people were injured in the blast, including fourteen soldiers.[37]
4. On April 9, 1999, a Kurdish suicide terrorist detonated himself near the district governor's car in the city of Yuksekova in southern Turkey. Two people were killed and four were injured, including the governor and his bodyguard, the chief of the local police, and passersby.[38]
5. On June 7, 1999, a young Kurdish woman who was a member of the PKK carried out a suicide attack at a police station in one of the cities in southern Turkey.[39] The woman detonated herself at the entrance to the police headquarters and caused injuries to eighteen people, including the local chief of police. This attack came in retaliation for the Turkish court's death sentence vis-à-vis the PKK leader Abdallah Ocalan, and was one of a series of attacks (a total of twenty) perpetrated in response to the arrest and sentencing of Ocalan in a Turkish court.

Professor Ergil presents two interesting examples of female Kurdish suicide attackers: one who carried out the attack and the second who reconsidered:[40]

• Leila Kaplan carried out a suicide attack at the entrance to a police station in the city of Adana, Turkey. Three policemen were killed, nine were injured, and three passersby were hurt. An investigation of the attack indicates that Leila did not volunteer for the mission. The mission was first offered to another female member of the PKK named Turkan Adiyaman. Turkan refused, and was executed by organization members in front of Leila's eyes. Afterwards, Leila was offered the mission and she "accepted the offer" and carried out the attack.

- Elif Mavis was born in France in 1980 to an emigrant Kurdish family from southern Turkey. She was influenced by the PKK propaganda in the high school where she studied in the city of Creil in France and joined the organization. During her membership in the organization she underwent ideological training in France, Holland, and Germany. In Germany, organization activists tried to recruit her for a suicide mission in Istanbul. She refused, and heavy pressure was placed on her to change her mind. Elif "stuck to her guns" and fled to Istanbul where she was arrested by Turkish authorities immediately upon her arrival.

Chechen Terror and Suicide Attacks

Terror serves as an important tool in the Chechen struggle for independence from Russia. Chechen terror activity has been waged on several fronts since the early 1990s:

- Terror activity in Chechnya against entities recognized as collaborators with Russia, and against Russian targets on Chechen soil.
- Terror activities in the republics neighboring with Chechnya (Dagestan, Ingushetia) to assist local Islamic organizations in their struggle against the pro-Russian regimes in these republics, and against Russian targets.
- Terror activity in Russia (including the heart of Moscow).
- Terror activity in the international arena (hijacking of sea vessels and airplanes and forcing them to land in foreign countries).

Chechen terror uses a wide range of modi operandi:

- Kidnapping of hostages
- Detonating explosive charges and car bombs
- Hijacking planes, sea vessels and buses
- Suicide attacks

Information and security entities in Russia emphasize the link between Chechen terrorists and the international Islamic terror of the Afghan "alumni," such as Emir Katab and Osama Bin-Laden.[41] Chechen terror served as a central pretext for the Russian invasion of Chechnya in 1999, a step that had the backing of the Russian general public and the understanding of the international community.[42] The Chechen terror in 1999, which strayed beyond Chechen borders, was perceived by the Russian public and Russian decision-makers as a threat against Russian security and a departure from "the rules of the game," which had been accepted up to that time in the Chechen-Russian struggle.[43]

In the eyes of Western countries, the series of attacks against innocent civilians generated a process of de-legitimization vis-à-vis the Chechen struggle, and at the very least a condemnation of the use of terror. Therefore, it is reasonable to state that the series of attacks in 1999 caused grievous damage to Chechnya, and granted legitimization to the invasion, to the destruction of the state, and to the loss of all of its achievements during the war (1994-1996).

Russian security agencies encountered difficulty in handling the Chechen terror for several main reasons:

- The weakness of the Russian intelligence and thwarting agencies in light of the reforms, changes, and budgetary cuts introduced in the ranks of the Russian security system (the dismantling of the KGB, the establishment of the FSB, and more).[44]
- Lack of coordination between the various entities dealing with terror— The FSB, the Ministry of the Interior, the Defense Ministry, the Russian Army, the police, etc.
- The scope of the arena. The terrorists could attack at any location throughout Russia.
- The Chechen adversary was well acquainted with Russia and its security capabilities, and it had considerable experience in guerrilla and terror activities against Russia (and the USSR in the past).

Therefore, during most of this period, Russian authorities generally failed to thwart terror activities. However, in some of the cases, mainly in kidnapping incidents, the Special Forces (particularly the "Alpha" counter-terror unit) demonstrated impressive operational capabilities, which enabled the liberation of hostages.

Bombing Attacks against Civilian Targets in Russian Cities

In the months of August-September 1999, a series of grave terror attacks took place against civilian targets in Russia, with the emphasis on Moscow, the capital.[45] According to the Kremlin's claims, the attacks in which Chechen terrorists detonated powerful explosive devices and car bombs were directed against residential buildings, shopping centers, markets, and at subway stations in Moscow. In this series of attacks about 300 Russian citizens were killed and hundreds were injured.[46]

The Russian security agencies made a huge effort to try and thwart the attacks and apprehend the perpetrators. However, despite widespread arrests (reaching about 11,000), it is doubtful whether the entities responsible for the attacks were caught.[47]

According to Russian security agencies, after the failure in Dagestan, the commanders of the Chechen rebels, Sjamil Besayev and Emir Katab, dispatched about thirty terrorists (divided into four cells) who carried out terror attacks at four different focal points:[48] Moscow, St. Petersburg, Rostov-on-Don, and Dagestan.

At the end of September 1999, the Russian security services (the FSB) reported the discovery of a Mercedes van loaded with eleven tons of explosives, as well as the detection of seventy-six backpacks containing explosives in an apartment in Moscow. These forces suspected that the explosives were designated for the perpetration of additional attacks by the Chechen terror networks. Chechen President Aslan Maskhadov and Emir Katab denied Chechnya's involvement in the series of attacks. An unknown terror organization called "The Dagestan Liberation Army" claimed responsibility for two of the attacks. However, Russian security entities were skeptical about the organization's very existence and raised the supposition that this was merely an attempt to conceal the identity of the true perpetrators—Chechen terrorists.[49]

Suicide Attacks in Chechnya

Prior to the terror attack at the Moscow theater in October 2002, Chechen suicide attacks were perpetrated only in Chechnya itself, and they were directed mainly at security forces and/or government and Russian security facilities. The suicide missions were generally carried out by a single suicide attacker equipped with an explosive device or a bomb belt, or driving a car bomb and detonating himself with the vehicle when approaching his target.

In June 2000, suicide attacks were first perpetrated in the framework of the Russian-Chechen conflict.[50] On June 2, two Chechen suicide terrorists, a man and a woman, detonated a truck loaded with explosives near the barracks of the Russian elite unit (OMON) in the city of Alkhan-Yurt. The truck rammed the gates and exploded near the building. Immediately after the explosion, a Chechen force opened fire at the building. According to Russian reports, two people were killed in the attack and five were wounded. On the Internet site of the Chechen isolationists it was reported that the attack had been carried out by a lone suicide terrorist named Barayev, and that he had caused the deaths of twenty-seven Russian soldiers. Barayev was the cousin of one of the senior Chechen commanders (Arbi Barayev). The site stated that this was a message not only for Russia but also for Muslim brethren worldwide, to come to the aid of their brothers in Chechnya.

On June 11, 2000, a deserter from the Russian army who had converted to Islam and joined the Chechen rebels perpetrated a suicide attack using a car bomb loaded with explosives against a Russian checkpoint near Khanakala. Two Russian soldiers from the OMON unit were killed in the attack.

Following these attacks, the Islamic rebels in Chechnya adopted this modus operandi as part of their action pattern in the struggle against Russia. In the first week of July 2000, suicide attacks against Russian military and civilian targets were carried out in four Chechen cities.[51] The Russians claimed that forty people perished in these attacks, while the Chechen rebels maintained that hundreds of Russians were killed.[52]

The attack at Argon. The most severe attack occurred in the city of Argon, which is located several kilometers east of Grozni, the Chechen capital. A truck loaded with explosives and driven by a suicide terrorist detonated near a hostel that served as the barracks for Russian policemen. Thirty people were killed and eighty-one were injured in the blast.

The attack at Gudmares. At the city of Gudmares, a truck loaded with explosives and driven by a suicide terrorist detonated near the governor's building in the city, which was populated by Chechens loyal to the Russians. Soon after the explosion, a force of Chechen rebels opened fire on the building. In the combined attack, five Russian soldiers were killed as well as eight civilians, and many were wounded.

The attack at Urus Martan. A truck packed with explosives and driven by a suicide terrorist rammed the gate near a Russian army barracks and detonated. Two Russian soldiers were killed in the attack.

The attack at Novogrozni. A truck packed with explosives and driven by a suicide terrorist rammed the gate near a building inhabited by Russian soldiers and exploded. Three soldiers were killed and twenty were wounded.

The attack of a female suicide terrorist in Urus Martan–2001. On November 29, 2001, a young Chechen woman named Louisa Gazoaba carried out a suicide attack in the city of Urus Martan. In this attack General Gadzhiev, the regional commander of the Russian army, was killed. Two other officers and the general's bodyguards were injured. The female suicide terrorist approached the general and several other military men who were standing near the Russian army headquarters. The young woman asked the general if he recognized her. He replied that he did not have time to talk to her, at which point she detonated the bomb belt concealed beneath her clothing. The exact motives of the young woman who detonated herself are not clear. However, it is a known fact that her husband, her two brothers, and a cousin were all killed during the Russian invasion of Chechnya.

The attack at the theater in Moscow, October 23-26, 2002. On October 23, 2002, approximately fifty terrorists overtook a theater in Moscow during a play, and nearly 1,000 people were taken hostage.[53] The Chechen terrorists were armed with light weapons including grenades, explosive devices, and belt bombs. They booby-trapped the building and threatened that if Russian forces attempted to overtake it, they would detonate themselves along with their hostages. In exchange for releasing the hostages, the Chechens demanded "cessation of the war and withdrawal of the Russian forces from Chechnya." Upon learning about the attack, Russian authorities immediately surrounded the building with military and police forces, which began negotiations with the Chechens. The Chechen terrorists screened the hostages and released the Muslims as well as eighteen children.

The group of terrorists was headed by Mubarak Barayev, a nephew of one of the Chechen commanders, Arbi Barayev, who had been killed by Russian forces a year earlier. The number of women among the terrorists was prominent; they were clad in "Islamic dress" and were equipped with belt bombs. During the terror attack, a videocassette was handed over to broadcasters showing the terrorists prior to their departure on the mission. The preliminary filming and the terrorists' introduction as "shahids" testified to their intention to perpetrate a suicide attack, or to convert the bargaining attack (the taking of hostages) into a suicide attack, in the event of any Russian attempt to release the hostages.

Preliminary findings of the investigation indicate that the mission had been planned for several months. In the framework of preparations for the attack, the terrorists purchased the theater's snack bar and under the camouflage of renovation work planted all of the required equipment for the mission: belt bombs, explosive devices, and light weapons. On the evening of the attack, the terrorists acquired tickets for the play and entered the hall like other members of the audience.[54] The investigation also indicated that some of the terrorists were of Arab descent and apparently had contacts with Arab embassies in Moscow and with entities in the Middle East.[55]

During the three-day siege at the Moscow theater, the Chechen terrorists allowed the hundreds of hostages to use their personal cellular phones in order to calm their families and pass on the terrorists' demands. What they did not know, so Russian observers believe, is that Russian security services eavesdropped on the calls and gathered essential information that put an end to the hostage crisis.

Security sources in Moscow, which helped to formulate the mission to release the captives, revealed that the relative freedom granted to the hostages by the terrorists was the source of the kidnappers' failure. A senior security source noted that agents of the Russian secret service intercepted scores of telephone calls made by the hostages right after the attack and realized that these would constitute an important source of information about events unfolding inside the theater. When calls were made by the hostages to their families, Russian agents first determined if there were any terrorists in the vicinity of their loved ones on the other end. When it became clear that there were none, the family members handed over the phone to security officers who asked the caller to answer "yes" or "no" to questions regarding the terrorists, thus avoiding the arousal of any suspicion on the part of the Chechen terrorists.[56]

The Russian foreign minister, Igor Ivanov, described the incident, as "a link in the chain of terror acts planned and coordinated at one center outside of Russia."[57]

After fifty-eight hours of siege and negotiations, when near the end of the ultimatum set by the terrorists shots were heard inside the building, Russian security forces burst inside. The forces stormed the building at 5:15 a.m., right before dawn. The first stage of the rescue mission consisted of pumping anesthetizing gas into the building. It is not clear whether the "Alpha" counter-terror unit pumped the anesthetizing gas into the area of the huge theater via the air conditioning system or whether they lobbed gas grenades. However, it is clear that everyone who was inside the building at least lost partial consciousness. The gas appeared to have an immediate effect: scores of terror-ists—some of them women wearing belt bombs ready for activation—did not even succeed in pressing the switch grasped in their hands.

The commando fighters streamed into the building from the basement, while a diversionary force stormed through the main entrance. Already on the first day of the kidnapping, workers were seen digging openings into the sewage system and heating pipes. Now it appears that they were preparing means for rapid access into the structure. Dozens of Chechens were ruthlessly mowed down. Witnesses stated that some of them were executed on the spot with one shot in the head.

The fighters feared that the huge quantities of explosives placed by the terrorists in sensitive spots would bring down the building on the heads of the hundreds of hostages. The Special Forces succeeded in preventing this horrifying scenario.[58] "We succeeded in preventing mass slaughter," declared Vladimir Vasiliev, the Russian deputy minister of the interior. As a result of inhaling the gas, over 100 hostages were killed, and almost all of the rest were injured, and subsequently hospitalized with various levels of injury.

The majority of the abductors were killed on the spot as the result of inhaling the gas and the shots fired by the Russian soldiers, although there are reports that several of them were taken alive, including a female terrorist who succeeded in passing herself off as a hostage, and was therefore taken to the hospital.

"We do not dismiss the possibility that next time a group of Chechen rebels may attempt to overtake a nuclear facility," warned the representative of the exiled Chechen leader Aslan Maskhadov. The representative, Ahmed Zakayev, told journalists that though the chosen representatives of Chechnya are willing to reach a political resolution with Moscow, they cannot control the desperate extremists. "We cannot promise that another group will not act on Russian soil," he stated. Zakayev stressed that the attack on the theater in Moscow was carried out without Maskharov's knowledge. "What happened was the act of desperate people and the result of the continuous war," he added.

When addressing the possibility that the next group of rebels might take over a nuclear facility, Zakayev said "the consequences in that case would be disastrous not only for Russia and Chechnya but also for all of Europe." He emphasized that the Russian leaders would bear the responsibility for that type of attack because they were unable to put an end to the violent acts in Chechnya.[59]

The Suicide Attack at Zamenski, North of the Chechen Capital of Grozni[60]

On May 12, 2003, a truck driven to the site by two suicide terrorists drove rapidly towards a building that housed the local offices of the Russian security services. Soldiers guarding the compound tried to stop the truck by shooting at it, but it continued to race down, burst through the security roadblocks, and exploded. The building was razed completely by the blast, and eight structures were damaged. The spokesperson of the Chechen Ministry of Interior announced that forty people were killed, including the two suicide attackers, and over 100 were injured.

In response to the attack, Russian President Vladimir Putin declared that nothing would stop the Kremlin's peace plan for Chechnya. "We cannot and will not allow something like this to happen," he averred.

A Suicide Attack in the Town of Ilishkan-Yurt

On May 14, 2003, at least fourteen people were killed and 145 were injured in a suicide attack at the town of Ilishkan-Yurt (its Russian name is Byelorechye). A female suicide bomber detonated herself with a suicide belt during the celebrations marking the birthday of the prophet Muhammad. It appears that the suicide bomber intended to kill the pro-Russian Chechen administrative director, Akhmad Kadyrov, who was delivering a speech on stage at the time. Kadyrov himself emerged unscathed, but four of his bodyguards were killed.

The suicide attacker was Shakhida Baimoratova, 46, whose husband was killed in the skirmishes with the Russians in 1999. The Interfax news agency maintained that Shakhida was affiliated with a group of Chechen rebels headed by Shamil Basayev.

An Attack near the City of Mozdok[61]

On June 5, 2003, a female Chechen suicide attacker detonated herself on a bus full of Russian civilians and Air Force employees. The attack took place near the city of Mozdok in northern Chechnya while the bus was en route to a Russian army base. Nineteen individuals were killed in the blast and others were wounded. A leading Chechen rebel, Aslan Maskhadov, denied any involvement of the Chechen rebels in the attack, but Russian authorities unequivocally attribute the attack to the rebels.

Blast near Chechen Government District in Grozni[62]

On June 19, 2003, a day before the republic's temporary legislature was to meet for its first session, a truck packed with explosives blew up near a Russian government compound in the Chechen capital of Grozni. Chechen officials estimated that the blast killed two bombers and injured at least thirty-six bystanders. Alexander Khityanik, a police official in Grozni, told NTV television that the suicide bombers—a man and a woman who were riding in the truck as it sped toward the police building—were killed in the explosion. Security sources said the truck carried the equivalent of 1.6 tons of TNT. The blast left a crater some three meters wide by four meters deep in the road outside the police headquarters. Surrounding buildings included the headquarters of the police organized crime unit and the region's electricity utility.

Suicide Blasts Target Moscow Rock Festival[63]

On July 5, 2003, two women strapped with explosives blew themselves up at the entrance of a popular Moscow rock festival, killing at least sixteen people and injuring sixty. The attack targeted the annual Kryiya (Wings) rock festival held at the Tushino airfield on the outskirts of the capital. The rock festival is a popular event and some 40,000 spectators—mostly young people—were in attendance at the time. Police said that the bombers worked as a team, with the first detonating her explosives when she was stopped by security guards at the ticket booth entrance to the festival. It is unclear what aroused the guards' suspicions, though a police spokesman said that the bombers appeared agitated and "tried to get in too fast." After the first blast, police tried to direct throngs of people who had been waiting to buy tickets to a nearby exit, and it was there that the second blast occurred. Most of the casualties were from this second explosion. Although no organization claimed responsibility for the bombings, Interior Minister Boris Gryzlov said suspicion pointed to Chechen rebels. Local news reports said that Chechen identity papers had been found at the bombing site and First Deputy Interior Minister Rashid Nurgaliyev said that one of the bombers had been identified, apparently by means of documents found at the scene. Police estimate that the bomb belts used in the attack were packed with close to a kilogram of explosives.

Suicide Attack at Russian Military Hospital[64]

On August 3, 2003, at least fifty people were killed when a Chechen suicide bomber detonated a truck laden with explosives in a Russian military hospital compound in the North Ossetia region. The four-story building in the city of Mozdok was reduced to rubble. The hospital, near the Chechen border, was treating many soldiers who had been injured in the long war between the Russian military and Chechen rebels. Some 150 people were housed there at the time of the attack.

Following the attack, the head of the destroyed military hospital, Lt. Col. Artur Arakelian, was arrested on charges of criminal negligence and failure to carry out an order. Sky News quoted Russian Defense Minister Sergei Ivanov as saying that recent orders to block access to the hospital to unauthorized vehicles had not been implemented.

Suicide Attack on a Train in Russia[65]

On December 5, 2003, before 8 a.m., an explosion tore through a packed morning commuter train just outside Yessentuki station in the Stavropol region to the north of Chechnya, killing thirty-six people and injuring 150. Both the FSB and the Interior Ministry said a woman appeared to have detonated the explosion, which sliced the train's second carriage in two. It was the second such attack in three months on the train line. On September 3, 2003, an explosion had ripped through a train the Stavropol region, killing six people, but it was not clear if it was a suicide attack.

Suicide Bomber Strikes near the Parliament in Moscow[66]

On December 9, 2003, a bomb exploded at mid-day near the Russian Parliament in Moscow, killing five people and wounding fourteen. The blast occurred outside the prestigious National Hotel, across from the gate leading into Red Square and the Kremlin. Moscow Mayor Yuri Luzhkov told reporters that two women had walked up to a passerby and asked, "Where is the Duma?" (The Duma refers to the lower house of Parliament.) Very shortly afterwards an explosion ripped through the area, strewing broken glass and body parts across the street. The detonation was a relatively small one—equal to about 5 kilograms of TNT according to local police sources. However, more undetonated explosives were found on the headless body of the attacker. A second undetonated suicide belt similar to those worn by Chechen suicide bombers was found on the body of a second woman.

Luzhkov speculated that the bomb had exploded prematurely in front of the National Hotel. The attack occurred shortly before President Vladimir Putin addressed regional leaders meeting at the Kremlin to commemorate the tenth anniversary of the nation's constitution.

The ITAR-TASS news agency quoted an unnamed security official as saying Russian authorities had identified one of the bombers as a woman for whom they had been looking since July. "She went through training in one of the[Chechen] rebel camps," the official noted.

Attacks Perpetrated by Al-Qaida[67]

Al-Qaida itself has perpetrated only a small number of all of the attacks carried out by terror organizations affiliated with the Sunni Islamic Fundamentalist stream. Al-Qaida, which for years supported a long series of Islamic terror organizations and cells behind the scenes, initiated direct action related to attacks only after its formal declaration regarding the establishment of an organizational umbrella framework called "The International Islamic Front for Jihad against the Crusaders and the Jews" (February 1998). From this point on, Al-Qaida assumed the leading role in perpetrating terror attacks, while beforehand the organization had been satisfied with the provision of training and the offering of operational and logistic support for terror activities perpetrated independently by Islamic terror organizations and cells worldwide.

The first operations by Al-Qaida members were the suicide attacks at the U.S. Embassies in Kenya and Tanzania in August 1998. While these attacks were planned over a five-year period prior to their actual execution, the timing was chosen by the Al-Qaida command in Afghanistan and was meant to demonstrate the Islamic Front's intention to realize its declarations and lead the Jihad assault undertaken by Bin-Laden at the time of its establishment and the announcement of the fatwa (the religious ruling) of February 1998. The next Al-Qaida attack was also a direct assault carried out by two suicide terrorists navigating a dinghy loaded with explosives that hit an American destroyer, the *USS Cole*, while the latter was moored at the port of Aden in Yemen for the purpose of refueling and restocking. The pinnacle of the Al-Qaida attacks was the combined terror attack in the United States against the Twin Towers and the Pentagon, the aim of which was to strike a heavy blow at the very heart of the American nation and its symbols of power, and incite a global battle between Islam and the West.

The Attacks in Kenya and Tanzania (August 7, 1998)

On August 7, 1998, at 10:00 a.m., a car bomb carrying about three- quarters of a ton of explosives was detonated near the United States Embassy in Nairobi. The car was driven by one of two suicide terrorists (one of whom, Al-Awali, survived because he had gotten out of the vehicle to pursue the embassy guard who was fleeing). As a result of the explosion, 213 people were killed, the majority of whom were Kenyans, as well as a dozen American citizens who were embassy employees. Over 4,000 people were injured. Simultaneously, an additional suicide attack was perpetrated by the same organization near the U.S. Embassy in Dar A-Salaam in Tanzania. Eleven people were killed and scores were injured. These attacks signaled Al-Qaida's intention to perpetrate indiscriminate mass slaughter in attacks against American targets throughout the world, and reflected its characteristic modus operandi, as it was to be expressed subsequently in September 2001 in the United States.

The apprehension of a number of key activists involved in the terror network responsible for the planning and execution of the attacks led to a string of arrests and the preparation of a detailed charge sheet, which clearly indicated the direct responsibility of the organization headed by Bin-Laden for the terror campaign in east Africa. The investigation's findings offered a unique preliminary opportunity to closely observe the organization, thus providing in-depth knowledge of its modus operandi.

The Attack in Kenya. The terror cell that perpetrated the attack in Nairobi was composed of a small nucleus of six to eight activists under the command of Harun Al-Fazul, an Al-Qaida member born in the Comoro Islands.[68] The original plan had been to drive a car bomb into the embassy's underground parking, detonate it with the help of suicide drivers, and bring the building down upon its inhabitants.[69]

The terror team included three people who drove to their destination in two vehicles. The first car was driven by the mission commander Fazul Abdallah, known as Harun al-Fazul, and served as an escort vehicle for the car bomb. The second carried the two suicide bombers, the driver who committed suicide and his escort Rashid Daoud Al-Aewali, who survived the attack, and, after being apprehended, was extradited by Kenya to the United States, where he would stand trial. The car bomb driver, an Egyptian by origin, tried to enter the embassy's underground parking facility, but was unable to do so because of the Kenyan guard's refusal to open the embassy's gates. His attempt to circumvent the barrier was prevented by a car driving up from the underground parking area that blocked his way. Awali (the surviving driver) threatened the guard and demanded that he open the gate, but when the latter refused, he lobbed a stun grenade at the guard and proceeded to run after him, moving away from the vehicle. The driver detonated the bomb in a compound containing three buildings, about ten meters away from the embassy wall. The explosion resulted in a large number of casualties and the collapse of several buildings near the embassy. The embassy building itself, the attack's main target, did not collapse although it was damaged.

Preliminary preparations for the attack had begun in 1993.[70] Senior Al-Qaida personnel, including Bin-Laden and his assistant, the military commander Abu-Hafez, participated in the planning. The team consisted of eight members. Preparations for the attack were divided into several stages: As noted, the first stage was in 1993 when Bin-Laden conceived the idea and sent his representatives to Kenya. One of them was Muhammad Ali, a former sergeant in the U.S. military who subsequently served as a state's witness in the trials of the attack perpetrators in Kenya and Tanzania held in New York, and who confessed that he had met with Bin-Laden and given him photographs of the embassy in Nairobi. Bin-Laden sent several emissaries to Kenya with the aim of learning the lay of the land. They married local women and took work enabling them to gather qualitative information about the potential targets, mainly the U.S. and Israeli Embassies.

The second, more advanced stage of preparations in anticipation of the attack, was launched in May-June, 1998 (about two months before the attack). The decision was made following Bin-Laden's public declaration in an interview with ABC in which he threatened to perpetrate mega attacks against U.S. targets in retribution for the U.S. anti-Islamic policy. The practical preparations for the attack were administered from the network headquarters in the target country, the "Top-Hill" Hotel in Nairobi. Network members also rented a house in Nairobi where they hid the weapons; explosives, stun grenades, and handguns smuggled into Nairobi from the Middle East via the Comoro Islands. A short time prior to the attack, three cell members gathered intelligence about the U.S. Embassy in Nairobi, and when all preparations were in place, the date for the attack was set.

Several days prior to the attack date most of the network members left Nairobi, with the exception of Harun Fazul, the team's commander, who escorted the car bomb with the suicide terrorists to the target in order to personally supervise the operation. After the explosion, Harun returned to the safe house to cover their tracks and then disappeared.

The attack in Tanzania. On August 7, 1998, a car bomb exploded near the U.S. Embassy in Tanzania. Eleven people were killed in the explosion and eight-five were wounded, all local residents. The Tanzanian cell consisted of six members and additional individuals who assisted in the preparations for the attack in various stages of the planning. Members of the team, which was composed of a variety of nationalities including Kenyans, Tanzanians and Egyptians,[71] underwent training in Afghanistan in the course of 1994.

With the help of local collaborators, the team members rented a private safe house two months prior to the attack. The house was located outside of the city and was used for storage of the car bomb (a van) and the purchased weapons. The van had been bought two months earlier and was rigged as a car bomb a short time before the attack. The cell members collected preliminary information about the routine procedure for cars delivering water to the embassies, and took advantage of the information to infiltrate a car bomb into the embassy. The suicide bomber arrived separately in Dar-A-Salaam and was kept at a safe house.

On the day of the attack, the suicide driver of the car bomb drove to the embassy building and followed the water truck that arrived at its entrance. When the water truck was about to enter the premises, the car bomb drew up close and the suicide driver detonated the van that was loaded with a quarter ton of explosives.[72]

The African continent was chosen for these attacks because it was deemed a relatively easy site for terror activity due to the limited capabilities of the local security forces to perform surveillance of the preparations and of the Al-Qaida activists who had already arrived on the continent at the end of 1993. The slack local security and the ease of traveling to and from Africa were perceived as advantages. In addition, the level of security at the U.S. Embassies in Africa turned U.S. Embassies on this continent into attractive targets.

The Attack on the USS Cole

On October 12, 2000, the destroyer *USS Cole* was attacked by a boat bomb containing over half a ton of explosives. The boat bomb was navigated by two suicide attackers from the Al-Qaida organization. Seventeen American sailors perished in the explosion and thirty-five were wounded. The boat bomb was disguised as a service boat on its way to handle technical repairs aboard the American destroyer. The two suicide terrorists were dressed in white coveralls and therefore did not arouse suspicion. They tried to draw up alongside the vessel's stern in order to wreak as much damage as possible, but were unable to do so and finally detonated the boat near the destroyer's center.

On April 2, 2001, Yemen's minister of interior announced that local security forces had apprehended six terrorists who would be brought to trial; three of them reportedly had been directly involved in the attack and another three had served as collaborators. As stated above, two additional members were killed in the attack (the suicide bombers), and another two are still at large.[73] It appears that preparations for this attack were launched about eighteen months prior to its execution. Initially, the chosen target was the *USS Sullivan* that docked in the Aden port on January 3, 2000. Preparations for the attack started in mid-1999, but due to a miscalculation regarding the boat bomb's load capacity it sank because of an overload of explosives. Therefore, the attack was postponed for ten months.

Preparations for the two attacks, both the one in January and the other in October 2000, were supervised by two central Al-Qaida activists. The commander of the first attack was a man of Saudi origin who carried several IDs and had many aliases, including Abd Al-Rahaman Hassin al-Nashiri, also known as Muhammad Omar Al-Harazi, and the second was Jamal al-Badawi. Al-Nashiri, the more senior of the two, escaped after the attack, while al-Badawi was arrested in Yemen. Nashiri was eventually arrested in November 2002 and extradited to the United States.

According to an FBI document, al-Badawi confessed that he had traveled to Afghanistan in 1997, undergone training in Bid-Laden's camps, and pledged his loyalty oath. There he met his future accomplices in the attack, including Yemen-born Tawfik Al-Atrash, known by the code name of "Khaled." In June 1999, Khaled sent two of his men to meet al-Badawi. They asked him to travel to Saudi Arabia in order to purchase the boat that served as the boat bomb. The boat was bought with false documentation in order to conceal the identity of the buyers, and the vessel was ultimately presented to the two suicide bombers.[74]

Following the attack, several declarations claiming responsibility were announced in the name of unfamiliar organizations, including the "Islamic Deterrent Forces." According to their announcement, the organization called the Brigades of the Al-Aksa Intifada's Martyrs perpetrated the attack in order to "defend the honor of the Islamic nation and avenge the blood of the Muslim people subdued in Palestine due to American aid."

The Deterrent Forces stated that the attack was a gift to Al-Aksa and "a means to promote the objective of flying the Palestinian flag over our people in Palestine." The attack was meant "to defend the honor of the Islamic Arab nation so that America will know the price of its attempt to achieve hegemony over our lands through its warships and military bases on our lands (Yemen)." The declaration ended with a warning to the United States not to aid and abet the Zionist entity.[75]

Rifai Taha, one of the most senior members of the Jama'a al-Islamiya, who was first presented by the *A-Zaman* newspaper as Bin-Laden's spokesman,[76] denied that Bin-Laden was involved but welcomed the attack. Taha stated,

> this was a great campaign perpetrated against the United States, which is a country that harms our lands, our people, our treasures and our honor in Palestine. The lessons to be drawn from this attack are that even the powerful have weaknesses. The practical conclusion is that the United States was forced to have its destroyer towed in the dead of night and moved secretly, as well as raise the alert level in the U.S. Navy in the Gulf.[77]

In his announcement to *Al-Sharq al-Awsat*, Rifai Taha added that the operation had cost $5,000, but the damage caused to the American defense system was valued at hundreds of millions of dollars. He added,

> the attack had been carried out against a fortified military target, which in contrast to the condemnations we absorbed for action taken against civilian targets, cannot trigger criticism because this is a military target belonging to a hostile country which aids and abets the enemy.[78]

As is their wont, in retrospect the Al-Qaida leaders attempted to attribute this operation as well to their aspiration to aid the Palestinians in their struggle against Israel. It is noteworthy that this attack was perpetrated during a period when Israel and the Palestinians were involved in political negotiations and were cooperating in the framework of the Oslo Accords, before the renewed violence erupted between them in September 2000.

The Terror Attack in the United States on September 11, 2001, and the Phenomenon of Suicide Terror[79]

The terror campaign in the United States was primarily the act of suicide terrorists. As such, it was based on the willingness of its participants to take part in an act of collective suicide. Although Al-Qaida and other Islamic terror organizations that identify with the Global Jihad stream had already perpetrated previous suicide attacks, the assault on September 11 constituted an unprecedented event, both from the aspect of the number of casualties and from the aspect of method. The ability to perpetrate an attack of this sort was the direct product of Bin-Laden's terror industry in Afghanistan, which worked to cultivate a "pool" of fighters willing to carry out suicide attacks in the name of Global Jihad. Although Bin-Laden claimed that most of the participants learned about the mission's details only a short time before the attack, it is clear that it was based on the preliminary preparation of the participants and their willingness to participate in a suicide attack, whatever its character. This supposition is corroborated by a videotape filmed about six months prior to the attack, in which one of the suicide terrorists expressed his fierce desire to participate in a suicide attack and die the death of a martyr.

Various groups doubted the proof of Al-Qaida's responsibility for the attack, but the initial assessment that Bin-Laden was, indeed, responsible was confirmed by Bin-Laden himself, who confessed to prior knowledge of the attack, but noted that he had preferred to wait for the results.[80] He stated that he, who had been the "optimistic" one among his accomplices to the attack, predicted the collapse of "only" four floors in each of the "Twin Towers" targeted by the attack, and the consequent death of thousands of victims. He confessed that he had not expected the success to be so "great" and did not foresee that both towers would crumble. The attack against the Pentagon and the White House or the Capitol (one of which was apparently the fourth target) was meant to complete the frontal attack against the United States. He also revealed the fact that Muhammad Atta was the commander of the entire group and that most of the suicide attackers did not know about the action plan until immediately prior to its execution.[81]

What Were the Objectives of the Attack?

As is characteristic of many other terror attacks, this attack was also meant to achieve several goals simultaneously:

• Provocation
  In Bin-Laden's eyes, the primary, concrete, and operative goal of the attack against the United States was the multiple deaths and massive damage anticipated by the planners, aimed at dragging the United States into an overall and indiscriminate war against the Muslim world. It was meant to corroborate the concept that Bin-Laden had endeavored to disseminate among the Islamic States and Muslims worldwide regarding the struggle between the West's "evil culture" and the Muslims' "just culture"—the inevitable battle when the "American despots and tyranny confronted Islamic purity."[82] Bin-Laden and his people had expected the United States to declare a total war against the entire Muslim world. They hoped that this period would create a dichotomy between two completely rival camps, which would act according to the popular rule of "choose which side you are on." The first camp would be composed of the United States and a handful of Western states that would join her, while the second camp would include the entire Muslim world that would come to his aid because it felt oppressed or alienated by the antagonistic West.

Bin-Laden believed that in any event the attack perpetrated by his people would expand his small group of supporters to a much larger camp than the one at his disposal prior to the attack. This great provocation was designated to "squeeze" from the United States a set of counter-responses that would unmask its true face before the Muslims, in particular, and world opinion, in general, that is, that in contrast to its pretensions and declarations the United States is ultimately and fundamentally anti-Muslim, anti-democratic, and anti-humane.

- Achieving "propaganda by the deed"[83]
Bin-Laden and his men sought to prove the ability of the "Islamic fighters" to deal a mortal blow to American society and its power symbols, thus exposing the weakness and vulnerability of the American superpower before the members of Al-Qaida and its followers in the radical Islamic camp. In a television broadcast on Al-Jazeera in December 2001, Bin-Laden pointed out the achievements of the attacks against the United States, including the exposure of America's weakness and vulnerability, by a handful of Muslim fighters. "The war in Afghanistan has exposed America's weakness. Despite the clear technological advantages of its war machine, it cannot defeat the Muslim mujahidin." The second achievement that he noted was the exposure of what he referred to as "the Crusader hatred for Islam."[84]

Reinforcement of this intention can be found in the videotaped testimony of al-Hiznawi, one of the nineteen suicide attackers, which was filmed six months prior to the attack, in which he read out his will and stated: "America is nothing beyond propaganda and a huge collection of exaggerated and false declarations. The truth is what you see. We have killed them (the Americans) outside of their country, thank God, and we are killing them in their homes."[85]

- Accelerating the recruitment of new volunteers for the Global Jihad organization.
- Bin-Laden stated this clearly: "The acts of these young men in New York and Washington render unimportant all the speeches delivered anywhere else in the world. Their speeches (meaning their deeds) were clearly understood by all the Arabs and non-Arabs as one.... The number of people who embraced the Islamic faith after the campaign was greater than the number that has grasped Islam in the past eleven years."[86]
- The killing of as many American citizens as possible.
- As stated above, the most "moderate" estimate of the planners was at least
- Dealing a heavy blow to the American economy.
- Damaging the symbols of the American culture—which serve as role models for members of the Western civilization, their bitter enemy.

The September 11, 2001 Attack[87]

On September 11, the most deadly terror attack in the annals of international terrorism was perpetrated against targets symbolizing the military and economic power of the United States, and had a dramatic impact on international relations. Some three thousand people from eighty different countries were killed in the attack, most as a result of the deliberate ramming of two commercial airplanes, flown by suicide pilots, into the Twin Towers in New York City. The two tall buildings collapsed, causing the death of approximately 2,500 people who were in the buildings at the time or were participating in rescue efforts to extricate people trapped in the burning buildings.

Another target under attack that also had symbolic significance was the Pentagon in Washington, which was severely damaged by a third plane flown by the suicide pilots that crashed into it. The intention of the hijackers of the fourth plane apparently was to crash into the White House, but their efforts were thwarted due to the heroic struggle of the plane's passengers who were informed through telephone calls made from the plane to their families of the fates of the other planes, and of the hijackers' intention to crash into a selected target within the United States. The decision of the aircraft's passengers to attack the hijackers and prevent them from carrying out their scheme even at the expense of their own lives caused the plane to crash in an unpopulated area of Pennsylvania, thus saving many lives.

In all four hijacked airplanes, a total of two hundred and forty-six passengers and crewmembers perished. This number does not include the nineteen suicide hijackers. On the ground, another 2,750 people died. The terror attacks in the United States also resulted in heavy direct and indirect damages, amounting to billions of dollars, to the American economy in particular, and world economy in general.

Preparations for the Attack

Even now, over a year after the attacks, many details connected to the preparations that are still unclear or classified. However, in light of past experience, particularly when dealing with highly fatal, mega terror attacks (like the detonation of the Pan American flight 103 over Lockerbie, perpetrated under Libyan sponsorship, and the attacks in Kenya and Tanzania under Bin-Laden's command), most of the facts related to the perpetrators and their modus operandi ultimately do emerge. The confiscation of many documents and the apprehension of senior Al-Qaida members during the offensive in Afghanistan, as well as the intensive manhunt for the fleeing Al-Qaida leaders, will undoubtedly reveal the planning and implementation details related to this operation.

Despite the existing gaps connected to the operational planning of the terror attack in the United States, it is possible to sketch a fairly clear overall picture of the preparations for the campaign and its execution.

It is evident that the attacks were part of a well-planned and orchestrated terror strategy, which was designed and financed by the Al-Qaida command headquarters. The idea of detonating buildings with symbolic significance through the use of suicide pilots was the brainchild of Ramzi Yusuf and his comrade Abd al Hakim Murad in the early 1990s; they had planned to crash into the CIA headquarters at Langley in Virginia. This idea also occurred to members of the Algerian GIA terror cell who hijacked a French plane en route from Algeria to Marseille in December 1994 with the intention of crashing it into the Eiffel Tower in Paris.[88]

The idea was embraced by Muhammad Attef, Al-Qaida's military commander, who turned it into a practical plan at the end of the 1990s and executed it in September 2001 (Attef was killed in the bombings of the coalition forces in Afghanistan in November 2001). The "Hamburg Group," led by the Egyptian Muhammad Atta, was deemed by the Al-Qaida headquarters to be the most suitable team to turn the diabolical idea into an operative plan.

Preparations for the attack in the United States, which took two years, apparently commenced in 1999, after the training of the Hamburg Group, which, upon its return to Germany, became the terror cell to lead the mission. Hamburg, a city in northern Germany, was chosen as the base point for preparations prior to departure for the country of destination, the United States. The German Group was recruited from among worshippers at the El-Quds mosque in Hamburg, which, like other central mosques located in various capitals throughout Europe, served as an enlistment site for Muslim youths with radical leanings in order to mobilize and send them for training to Afghanistan, in preparation for an active role in the Global Jihad.

The Hamburg Group included six activists, some of whom studied at the technical college in the city. All six lived in one apartment house in Hamburg; some even shared the same apartment.[89] Three of the six cell members ultimately took part in the suicide operation and actually piloted three of the four hijacked airplanes. The three other members of the cell served as collaborators, because two, who were apparently supposed to be part of the group of suicide pilots were refused entry visas to the United States. This fact induced the attack planners to expand the circle of pilots and to use one pilot who was not initially a member of the Hamburg Group.

The three collaborators, members of the Hamburg Group, left Germany for Pakistan about a week before D-day, and from there continued on to Afghanistan where all traces of them were lost. All three are fugitives from justice.

The second group to take part in the attack in the United States was based on the "Saudi Group." This group was composed of sixteen activists (fifteen of whom were of Saudi descent). Their training was conducted separately from the Hamburg Group. The two groups were strictly compartmentalized and neither was aware of the existence of the other. The role of the Saudi

Group (with the exception of the pilot Hanjur) was to serve as "musclemen" and bodyguards to the hijacking pilots during the mission. The Saudi Group, whose members were aged 20-29, was completely compartmentalized from the objectives of the assault, and its exact details were provided (it is not clear if this applies to all of them and what the level of information was) immediately before its execution.[90] Nevertheless, it appears that at least some of the members did not know, but they had consented to take part in suicide missions on behalf of the Global Jihad.[91]

The Hijacked Airplanes

The terror campaign of September 11 began in the early hours of the morning, a short time after the airplanes took off from three different airports on America's East Coast. All of the hijacked aircraft were en route to distant airports on the West Coast. The hijackers intentionally chose long flights in order to ensure that the planes would be carrying large amounts of fuel and a small number of passengers. The copious amount of fuel would enhance the effect of the explosion upon impact, while the relatively low number of passengers would ensure the hijackers' ease in overwhelming them if any opposition were to arise on their part.

The four airplanes that crashed were hijacked by four trained teams of terrorists who were affiliated with the Al-Qaida organization. The group of terrorists was divided into four teams, and numbered a total of nineteen men, aged 20-33. Fifteen of the assailants were of Saudi origin, one was Egyptian, another was Lebanese, and two were from the United Arab Emirates. Each of the four teams had at least one trained and certified pilot.

American Airlines flight 11. The first hijacked plane was an American Airlines Boeing 767, flight 11, which took off at 8:02 a.m. from Boston for Los Angeles. The hijacked aircraft rammed into the northern tower of the Twin Towers at 8:45 a.m. Eighty-seven passengers and crewmembers were killed in the crash.

Ramming of the plane into the northern tower caused its collapse at 10:29 a.m., New York time, about an hour and forty-five minutes after the initial collision.

The plane was manned by five hijackers:

Muhammad Atta, head of the network and commander of the entire operation. Atta, a thirty-three-year-old Egyptian citizen, had arrived in the United States in anticipation of the hijackings on July 29, 2001, and had a pilot's license issued in the United States.

Abd al-Aziz Al-Omri, a twenty-nine-year-old Saudi Arabian (who apparently had a pilot's license).

Wa'al A-Shahri, a twenty-eight-year-old Saudi Arabian.

Wali A-Shahri, a twenty-five-year-old Saudi Arabian.

Stam A-Sukami, a twenty-five-year-old Saudi Arabian.

United Airlines flight 175. The second hijacked Boeing 767, United Airlines flight 175, left the Boston Airport on en route to Los Angeles and crashed into the southern tower of the World Trade Center at 9:03 a.m. (New York time), some eighteen minutes after the collision of the first plane. This crash resulted in the death of fifty-one passengers and nine crewmembers. Ramming of the plane into the southern tower caused its collapse at 9:50 a.m., about forty-seven minutes after the aircraft hit the building.

The plane was manned by five hijackers:

Marwan A-Sheikhi, the twenty-three-year-old pilot, born in the Gulf Emirates, who arrived in the United States in anticipation of the attack on May 2, 2001.

Hamza al-Ramdi, a twenty-one-year-old Saudi Arabian.

Mahnam A-Shahri, a twenty-two-year-old Saudi Arabian.

Ahmad al-Ramdi, a twenty-one-year-old Saudi Arabian.

Faiz Ahmad, a twenty-four-year-old native of the Gulf Emirates.

American Airlines flight 77. The third hijacked plane was an American Airlines Boeing 757, flight 77, from Washington to Los Angeles. It crashed into the Pentagon building in Washington, D.C. at 9:39 a.m. (Washington time), about an hour and twenty-four minutes after takeoff. As a result of the crash, fifty-nine people were killed, including fifty-three passengers and six crewmembers. In addition, one hundred and eighty four people were killed on the ground in the Pentagon.

There were five hijackers on board:

Hani Hanjur, a twenty-nine-year-old Saudi Arabian and the team's commander. He was a licensed commercial pilot and qualified for his license in the United States. Hanjur had resided in the United States for about ten years prior to the attack. He returned from Saudi Arabia to the United States in December 2000 in anticipation of the attack.

Khaled al-Midkhar, a twenty-six-year old Saudi Arabian.

Salem al-Hazmi, a twenty-year-old Saudi Arabian.

Majed Makdad, a twenty-four-year-old Saudi Arabian.

Naaf al-Hazmi, a twenty-five-year-old Saudi Arabian.

United Airlines flight 93. The fourth hijacked plane was a United Airlines Boeing 767, flight 93, en route from Newark Airport in New Jersey to San Francisco. The plane took off at 8:10 a.m. and crashed at 10:10 in an open field in Pennsylvania. The target apparently was the White House.'As a result of the crash forty-four people perished, including thirty-seven passengers and seven crewmembers.

There were four hijackers on board:

Sa'ad al-Ramdi, a twenty-two-year-old Saudi Arabian with a pilot's license.

Ziad Samir Jarah, a twenty-six-year-old Lebanese citizen.

Ahmad al-Hinzawi, a twenty-one-year-old Saudi Arabian.

Ahmad al-Nami, a twenty-four-year-old Saudi Arabian.

An Analysis of the General Characteristics of the Suicide Group in the September 11 Attacks in the United States

The suicide group was made up of at least two teams, or to be more accurate, two cells that acted independently of one another and apparently underwent separate integration processes without any contact between them, under the supervision of the Afghanistan headquarters.[92] Also noteworthy is the fact that we have far greater information about the Hamburg Group, which acted as a separate unit and bonded around the dominant personality of Muhammad Atta, the Egyptian who was the oldest member of the group and was chosen by Al-Qaida to command the entire mission.

Most of the details that we have about the preparations of the group are based on written or filmed wills of several of the participants, the testimony of the acquaintances of the suicide attackers, and information revealed in the media as a result of journalistic investigation. Also worthy of mention is the fact that there is limited information regarding the biographical details and personal characteristics of most of the hijackers, particularly those who were affiliated with the Saudi Group.

The age range of the suicide attackers in the United States was between 20 and 33. The suicide attackers from the Hamburg Group were students, educated individuals from prosperous families, who had lived in the West for several years, and appeared to have promising futures. It is clear that the participants in the attack were people who differed from each other in personal aspects as well as background. The Saudi Group was made up of fifteen young men, some of them in their early twenties.

The suicide attackers in the Hamburg Group shared an apartment and a residential building for a long period of time and acted jointly as a cohesive group that had trained itself for the attack from the operational aspect, apparently focusing on mental preparations which included the embracing of a religious Islamic lifestyle, joint prayers, and mutual support. This characteristic of group preparation and influence among suicide attackers has also been evident among suicide attackers in Israel; for example, when three Hamas members sharing an apartment carried out suicide attacks one after the other.

It is reasonable to assume that the significant difference in ages between the Egyptian Muhammad Atta, head of the Hamburg Group on the one hand, and the twenty-three-year-old Marwan A-Sheikhi and twenty-six-year-old Ziad Jarah on the other, aided Atta in leading his team members along the route he had navigated, thanks to his dominant personality and the support he received from the Al-Qaida headquarters in Afghanistan.

Mental Preparation of the Suicide Attackers Immediately before the Attack

Part of the solution to the riddle of how the hijackers were persuaded to take part in the suicide attack can be ascertained, at least at this stage, from letters found in the bags of three of the nineteen suicide attackers (two from the German Group and one from the Saudi Group), on three different airplanes and on a videocassette, in which Saudi Arabian al-Hiznawi reads out his will on film six months prior to the attack. One of the letters was found in the luggage of Muhammad Atta which was not loaded onto the airplane. Similar letters were found at the crash site of United Airlines flight 93 in Pennsylvania and in the luggage of Nawaf al-Hazmi, who participated in the hijacking of American Airlines flight 77 that rammed the Pentagon. The letters clearly indicate that the hijackers, and certainly the cell leaders and apparently others, were issued detailed guidelines in writing and perhaps orally as well, regarding how to prepare for a suicide operation and how to behave during the attack.

In these letters, the suicide attackers asked God to forgive them their transgressions and requested permission to glorify His name in any way possible. The letters specified the exact behavior expected of them the night before their deaths. The hijackers were commanded to engage themselves in prayer, fasting, and seeking God's direction, and to continue reading the Koran and purifying themselves in anticipation of their ascent to heaven and meeting their maker.

The suicide attackers were instructed to remain calm, to refrain from showing tension, and to internalize the fact that they were going to a better and happier place, and that the life awaiting them after their physical death was eternal life in the Garden of Eden. They were told to draw inspiration from their situations, because if they knew the reward awaiting them after death they would request to die on their own, because the Garden of Eden, which has become even more beautiful in anticipation of their arrival, awaits them....[93]

In addition to mental preparation, the letters included practical instructions regarding preparations for the attack from the operational point of view. For example, they were instructed to prepare the necessary equipment for the mission, to verify that they were not under surveillance, that their box-cutters were sharp, and that they had their passports on them. The letters included instructions regarding their behavior when boarding the plane, including reciting a prayer to the Prophet Muhammad and to Allah so that they might illuminate their way.[94]

Additional testimony regarding the mode of preparation of the September 11 suicide terrorists can be found in the videocassette that was aired in April 2002, in which Haznawi (who participated in the hijacking of the airplane that crashed in Pennsylvania) is taped. From the text it is possible to glean the worldview of the suicide attacker and his perception of the act of suicide as an expression of God's will, and his envisioning of his (the individual's) role and duty to die in order to promote the world Islamic system and realize God's commandments.[95]

Suicide Attacks Perpetrated by Al-Qaida after
September 11, 2001

The Al-Qaida organization and the Taliban regime absorbed a crippling blow during the American offensive in Afghanistan. Nevertheless, Al-Qaida infrastructures worldwide continued to function and attempt to perpetrate attacks, even after the eradication of the organization's infrastructure in Afghanistan.

The Incident of Richard Colvin Reed ("The man with the Explosive Shoes")

On December 22, 2001, a suicide bomber named Richard Colvin Reed attempted to detonate American Airlines flight 63, which was en route from Paris to Miami. His shoes were loaded with about two hundred grams of explosives, which he attempted to ignite in his effort to blow up the aircraft along with its 196 passengers and crewmembers about two hours before the scheduled landing in Miami. Only the alertness of a flight attendant, who was summoned to Reed's seat by a suspicious passenger, and the terrorist's neutralization with the help of other passengers, prevented a grave disaster.[96]

In his interrogation, Reed claimed that he was acting alone, but it is evident that he was a member of a terror cell affiliated with Al-Qaida, which sent him on the mission. His interrogation revealed that he was in constant contact with Pakistan via the Internet and apparently received instructions from his operators in this way.[97] His personal background indicates a familiar pattern of activity of recruiting British citizens who had converted to Islam into the ranks of Al-Qaida and into terror cells supported by the latter.

The attempted attack by Reed serves as indisputable evidence that Al-Qaida and its affiliated terror cells have not abandoned their intention to perpetrate additional deadly mega attacks. It testifies to the fact that despite the heavy blow sustained in the onslaught of the international allied forces led by the United States, Al-Qaida's ability to persevere in the perpetration of grievous terror attacks (particularly against transportation targets) has not been impaired. This also bears witness to the action pattern of Al-Qaida-affiliated terror cells, which is based on the activity of small terror cells, consisting of three to five members, with the capability to cause severe damage.

The alertness of the crewmembers and passengers, which helped to thwart the attempted attack, provides additional evidence that public alertness and its response play an important role in the war against terror. [98]

The Suicide Attack near the Ancient Synagogue in Djerba, Tunisia

On April 11, 2002, a suicide driver blew up an oil tanker near the ancient synagogue in Djerba. The driver, a Tunisian from an emigrant family living in France, aimed the fuel truck carrying explosives so that it would hit the synagogue and a group of tourists visiting the site, and detonated the explosives. The attack left nineteen dead, fourteen of whom were German tourists.

"The Organization for the Liberation of the Holy Sites" and the "Al-Qaida al-Jihad" organization claimed responsibility for the attack in letters sent to the *Al-Hayat* and *Al-Quds al-Arabi* newspapers, and stated that the act was an expression of solidarity of Moslems throughout the world with their Palestinian brothers' struggle.[99] As mentioned earlier, the responsibility for the attacks in Kenya and Tanzania was also claimed by The Organization for the Liberation of the Holy Sites, while the name "Al-Qaida Al-Jihad" is the name of the organization whose foundation was declared by Bin-Laden and his deputy Aiman A-Zawahiri in June 2001, when they announced the de jure consolidation of the Al-Qaida and Egyptian Jihad Organizations.

In an interview, Abd Alatim Al-Mohajar, one of the leading military leaders of the Al-Qaida organization, confirmed that Al-Qaida members carried out the attack at the synagogue in Djerba. Al-Mohajar stated that the perpetrator was Nawar Saif A-Din A-Tunisi, one of Al-Qaida's fighters, and that in the organization he was called "Saif."[100] An investigation of the incident indicated that the suicide terrorist had connections with terror cells in France, Germany, and Canada. Nawar was an Afghani "alumnus" and he had begun his preparations several months prior to the deed. A search of his apartment yielded telephone numbers of Binalshibh, a prominent leader of the terror cell in Hamburg, whose other members were among the pilots who perpetrated the terror attack in the United States.[101]

In light of the violent clash between Israel and the Palestinians, and bearing in mind the severe blow which Al-Qaida sustained in Afghanistan, Bin-Laden and his men recognized the potential support among Moslems worldwide for carrying out attacks against Israel and Jews. In view of this situation, massive terror attacks against Israeli and Jewish targets around the world, but mainly in Israel, have become a strategic objective in their eyes. Therefore, it should be anticipated that Al-Qaida will make a concerted effort to realize these intentions, along with attacks against other Western targets, particularly those connected to the United States and her allies.

The Attack against the French Oil Tanker Limbourg Opposite the Shores of Yemen on October 6, 2002[102]

The French oil tanker *Limbourg* moored opposite the Yemen coast, after having been loaded with oil at an Iranian port, with the intention of loading additional oil at the port of Debbah in the Hadhramaut region of Yemen. When the tanker was about 5 kilometers off the coast of Yemen, a huge blast occurred, igniting the ship. After the crew's attempts to extinguish the fire proved to be ineffective, the tanker was abandoned. In the explosion and subsequent fire twelve crewmembers were injured, and one crewmember was declared missing. An officer on the tanker's crew said that he had seen a small boat rapidly approaching the tanker's side. He believes that the smaller boat's collision with the tanker's side is what caused the explosion. The ship's captain claimed that the explosion that split the tanker's side was external rather than internal.

Yemenite authorities originally claimed that the fire was caused by an accident. Yemen's Transportation and Shipping minister stated that the explosion was caused by an oil leak from one of the tanks on board, but managers of the French company that had hired the tanker's services dismissed this explanation. The spokesperson for the French Foreign Ministry announced that the matter was being investigated and it was too early to determine the cause of the collision.

On October 10, 2002, the "Islamic Army of Aden and Abyan" dispatched an announcement to the media in which it claimed responsibility for hitting the tanker and noted that the attack was meant to avenge the execution of the organization's leader Zin al-Abadeen al-Midhar by the Yemenite authorities two years earlier. This announcement stated that the attack also came in protest against the U.S. forces and the American intention to initiate an assault against Iraq; according to the organization, the oil transported by the French tanker was designated for this purpose.[103] A French research team that visited Yemen discovered wreckage of fiberglass near the tanker that apparently was part of the boat bomb that collided with it.

Once the organization had claimed responsibility, official Yemenite entities acknowledged the possibility that the incident had been a terror attack, although they rushed to qualify the statement with the declaration that it was yet too early to determine this unequivocally.

This was the first attack to be carried out in the Yemenite arena against a Western target after September 11, and after Yemen had joined the United States in the global war against terror. The ability of Al-Qaida or any other radical Islamic organization to carry out a maritime attack of this sort, at a time when Yemenite authorities were purportedly taking resolute action against Islamic terror entities, constituted a significant blow to Yemenite credibility, and may have a negative impact on this country's future relations with the United States and the West. The attack's target, a French tanker, constitutes an innovation vis-à-vis the targets of attacks in this arena, and conveys the message that the Islamic terror organizations do not distinguish between French targets and American or British targets.

The Terror Attack on the Island of Bali, October 2002

During the night hours of October 12, 2002, a lethal terror attack was perpetrated on the Island of Bali, Indonesia, killing about 200 people and injuring about three hundred. Most were Westerners who had come to the island on vacation. The attacks were focused on two popular nightclubs on the Kota coast, which is considered a central tourist attraction. The attacks apparently were perpetrated through a suicide terrorist and a car loaded with TNT that detonated within seconds of each other, demolishing the discotheques, causing the ceilings to collapse and igniting a huge fire that caused most of the fatalities aside from inflicting considerable environmental damage. About half of the victims were Australian nationals, who visited the island in droves, as well as tourists from the United States, Germany, and Britain.

Prior to this, two bombs had been detonated near the American and Philippine consulates. No organization claimed responsibility, but based on the investigations and arrests conducted afterwards it appeared that the Indonesian Jama'a al-Islamiya was responsible for the attacks. It was also announced that Abu Baker Bashir, head of the Jama'a al-Islamiya, had been arrested by Indonesian police following the testimony of Omar Faruk, a senior member of the southeastern Asian terror organization arrested in June 2002, who divulged incriminating testimony regarding Bashir's involvement in the Asian terror system. In November 2002, an additional suspect named Amrozi confessed to involvement in the terror attacks on Bali, noted that the cell had included six to ten activists, and stated that their objective was to perpetrate a lethal attack against Americans. Amrozi's interrogation subsequently led the arrest of a senior activist in the Jama'a al-Islamiya named Imam Samudra.

The Indonesian police announced on November 22, 2002 that Samudra, one of the main suspects in the planning of the attacks in Bali, had confessed during his interrogation to the planning and collaboration in the perpetration of the attacks. Following his arrest, authorities were able to apprehend three additional suspects.

Imam Samudra, who underwent training at the camps in Afghanistan, was a member of the Jama'a al-Islamiya terror organization. He is suspected of planning the attack on October 12 and assisting in the assembly of the bombs that detonated the discotheque and the bar, which at that time were teeming with tourists. The chief of Indonesian police, General Bahatiar, reported that Samudra was arrested in the city of Mark on the island of Java. As mentioned above, thirty-five-year-old Samudra was a senior member of the Jama'a al-Islamiya and followed the instructions issued by Riduan Isamudin Khambali.

According to police, Samudra learned how to assemble explosive devices in Afghanistan and was also suspected of involvement in a series of explosions in churches in Indonesia during 2002. Victims of the attack were Indonesian (one of the largest Muslim countries in the world), and Australian (whose citizens constituted the majority of the fatalities). Before the Bali attack, Indonesia did not make any outstanding effort to join the global efforts against terror mainly because it had never suffered in the past from attacks initiated by Afghan alumni. But the lesson that has repeated itself again and again is that no country and no citizen of the world are immune to the long arm of terror. It perpetrates attacks in different countries and hones the need for cooperation among all of the countries worldwide in order to neutralize the poison of "this diseased evil."

Car Bomb near Marriott Hotel in Jakarta, Indonesia[104]

On August 5, 2003, at 12:30 p.m., a huge blast tore through the Marriott Hotel in the Indonesian capital of Jakarta, killing at least ten people and wounding eighty-three. The blast appeared to be timed to coincide with the noon lunch hour; the area of the hotel hardest hit was the restaurant. National Police Chief General Da'Bachtiar said that the explosion originated in a locally made Kijang van that had pulled up in front of the hotel. The attack coincided with a series of high-profile trials of suspected Islamic militants on charges related to the Bali bombings.

The Terror Campaign in Kenya against Israeli Targets[105]

On November 28, 2002, a terror campaign was launched against Israeli targets in Kenya:

* A car bomb driven by terrorists exploded at the Paradise Hotel in Mombassa.
* Two Strella (SA-7) shoulder missiles were fired at an Arkia airplane immediately after takeoff but missed their target.

Responsibility was claimed by an unknown organization called the "Palestine Army."

The organization released an announcement via Al-Manar, the Hizballah television station, in which it stated that the attack had been perpetrated to commemorate the 55th anniversary of the UN partition resolution (November 29). The announcement added that the organization's headquarters had decided that the entire world must hear of the suffering of Palestinian refugees, and therefore it was decided to send a cell to Kenya with the aim of attacking Israeli targets. The message ended with a statement that the attacks had gone according to plan. The leader of the Islamic Organization "Al-Muhajrun" in London, Omar al-Bakhri, stated that during the week preceding the attack the organization had issued a warning in chat sites on the Internet that an attack was about to be launched against Israeli targets in Kenya. In an interview with the Al-Jazeera TV network, Bakhri said, "our sources are based on open forums on the Internet." According to Bakhri the message was as follows; "Brothers, you will receive good news during the last twenty days of the month of Ramadan," and it was also stated that the target would be in East Africa.

On December 2, 2002, claiming of responsibility was published in several Internet sites identified with Al-Qaida under the signature of "Tanzim Qaadat al-Jihad," the political office. It would appear that it was Al-Qaida that was claiming responsibility although the style differed in its characteristics from earlier claims of responsibility issued by that organization.[106]

The announcement also stated that the attacks in Mombassa were aimed at "eradicating all of the dreams of the Jewish-Crusader alliance, meant to preserve their strategic interests in the region. The next mission, meant to deal an additional blow to the Israeli Mossad, will be like the blows that fell upon the synagogue in Djerba in the past." It went on to say that both attacks, the attack at the Paradise Hotel and the attempt to shoot down the Arkia plane, "were meant to clarify to Muslims all over the world that the mujahidin stand by their brethren in Palestine and continue in their path." The announcement also referred to the Jewish-American connection, saying that the attack was in retaliation for "the conquest of our holy sites" and Israeli acts in Palestine. "For killing our children, we will kill yours, for our elderly we will kill your elderly, and for our homes your turrets."

The attack at the Paradise Hotel. On the morning of November 28, 2002, some 200 Israeli tourists landed at the Mombassa Airport, Kenya. They disembarked from an Arkia charter flight and passed through the various checks and border control. They boarded two buses and five minibuses, which took them to the "Paradise Mombassa" Hotel, some 35 kilometers north of the city, where they were to spend the Hanukkah vacation.

It appears that already during the journey to the hotel, a green Mitsubishi Pajero jeep was following the convoy. After disembarking from the buses, the Israeli tourists registered at the hotel and most went to their rooms. At about 7:20 a jeep burst through the hotel's security gate and exploded in the hotel's lobby. The jeep was carrying about 200 kilograms of explosives and gas balloons,[107] and a kalachnikov was found in the jeep's wreckage. Thirteen people were killed in the attack; three Israelis and ten Kenyans, including dancers from a dance troupe that received the Israeli tourists at the entrance to the hotel. According to the various reports, sixty to eighty people were injured in the attack, including some twenty Israelis.

The firing of missiles at the Arkia plane. At about 7:30 a.m., on the same day, several minutes after the launching of the car bomb driven by suicide terrorists into the Paradise Hotel, two shoulder missiles were fired at Arkia flight 582, which had taken off from the Mombassa Airport in Kenya for Israel. Two hundred sixty-one passengers were on board, in addition to ten crewmembers. About a minute and a half after takeoff, at a height of 3,000 feet, passengers felt a thump against the aircraft's hull. Immediately afterwards, the flash of two missiles was identified near the aircraft. Crewmembers rushed to report to the security team on land, and the latter started searches in the area in an attempt to locate the missile launchers. No damage was reported to the aircraft.

A preliminary investigation launched by security personnel in Kenya and Israel indicates that the shoulder missiles fired at the Arkia plane were launched from a point 1 kilometer away from the takeoff area. The terrorists set up the ambush a few hundred meters outside of the perimeter fence surrounding the airport. The spokesperson for the Kenyan Police reported that a car, apparently a Pajero jeep, had been seen in the vicinity of the airport a short time prior to the launching of the missiles. "Three or four people with an Arab appearance were seen in the car, fleeing the area," added the spokesman.

Two missile launchers and two additional SA-7 (Strella) missiles were found hidden in the bushes outside of the airport's perimeter, several hundred meters from the fence. According to U.S. sources, the missiles found in Mombassa were from the same series and production line as the missiles fired by Al-Qaida at an American military plane in Saudi Arabia in May 2002.[108]

According to the assessment of the Kenya Police, the firing of the missiles and the attack perpetrated with a car bomb at the hotel were coordinated and carefully planned in advance. Searches carried out by police investigators in the area where the missiles were fired indicated that the attack was perpetrated from a hill with an excellent view of the airport, particularly the takeoff areas, which made the operation easier for the attackers. It was fortunate that the missiles missed their target as takeoff is considered the most vulnerable phase of a flight.

The Strella, developed about thirty years ago, is a relatively outmoded missile. It is used by armies and guerrilla organizations, and it is known that various entities in Africa also have some of these in their possession. The missile is considered uncomplicated to operate and in regular circumstances its capability to hit a passenger plane during takeoff—which is considered an easy target—is relatively high.

The Strella homes in on heat and is usually adjusted according to the heat waves emanating from the plane's engines or its landing and takeoff lights. The missile's effective range is defined at four to six kilometers, with a flight velocity of 580 meters per second, and its warhead's weight ranges between 1-1.2 kilograms.

The attempt to hit the Arkia plane in Mombassa, Kenya, is not the first time that terrorists have tried to fire shoulder missiles at Israeli aircraft, and it is also not the first attempt to be made in Kenya. In 1969 a Palestinian cell was apprehended in Rome. It had shoulder missiles in its possession and the intention was to shoot down an El Al plane. The cell was caught as the result of prior information obtained in a joint operation of the Italian security forces and the Mossad.

Suicide Attacks in Riyadh, Saudi Arabia[109]

On May 13, 2003, three car bombs were detonated by suicide terrorists in Riyadh, the capital of Saudi Arabia, several hours prior to the arrival of U.S. Secretary of State Colin Powell in Riyadh.

The well-coordinated and carefully planned attacks were carried out at two residential complexes and at a third complex populated by employees of Vinnel, the American consulting firm that is involved in the training of the Saudi royal guard under the command of the crown Prince Abdullah. In each of the residential complexes, the attack was launched by assaulting the local guards and infiltrating a booby-trapped car. The blasts also destroyed several private residences in the vicinity. Ninety-one people were killed, including twenty Americans and other foreign residents, and some 200 people were injured. (U.S., Swiss, Lebanese, Jordanian, and Philippine citizens were wounded, in addition to Saudis.)

An individual who identified himself as an Al-Qaida activist claimed in an email, which he sent to the Arab weekly *Al-Majla* in London, that his organization was responsible for the attacks.

The characteristics of the attacks and the precise synchronization of the three explosions could very well connect the attacks to Al-Qaida, but at the same time the organization responsible could have been an internal Saudi movement, which received its training, like many other terror activists, in Afghanistan or Pakistan.

At the beginning May, Saudi authorities announced that they had exposed a terror organization operated by radical Islamic entities connected to Al-Qaida. The Saudis claimed to have discovered large stockpiles of combat equipment designated for terrorists' use in attacks against Saudi targets, including the royal family, American, and infrastructure targets. In addition, the Saudis announced that they were seeking nineteen individuals suspected of terrorist activity. In practice, up until the perpetration of this series of attacks on May 13, not one of the terrorists was arrested.

The U.S. Embassy published a warning as a result of the information received from the Saudis, but despite all of the steps taken the brutal attacks could not be prevented.

In a speech delivered by President Bush in Indianapolis, he vowed to track down those responsible for the attacks:

These are murderers whose belief is hatred. We will find the murderers and they will learn the meaning of American justice. The murderous attack in Saudi Arabia against U.S. citizens and others reminds us that the war against terror continues.

Immediately after the attack, the FBI dispatched a team of investigators headed by John Pistol, a senior member of the U.S. counter-terror unit. The FBI has experienced difficulties in matters related to cooperation with the Saudis. In 1996, when a team of American investigators set out to investigate the attack at the Hobar Towers in which nineteen Americans had perished, the investigators complained about the Saudis' lack of cooperation, which caused relations between the countries to deteriorate. In any case, this time the Saudis announced that they would offer full cooperation. Thirty-five thousand

Americans reside permanently in Saudi Arabia and are employed as consultants to the Saudi Arabian army and as employees of infrastructure companies, including oil producers. In addition, 5,000 American soldiers are stationed on Saudi Arabian territory. However, Defense Secretary Donald Rumsfeld announced that most of these soldiers would leave Saudi Arabia by the end of the summer of 2003.

It appears that the attacks were designated not only to cause casualties among Western citizens in Riyadh and to facilitate their rapid departure from the country, but also to weaken the Saudi monarchy, which employs foreign citizens for the construction of the country's infrastructures. Without the skills of foreign citizens, the Saudi economy would sustain a heavy blow. For a long period of time, Saudi princes have been financing Al-Qaida in the hope that this will buy them and the monarchy some quiet. These attacks proved how mistaken they were. It appears that the attacks in Riyadh were perpetrated mainly by Saudi Arabians. Seventeen out of the nineteen people wanted in connection with these attacks are local Saudi citizens. It is logical to assume that they were known to the Saudi security services prior to the incidents, but it appears that no great effort was made to apprehend them prior to the attacks.

Suicide Attack on a Saudi Housing Compound[110]

On November 9, 2003, a powerful car bomb exploded shortly after midnight in the Muhaya housing compound near Riyadh's diplomatic quarter, which at the time housed mostly foreigners from Arab countries. The assailants, reportedly disguised as Saudi soldiers, shot their way into the compound and then set off explosives packed in a truck bearing security forces colors. According to one report, the attackers had positioned snipers on the ridge outside the complex that shot into the compound before the blast. The massive blast killed at least two people and injured at least fifty.

The Muhaya was at one time predominantly occupied by Westerners. However, a Saudi official said that the current complex occupants were "95 percent Arabs, Jordanians, Lebanese, Palestinians, and Egyptians." He said that the attack could have been the result of "poor reconnaissance," and the bombers may have thought the Muhaya housed more Americans and other Westerners.

At least one-quarter of the victims reportedly were children. The toll could have been worse as many of the compound's adult residents were not at home at the time of the bombing. During the Muslim holy month of Ramadan, Muslims fast until dusk and many go out after dark for an evening feast and shopping.

Saudi security forces have attempted to preempt terrorist attacks and had been involved in at least two confrontations with suspected militants. The

Saudi police reportedly uncovered a cell that was plotting attacks during Ramadam, and two suspects blew themselves up rather than surrender during a police raid in Mecca. The bombing took place just hours after a decision by the United States to shut down its embassy and two consulates, due to intelligence indicating that terrorists plotting attacks were moving into an operational phase.

Suicide Attacks in Casablanca, Morocco[111]

After midnight on May 17, 2003, a series of suicide attacks took place in the city of Casablanca, Morocco. The explosions occurred around 1:00 a.m., Israeli time. Thirteen suicide attackers detonated themselves at five different sites in the city, as follows:
• An attack against the Jewish community center Alliance.
• An attack against the Sapphire Hotel, (Israeli tourists were staying at the hotel).
• An attack against the ancient Jewish cemetery.
• An attack against a restaurant under Jewish ownership (near the Belgian consulate).
• An attack against the Spanish restaurant Casa Despania.

At least forty-one people perished in the attacks (including twenty-eight civilians and the thirteen terrorists). More than one hundred were injured (at least seven of the victims were foreign residents).

An additional terrorist, who was supposed to detonate himself with two of his fellow terrorists, reconsidered at the last minute, and was apprehended by the authorities. This terrorist was the main source of information that enabled security services to sort out the facts surrounding the attacks.

Morocco's security services have exposed the identity of most of the suicide terrorists who were responsible for the five attacks in Casablanca, as well as their affiliations. The following statement was made by the Moroccan minister of justice in an interview on Moroccan television: "They are Moroccan citizens, some of whom recently arrived from a foreign country," without mentioning the country involved.

According to the minister of justice, the terrorists were affiliated with a local radical Islamic group called "al-Sirat al-Mustakim" (the "just path" or the "path of good talismans"). This group, which has several dozen members, is a faction that split off from a larger militant group called "al-Salfia al-Jihadia." One of the spiritual leaders of the al-Salfia al-Jihadia is Muhammad Abd al-Wahab Rakiki, also known as Abu Hafez, who was imprisoned in 2003 for inciting violence against Western residents. Twenty-eight-year-old Abu Hafez is one of the "Afghan Arabs" who volunteered to fight in the jihad in Afghanistan. After the September 11 assault he expressed his support for the attacks against the Twin Towers in New York and the Pentagon in Washington, lauded Bin-Laden and called him a hero. In the course of the investigation thirty-three suspects were arrested, mostly activists from radical Islamic organizations. The investigation revealed that the explosives were supplied by a supporter of the organization, an engineer by profession.

Suicide Attacks in Istanbul, Turkey[112]

In the month of November 2003, Al-Qaida perpetrated a series of suicide attacks in Istanbul. The attackers belonged to a local Al-Qaida affiliate in Turkey, acting on orders from Al-Qaida headquarters (the head of the Turkish branch of Al-Qaida met with Bin Laden and received his blessing). The attacks in Istanbul took place on two dates: (1) November 15, 2003, two synagogues were attacked; (2) November 20, 2003, two British targets were attacked. A short summary of the attacks follows.

On November 15, two cars rigged with explosives and driven by suicide bombers blew up near two synagogues, killing twenty-three people and injuring approximately 300. Police sources in Istanbul reported that the vehicles in question were Isuzu vans, each rigged with 400 kilograms of explosives. Al-Qaida claimed responsibility in a message faxed to the London-based *Al-Quds* newspaper in which it claimed that the group responsible for the attacks was the Abu-Khafes al-Misri memorial organization. This was the alias of Muhammad Ataf, the former number three in the Al-Qaida hierarchy who had been killed in an American attack on the building in which he was dwelling in Afghanistan two years earlier. Al-Misri was one of the former commanders of the Egyptian Jihad organizations and a close confidant of Bin-Laden; his son, Mohammed, had married Bin-Laden's daughter. Before his death, Al-Misri had headed Al-Qaida's military branch.

The message stated: "The brigades (in memory of the Shahid Abu-Khafez al-Misri) were following Jewish intelligence agents; it soon became clear that five of the agents were present in Jewish houses of prayer in central Istanbul. The Mujahidin (the holy warriors) struck a lethal blow, the rest was accomplished with the aid of Allah."

Suicide Attacks against the British Consulate and the British Bank in Istanbul[113]

On November 20, two cars rigged with explosives exploded near a British bank in central Istanbul and near the British consulate. At least thirty-two people were killed and more than 500 people were injured; among the dead was the British consul to Turkey. Al-Qaida, most likely with the aid of a local terror organization, was responsible for the attacks. In a message published on November 22, the Al-Qaida organization demanded that "Turkish officialdom stop functioning as an agent of America, Britain, and their allies in the Zionist entity." "Until now we spoke with you in words, and attacked predetermined targets," the statement said. "However, if you fail to heed our warnings, we will speak in the language of explosives, and will send you cars full of death until you learn your lesson." The message was signed: The suicide organization in memory of Abu-Khafez al-Misri.

The organization expressed remorse for the attack against the bank and claimed that it was a "mistake," that the car had exploded in the wrong place, and that was why so many innocents had been killed and injured. "It hurts us, but the media bears responsibility. We warned Muslims to stay away from foreign embassies and establishments affiliated with the Americans, the British, and the Zionists."

The organization made reference to the attack on the British consulate, noting that the British consul Roger Short was a target for assassination because of "his expertise in anti-Islamic warfare." "We followed Consul Short, who was the most senior expert, and the mastermind of British policy in Iraq, Turkey, Syria, and Iran, and the Consulate in Istanbul functioned as his operational headquarters. We followed him and succeeded in killing him and his associates so that Britain would understand that its affiliation with the United States would only bring death and destruction."

In the message, Al-Qaida also demanded the release of the prisoners incarcerated in Guantanamo prison, and the cleansing of Arab lands from Americans and Jews. They threatened another "specialized attack" would be forthcoming and that "the enemy would not know when and where it would occur."

After the interrogation of Haroun Ilhan, a Turkish national who had been arrested because of his alleged complicity in the bombing of the British targets, it became clear that Al-Qaida had planned to blow up an Israeli cruise ship that was supposed to have docked at the tourist city of Alniyah on the Turkish Riviera. When the ship was delayed and did not make its planned stop, the terrorists decided to change their plan and to attack British targets instead.[114]

Suicide Attacks Perpetrated by the "Tamil Tigers" (LTTE) in Sri Lanka[115]

The Tamil Tiger" acts in Sri Lanka to achieve independence for the Tamil minority on the island, which constitutes 12.5 percent of the population. Sri Lanka is governed by the Sinhali majority. The organization was founded in 1972 and initiated a violent struggle against the government. In 1981, many of the organization's leaders were arrested, and its very existence was in question. A lesson learned from the 1981 events was the organization's decision to provide each fighter with a capsule of poison that he would swallow if there were a danger of his being arrested or falling captive.[116] This custom contributed to recognition that self-sacrifice is part of the organizational culture of the Tamil Tigers.

During their years of activities the Tamil Tigers perpetrated many attacks against army bases using trucks loaded with explosives, from which the drivers would leap seconds before detonation at the target. This method was found to be ineffective, however, due to malfunctions in the detonation of the explosive.[117] Following a heavy blow that it sustained from the Sri Lanka military at the organization's strongholds in the Jafna Peninsula, the Tamil Tigers began perpetrating suicide attacks in 1987. At that time, a truck bomb was driven by a man named Miller, who volunteered for the mission. Sixteen soldiers perished in the attack and twenty-two were injured. Miller was promoted to the rank of captain posthumously and became one of the organization's heroes.[118]

During the years 1987-2000, the organization perpetrated 168 suicide attacks with the aid of two hundred suicide terrorists. In most of the operations, more than one terrorist took part simultaneously.[119] The contribution of women who perpetrated suicide attacks was particularly prominent (about 30 percent of the total number of attacks). This organization is one of the few to set up a unit of suicide attackers called "the Black Tigers," whose attacks were particularly vicious and caused many hundreds of deaths.

The Tamil Tigers, which focused its suicide attacks on senior leaders in Sri Lanka's political and military establishment, is the only organization in the world to succeed in assassinating two leaders of state. The first was the Prime Minister of India, Rajiv Gandhi, who at that time was involved in a reelection campaign in Madras. The second was Sri Lanka President Primadasa, who was assassinated in an attack in which twenty-two other persons also died (May 1993). On December 17, 1999, the organization made an assassination attempt against Sri Lanka's President Chandrika Kumaratunga, via a female suicide terrorist who detonated herself at the president's front door. The president lost an eye in the attack, but survived.

The organization also acted against politicians affiliated with the Singhalese majority as well as pragmatic politicians from the Tamil minority, senior military personnel, sea vessels, command headquarters, and economic facilities such as oil centers. In the attacks, the LTTE demonstrated indifference to the killing of innocent bystanders and showed no compassion for anyone who happened to be in the vicinity of their target. The main motivating factors behind the Tamil suicide attackers were an aspiration for national independence, blind obedience to the charismatic leadership of the organization's leader Prabhakaran, and strong peer and social pressures.[120]

Examples of Suicide Attacks Perpetrated by the Tamil Tigers[121]

The assassination of Indian Prime Minister Rajib Gandhi. In May 1991, the organization assassinated Prime Minister Rajib Gandhi during an election campaign. A female suicide terrorist named Dhano, who was in the midst

of an audience at an election rally in Madras, approached Gandhi, supposedly to present him with a bouquet of flowers, and detonated herself with a
belt bomb concealed under her clothing. Eighteen people were killed including Rajib Gandhi.

The assassination of the Sri Lanka President Primadasa. In the framework
of his preparations for the attack, the assassin applied for a job in the maintenance team at the president's residence. Thus, he had free access, and was able
to come and go without arousing suspicion. On May 1, 1993, when the president was on his way to a press conference, the assassin approached him. The
bodyguards, who knew him, did not suspect him, and he detonated himself
near the president. In this attack, eleven other people were killed along with
the president of Sri Lanka.

The attack against the Central Bank of Sri Lanka. In January 1996, the
organization perpetrated a suicide attack with a truck bomb driven by a
suicide terrorist. The truck detonated near the Central Bank of Sri Lanka
in the capital of Colombo. Eighty-six people were killed and 1,338 were
injured, including foreign residents. The attack was not completely successful, however, as two organization members who were moving near the
truck bomb and were meant to secure its operation were apprehended by the
government and disclosed considerable information in the course of their
interrogation.

As a lesson learned from this incident, in subsequent attacks the organization required all participants in the activity (not only the suicide terrorist) to
wear belt bombs and activate them in the event that they might be taken
captive.

Support of Arab and Muslim Countries for Suicide Terror

Most of the leaders of Muslim and Arab states take a cautious and sometimes even ambivalent stand regarding the issue of suicide terror. On the level
of principle, there is overall consent that terror in general should be opposed,
and suicide attacks in particular should be condemned. Nevertheless, the
concrete position of the various countries stems from the particular view of
the political context of events and occurrences. Many of the leaders of the
Arab and Muslim world regard the Palestinian struggle against Israel as a
legitimate one. Therefore, violent acts perpetrated by the Palestinians in
this framework, including suicide attacks, are not condemned and are
perceived as legitimate acts. This is also true of other areas of conflict
worldwide, such as the conflict in the Kashmir region, Chechnya, and
others. While the perpetration of suicide and other attacks against a political adversary are received with understanding, albeit not with enthusiasm, domestic terror is perceived as an essential threat against Arab and
Muslim regimes, and these regimes do everything they can to fight a war to

the death against Islamic terror organizations that threaten their stability. Prominent examples are:

- Egypt—which is fighting a relentless war against Islamic terror organizations in Egypt, and has itself fallen victim to several suicide attacks.
- Saudi Arabia—which supports Islamic terror organizations like the Hamas, but ruthlessly subjugates any indication of radical Islamic subversion within its territory.

The policy of the majority of Muslim and Arab states vis-à-vis terror is characterized by ambivalence, due to their obligation to condemn terror in the international arena, on the one hand, and to avoid confrontations with the opposition and the general public at home, which usually identify with radical Islam, on the other hand. Despite what has been said, several countries openly and consistently support terror and suicide attacks, and they include Iraq, Iran, and Syria. Two of these countries appear in the American definition of the "axis of evil," which includes Iran, Iraq, and North Korea.

Iraq and Its Involvement in Terror

Following the September 11, 2001 attacks, the United States declared war against terror worldwide and regimes that support it. The U.S. president defined three countries as the axis of evil, which endanger world security because of their support of terror and their attempts to develop means for unconventional warfare, including nuclear weapons.

Iraq, one of the countries in the axis of evil, was liberated of Sadam Hussein's regime by the coalition led by the United States.[122] Iraq was perceived by the United States and its allies as a primary threat against world peace and security due to the combination of a dangerous and unrestrained ruler (as expressed in his invasion of Iran in 1980 and Kuwait in 1990), his support for international terror, and the arsenal of non-conventional weapons in his possession, which he did not hesitated to use during the Iraq-Iran war and even against his own country's Kurd population in Halabgeh.

Since the end of the first Gulf War in 1991, Iraq has been embroiled in an ongoing conflict vis-à-vis the United States and her allies, mainly in light of its attempts to preserve and even continue the development of its capabilities in the area of mass destruction while circumventing the efforts of supervisors acting in the country on the basis of the UN resolution. Against this background of incessant confrontations between Iraq and the United States, during this period (1991-2003), U.S. and British aircraft attacked targets in Iraq in retaliation for attempts by Iraqi air defense batteries to shoot down coalition planes flying in Iraq's airspace. The most prominent crisis between Iraq and the United States pertaining to the "supervisors' issue" took place in

1998 and culminated in a raid against Iraqi targets by U.S. and British cruise missiles and combat planes. During 1991-2003, however, Iraq continued to support international terror in general and Palestinian terror in particular, while taking steps to conceal its involvement in these activities due to a fear of exacerbation of the international sanctions imposed upon it.

Since the mid-1960s, Iraq has had a long history in the use of weapons of terror to promote its goals:

- The Israeli-Palestinian conflict
- The internal Arab conflict
- In the international arena against Iraq's foes.

Iraq viewed the Arab-Israeli conflict as an arena where it could reinforce its status as a leader of the Arab world's struggle against Israel. Iraq dispatched its forces to participate in three of the wars waged against Israel (1948, 1967, 1973), and has supported and activated Palestinian terror organizations since the 1960s (see subsequent elaboration).

Iraq used Palestinian and other terror organizations in its struggles against adversaries in the Arab and Muslim world. For example, in 1976 the Iraqis activated the Abu Nidal organization, which had split from the Fatah, in order to attack Syrian targets, and, subsequently, in 1978 to attack PLO members and offices.[123] Following the Islamic revolution in Iran (1979), Iraq aided the Iranian Mujahidin Halq in its struggle against the Islamic regime in Teheran.[124]

From the early 1990s, Iraq was involved in international terror incidents perpetrated by Palestinian terror organizations such as the Popular Front for the Liberation of Palestine (the Wadia Khadad faction), which acted against Western and Israeli targets, the Abu Ibrahim faction (15 of May Organization), and the Abu Nidal organization.[125]

The use of the terror tool or the decision to refrain from its use was dependent on assessments of the Iraqi regime as to the ratio of cost/benefit in this regard; thus, fluctuating levels of Iraqi involvement in terror are to be discerned during different periods.

Iraqi Involvement in Terror Activities against the United States (since 1991)

An assassination attempt against former President George Bush. On April 14, 1993, an Iraqi plot to assassinate former President George Bush (Sr.) during a visit to Kuwait was thwarted.[126] Sixteen suspects were arrested by Kuwaiti authorities, including two Iraqis, who had planned the assassination attempt. The assassins, acting on behalf of the Iraqi intelligence, smuggled into Kuwait a booby-trapped Toyota Land Cruiser loaded with about 80 kilograms of plastic explosives which were well concealed in the car, apparently by Iraqi sabotage specialists. Aside from the car, cell members smuggled additional explosives which were to have been planted at various locations throughout Kuwait city. Reportedly, the two Iraqi terrorists heading the cell, Ra'id al-Assadi and Wali al-Razli, were recruited by Iraqi intelligence in the city of Basra,[127] where, on April 10, 1994, they were given the car bomb and explosive devices by their operators who smuggled them into Kuwait during the night of April 13, the eve of Bush's visit to Kuwait.[128] Apparently, al-Razli intended to perpetrate Bush's assassination using the suicide car bomb. His accomplice al-Assadi was to transport al-Razli to the venue of the assassination near Kuwait University, where Bush and the Emir of Kuwait were scheduled to appear before a group of students.[129] The attack was thwarted due to the arrest of the cell members before they were able to carry out the plot.

The Iraqi intention to perpetrate suicide attacks against American sea vessels in the Persian Gulf.[130] Information divulged during the interrogation of an Iranian gunrunner apprehended in the Kurd region of northern Iraq (who was questioned by U.S. security personnel) on March 4, 2002, indicated that an Iraqi plot was afoot to attack an American sea vessel using a boat bomb. The arrested man, Muhammad Mantsur Shaab, claimed that Iraqi intelligence personnel had contacted him and asked for his assistance in perpetrating a series of attacks against U.S. sea vessels in the Persian Gulf.

He claimed that the Iraqis had planned a series of nine attacks, designed to occur over a long period of time. The Iraqis asked Shaab to purchase a boat with 400-ton capacity that would sail under the Iranian flag. He was also told to rent or purchase a large date farm at the mouth of the Shaat a-Arab River near the Iraq-Iran border, as well as several small and fast motorboats. The farm was to serve as a base for the preparations for the attack. The Iraqis had intended to transport the explosives on the motorboats for loading onto the bomb boat on the Iranian side of the river. After completing preparations, the vessel was to sail to the Persian Gulf with the aid of a crew that was not to be informed that the boat was loaded with explosives. Near the time of the attack, the Iraqi suicide team would arrive, take over command of the ship (after eradicating the original crew), and carry out the attack against American vessels in the Persian Gulf. The plot was foiled by Shaab's arrest in Kurdistan.[131]

Iraq and Al-Qaida

One of the main U.S. allegations to justify the 2003 war against Iraq was based on the latter's involvement in terror in general and its links with Al-Qaida (which had carried out the September 11 attacks) in particular. The United States regarded the link between Sadam Hussein's regime (along with its non-conventional weapons) and Al-Qaida as a serious threat against world peace and security. In the U.S. administration's view, this threat justified the campaign in Iraq. Sadam Hussein made every effort to renounce any link with Al-Qaida in particular and terror in general in the hope that this approach might undermine the legitimization of and support for the U.S. attack.

Bin-Laden, however, openly declared his support for Iraq and called upon the entire Arab nation to adopt a similar policy, although he did not imply that Iraq had been involved in his organization's previous activities. The Al-Jazeera television network broadcast a cassette of Bin-Laden's voice, in which he appealed to the Iraqi nation to remain steadfast and offered advice on how to withstand the U.S. aggression:[132]

> Our brothers, fighters of the Iraqi Jihad: Do not allow yourselves to weaken in the face of the lies that the United States spreads regarding its strength and their laser-guided smart bombs, as smart bombs have very little effect on mountainous terrain, inside foxholes, on flat plains and in forests.
>
> These bombs require prominent targets, but if the targets are inside well-concealed foxholes, then the smart bombs and the stupid ones as well, cannot reach them, except through indiscriminate bombing, which causes waste of the enemy's ammunition and funds.
>
> Dig many pits, as stated by Omar (the second caliph) who said: "Take advantage of the earth," meaning—use its length, because thus with the will and kindness of Allah you will be able to bring about the waste of all of the enemy's stockpile of bombs within several months. As to their daily production of bombs, this is a small amount which can be borne, with Allah's will. We also recommend to drag the enemy's forces into prolonged, continuous and attritional combat, while taking advantage of camouflaged defense positions in the plains, agricultural farms, mountains and cities. The thing which the enemy fears most is urban and house-to-house warfare, because it anticipates heavy and painful casualties in this type of fighting. We also stress the importance of suicide attacks against the enemy (in the source; alamliat alisteshadiya). These actions have inflicted upon the United States and Israel a disaster which they have never previously experienced in their history, thanks to Allah the Almighty. Also, we clarify that anyone who aids the United States from among the hypocritical sinners in Iraq, rulers of Arab states, and anyone who is pleased with their deeds and follows them in this crusader war by fighting alongside them or offering their bases for aid, or any other form of support given to them, even if it is only in the form of words in order to kill Muslims in Iraq, then he must be aware that he is a traitor and that he will be ousted from the Islamic community.

And Bin-Laden goes on to add:[133]

> The Muslims in general and particularly in Iraq must gird their loins and set out on a Jihad against this oppressive attack and they must take care to obtain ammunition and arms because this is their duty as the preservers of Allah's reverence. To quote the Koran: "Play their equipment and weapons, and they will acquire the friendship of those who have disbelieved, if they present you with their weapons and equipment and lean towards you as one man" (Sura Alnasa'a, verse 102).

Bin-Laden does not align himself with Sadam Hussein and his secular regime, but rather supports the Iraqi people which are forced to withstand the aggression of the Crusader-Jewish alliance. Bin-Laden regards the conflict between the United States and Iraq as additional proof supporting his claim that this confrontation stems from a conflict between cultures, with Iraq constituting an additional target in America's chain of targets whose goal is to take over the Muslim world.

Therefore, the U.S. offensive must not be regarded as America's desire to topple Sadam Hussein's tyrannical regime, but rather as a pretext and a justification for an American move whose true, long-term objective is to take over the Muslim world and its oil resources.

A member of the Iraqi National Council, Muhammad al-Adami, was interviewed on Al-Jazeera in response to the tape.[134] Al-Adami denied any connection between Iraq and Al-Qaida and claimed that the tape was an American fabrication. When asked for his reaction to Bin-Laden's advice to the Iraqis, he replied that Iraq had not asked for advice or instructions. Finally, he stated that the United States would stop at nothing to prove that there was a connection between Iraq and Al-Qaida, but the entire world would not believe the American lies, the purpose of which were only to justify a military offensive in Iraq.

Iraq's connection with Bin-Laden and Al-Qaida began during the first Gulf War when Bin-Laden fiercely condemned the policy of Saudi Arabia and the remaining Arab states that had joined the U.S.-led coalition against Iraq. As a result of this condemnation, Bin-Laden was expelled from Saudi Arabia and shifted his place of residence and focus of activity to Sudan. During his stay in Sudan, he developed ties with Iraq, which, at that time, maintained a friendly relationship with Sudan.[135]

In the mid-1990s, an organization activist named Abu Abdallah al-Iraqi was dispatched by Bin-Laden to request Iraqi aid in the training of organization members in non-conventional combat means.[136] The Iraqis consented and an unknown number of Iraqi instructors were sent to Afghanistan to train the Al-Qaida members.

Current information regarding Al-Qaida's ties with Iraq has focused on three areas to date:

- Iraq's connections with a radical Islamic organization called Ansar al Islam, which is linked with Al-Qaida and has strongholds in northeast Iraq.
- The presence of Al-Qaida's senior leader Abu Masab al Zarkawi in Iraq (possibly in the area under the control of Ansar al Islam).
- Iraqi affiliation with the Abu Sayyaf organization in the Philippines.

According to the assessment of U.S. security agencies, ties existed between the Baghdad rulers and the Ansar al Islam organization as well as with Zarkawi, who also appears to maintain ties with this organization. On the other hand, it is to be noted that Ansar al Islam was active in an area that is not under Iraqi control and the organization's leader adamantly insists that he had no links with Sadam's regime in Baghdad.[137]

Following the occupation of Iraq by U.S. and British forces, documents were discovered by a *Daily Telegraph* correspondent proving that Osama Bin-Laden's representative in Sudan had been invited to visit Baghdad in March 1998,[138] five months prior to Al-Qaida's attacks at the U.S. Embassies in Kenya and Tanzania. According to the documents, which included correspondence between Iraqi intelligence agents, the visit's objective was to forge ties between Iraq and the terror organization in order to promote future cooperation. Following the meeting, which was described as successful, the intention was for Bin-Laden to visit Baghdad as well (although this never occurred).[139]

On April 23, 2003, American forces arrested the former director of Iraqi intelligence Farouk Khijazi at the Iraq-Syrian border. In the past, Khijazi had served as Iraqi Ambassador to Turkey. The United States alleges that during his term as ambassador in December 1998 he personally met with Bin-Laden in Kandahar, Afghanistan.[140] Various sources also implicate Khijazi in the assassination attempt against President Bush, Sr. during his visit to Kuwait in April 1993. It would appear that Khijazi's interrogation could well shed some light on the links between Iraq and Al-Qaida as well as other terror organizations.

Radical Islamic Terror Organizations in North Iraq

The mountainous region in northeast Iraq near the Iranian border, which is populated with Kurds, constitutes a focal point for radical Islamic groups from among the Kurds and Al-Qaida members who have fled Afghanistan and found refuge there. Because of this, the region has been dubbed "the Kurdish Tora Bora," after the mountainous terrain in northeast Afghanistan where the Taliban and Al-Qaida forces fought the Northern Alliance and U.S. forces in Afghanistan.

This area has actually been outside of Iraq's direct control since 1991. It was roughly divided between the two large Kurd factions after the civil war that was waged during the years 1994-1996. The Patriotic Union of Kurdistan, the faction under the leadership of Jalal Talbani, controls the northeastern sector that is near Iran. The western sector is under the control of the Democratic Kurd Party, led by Massoud Barzani. An Islamic enclave was created in the area under Talbani's control and centered in a town called Khalabja. Talbani consented to this territorial concession in exchange for support received from the Kurd Islamic Movement during the civil war. However, this concession has since cost him dearly.[141]

The Kurd Islamic Movement is only one of several movements located in that region. Organizations like the Kurd Islamic League or the Islamic Union are socially active but do not take violent steps to disseminate their ideas. The Kurd Islamic Movement itself has split into several factions due to ideological disputes. The Kurd Hamas Organization, for example, which confronted Talbani's forces and set up its own center in the city of Khormal, seceded due to the consent of the Kurd Islamic Movement's leader to serve in Talbani's secular government.[142]

The Kurd Hamas is led by Omar Barzani, who was trained and fought in Afghanistan. In 2001, it merged with the Islamic Hitwahid Front, which is led by Mulla Abd al Rani Bazazi. Bazazi's movement was established in the mosques of the town of Arbil, which is under the control of Massoud Barzani, and from there moved to an area under Talbani's control. Its members flung acid at Kurd women who did not cover their faces with a veil. The members of this radical Muslim organization were also trained in Afghanistan and according to Kurd sources also maintained close ties with Bin-Laden.[143]

Another Islamic group was the "Second Sudan Unit," with about 400 fighters—the largest armed group in the Kurd Islamic Movement. Its members are Arab fighters who also underwent military training in Afghanistan. This group fights the main Kurd factions but also the Islamic Movement itself, because it is not "sufficiently radical."[144] The two groups—the Second Sudan Unit and the Tahwid—merged in September 2001 under the name of Jund al-Islam (the Islamic Army). It appears that Al-Qaida representatives attended the signing of the merge agreement and presented $300,000 to support the new organization.

The organization is equipped with a wide range of combat means including tanks and airplanes. It is composed of some 600 fighters, divided into six battalions, under the leadership of Abdallah a-Shafi, an Iraqi Kurd trained in Afghanistan who also fought in Chechnya. The organization has a religious advisory council, a radio station, and several leaflets. Since its establishment it has occupied several villages and towns along the Iranian border. In December 2001, some other small organizations joined the Jund al-Islam and created the organization Ansar al-Islam. It appears that the organization receives aid from Iran, Al-Qaida, and Iraq.[145] A member of the Iraqi intelligence who was arrested by Talbani's forces disclosed that he had been placed in charge of reinforcing the ties between the Iraqi administration and the members of the Ansar al-Islam organization. According to testimony that he gave in prison, Iraq offered the organization weapons so that it would take action against Talbani's Kurds. Some of the organization's wounded members were treated in Iran, which proves that this country also has ties with it. The smuggling of weapons and equipment from the Iranian border is routine in this area, but it should not necessarily be attributed to the authorities but rather to bribery and local criminal activities.

Ansar al Islam is the most important organization that maintains ties with "foreigners"—apparently some 150 Arabs and others who fought in Afghanistan and found refuge in Kurdistan (they are called foreigners by the Kurds because they are not from the area). The organization invaded the towns of Biara and Tawla and declared a Jihad against the "secular" Kurd authorities. In skirmishes between Talbani's men and the organization in September 2001, ten days after the attacks in the United States, organization members slaughtered forty Kurd Pashmarga fighters. They tied up the victims and videotaped the slaughter. According to eyewitness testimony, the organization members spoke Arabic and Persian. Later, organization members attempted to assassinate Brahm Slah, the prime minister appointed by Talbani. According to Slah, Bin-Laden chose this region as an alternative hiding place in lieu of Afghanistan, even before the war started there.[146]

The Ansar al-Islam organization has 700-800 members and is headed by Omar Mula Krikar, a religious cleric whose real name is Najem a-din Fraj. His ties with Afghanistan go back as far as the 1980s, to the war against the Soviet invasion. Krikar, forty-seven years of age, studied in Afghanistan under the Palestinian religious cleric Abdallah Azzam who was also the spiritual mentor and personal aide of Osama Bin-Laden.[147]

Krikar lived in Norway with his wife and four children and in the past moved freely throughout Europe, raising funds for Ansar al-Islam.[148] Last year, he was arrested in Holland and an extradition request was filed by Jordan, but he was ultimately released due to lack of evidence. He then returned to Oslo, Norway. The Norwegian authorities have recently launched proceedings to deport him from the country.[149]

In an interview with the London *Al Hayat* newspaper, Krikar claimed that his organization is not connected to Al-Qaida or to Sadam Hussein's regime.[150] Moreover, he claimed that his organization aspired to liberate Iraq from Sadam Hussein's regime, but, nevertheless, opposed the U.S. offensive against Iraq and would do anything in its power to prevent it. As to Bin-Laden, he stated that the former was a good and devout Moslem and subsequently refused to take a stand regarding the terror activity perpetrated by Al-Qaida.[151] Krikar's brother, Khaled, is responsible for the organization's funds and budgets. Despite Krikar's denials, there exists information testifying to the organization's links with Baghdad. The liaison between the Iraqi authorities and the organization is Abu Wa'al, also known as Saadon Mahmad Abd Allatif Alaani.[152]

In a speech delivered to the Security Council, Colin Powell claimed that Ansar al-Islam developed and produced non-conventional combat means (particularly toxins) at a facility in northern Iraq, and that Al-Qaida activist Zarkawi was also involved in this activity. The Ansar al-Islam organization refuted these allegations and even allowed twenty journalists to visit the base mentioned by the Secretary of State in order to disprove these accusations. The journalists who visited the site did not discover any evidence of the presence of an infrastructure for the production of non-conventional combat means, but, nevertheless, they noted that the behavior of their hosts had been suspicious and they were barred access to parts of the base.[153]

During the U.S. offensive in Iraq, camps and facilities belonging to the organization were bombed, the majority of the Ansar al-Islam activists withdrew to the mountainous terrain near the Iranian border, and Kurd forces overtook most of the organization's known strongholds in the area, with the help of special American forces. In some of the organization's bases that fell into Kurd hands documents were found that attested to its connections with Al-Qaida, and to the fact that at least 150 people had come from various places worldwide (Yemen, Turkey, Pakistan, Iran, Algeria, Palestine and more).[154]

The Terror Infrastructure of Abu Masab al-Zarkawi

In a speech delivered by Colin Powell at the UN's Security Council, the U.S. Secretary of State accused Iraq of training members of Al-Qaida and of offering them refuge in that country. He claimed that an international terror network operated by Abu Masab al Zarkawi is affiliated with Al-Qaida and functions out of Iraq.[155] Powell also claimed in his speech that Zarkawi's international terror network is composed of several terror cells active in France, Britain, Spain, Italy, Germany, and Russia, and that some of Zarkawi's terror cells were involved in the preparation of non-conventional combat means such as the ricin laboratory exposed in London.

Recently, several Al-Qaida activists who belonged to the organization were arrested; their testimony indicates that Zarkawi's terror network is also linked to another terror network that the organization operates at several European sites.[156] To date a total of 116 individuals suspected of links with or membership in these networks have been arrested.

Zarkawi's real name is Ahmad Fadel Nezal Khaleila, and he is a Jordanian citizen of Palestinian descent. Zarkawi is considered an expert in matters of chemical and biological warfare. At the end of 1999, a cell that had been operated by Zarkawi was arrested in Jordan; it had planned to perpetrate a series of attacks against Israeli and American targets on the eve of the millenof nium. Following the exposure of the affair, Zarkawi was sentenced to death in absentia. He succeeded in fleeing from Jordan, and arrived in London where he stayed a few months until being summoned by Bin-Laden to Afghanistan to run one of his organization's training camps.[157]

When the U.S. offensive began in Afghanistan after the September 11 attacks, the Americans relentlessly pursued Zarkawi and almost managed to terminate him. In one of the bombing attacks, Zarkawi's leg was injured. Despite the injury, Zarkawi fled to Iran. In the light of U.S. accusations that Iran was collaborating with Al-Qaida activists, Zarkawi moved from Iran to Iraq, where he was given medical treatment. After the treatments he visited Syria, Lebanon, and Iran.[158] During his stay in Iran, Zarkawi masterminded an attempt by three suicide terrorists to infiltrate Israel via Turkey.[159]

Since 2001, Zarkawi has been Al-Qaida's commander on the Kurdistan front, which leads to the possibility that he is cooperating with Ansar al-Islam. Zarkawi's name was also mentioned in connection with an investigation initiated by Jordanian intelligence in the matter of the murder of U.S. diplomat Lawrence Foley in Amman in October 2002. Two suspects who were arrested in connection with the murder—a Libyan named Salem Saad Bin Soyd and a Jordanian named Yasser Fatkhi Ibrahim—were given $18,000 for the assassination. When apprehended, the two revealed their affiliation with Zarkawi. Turkish intelligence succeeded in taping a conversation on a cellular phone conducted by one of Zarkawi's aides with the assassins prior to the deed. Turkish authorities arrested the aide and conveyed the information to Jordan and the United States. Information that Zarkawi was to be found in the Kurd region apparently was obtained from Syrian intelligence.[160]

According to U.S. sources[161] it is possible to indicate additional links between Al-Qaida and Sadam Hussein's regime:

- Over the years, starting from the early 1990s to date, members of the Iraqi intelligence have met Al-Qaida activists at least eight times.
- In 1998, the Iraqi Ambassador to Turkey traveled to Afghanistan and met with Al-Qaida activists.
- According to an Iraqi defector, Iraq dispatched document forgery experts to Al-Qaida in Afghanistan in order to train organization members in this area.
- During the years 1997-2000, Iraqi instructors taught Al-Qaida activists about biological and chemical warfare.

Iraq's Ties with the Abu Sayyaf Organization in the Philippines

Another focal point for Iraqi involvement in terror has been exposed in the Philippines. The Philippine authorities deported an Iraqi diplomat suspected of ties with the Islamic terror organization Abu Sayyaf (which cooperates closely with Al-Qaida).[162] In an interview with one of Abu Sayyaf's senior members, it was disclosed that the organization receives annual financial support of $20,000 from Iraq.[163]

Abu Sayyaf is a radical Islamic organization that has been conducting a struggle to establish an independent Muslim state in the southern Philippines since the 1970s. In the framework of the global war against terror, the United States sent special forces to the Philippines whose role was to assist the government in its war against Islamic terror organizations in the southern part of the country.

Iraqi aid for the Iranian Mujahidin Khalq

Since the outbreak of the Iraq-Iran war to date, the Iranian Mujahidin Khalq organization, which is active against the Islamic regime in Iran, has enjoyed Iraqi patronage and aid. The organization's main logistic and operational infrastructure is situated in Iraq, and it operates with the blessings and sponsorship of the authorities. Attacks perpetrated by the organization in Iran have sometimes exacerbated the tension between the two countries and even triggered the Iranian shooting of Scud missiles at the bases of the Mujahidin Khalq in Iraq in 1999 and 2001.[164]

Iraqi Aid for the PKK (The Workers' Party of Kurdistan)[165]

The regime in Baghdad was involved in constant conflict with the Kurd population in northern Iraq, which demanded autonomy or at the very least improvement of the political and economic status of the Kurd population in Iraq. While on the home front the Iraqi regime ruthlessly suppressed any expressions of Kurd isolationism, Iraq supported and assisted Kurd organizations acting against the regimes in neighboring states.

During the Iraq-Iran war, Iraq assisted Kurd factions acting against the Islamic regime in Iran with the aim of achieving Kurd autonomy in northwest Iran. The objective of this aid was to tie down Iranian forces by compelling them to contend with Kurd terror and guerrilla warfare, thus weakening the Iranian forces at the main fighting front vis-à-vis Iraq. This aid was granted at a time when Iraq was ruthlessly suppressing its own Kurd population by using chemical weapons against this population in Khalabja.

Against the background of Turkey's support for the U.S.-led coalition during the first Gulf War (1991), Iraq assisted the PKK terror organization which aspired to obtain Kurd autonomy in Turkey. This aid was meant to serve as retaliation against Turkey due to its anti-Iraq policy, however, in the mid-1990s the relationship between the countries improved and Iraq's support for the PKK diminished.

Iraqi Involvement in Palestinian Terror during the Al-Aksa Intifada[166]

The Iraqi regime under Sadam Hussein regarded the perpetuation and escalation of the conflict between Israel and the Palestinians as leverage to promote its own strategic goals. Iraq aspired through unrestrained and radical Iraqi support for the Palestinian struggle—in light of what Baghdad and the Arab street talk perceives as the "failure" of the Arab countries—to boost its status in the Arab world. Iraqi propaganda labored at its description of the ties and links between the Israeli-Palestinian conflict and the ongoing controversy between the United States and Iraq (the connection between "the mother all wars" that Iraq waged against the United States and the Palestinians' Al-Aksa Intifada against Israel). Against the background of the U.S. offensive in Iraq, the Iraqi propaganda placed even greater emphasis on the link between American aggression and Israeli aggression, both of which were considered illegitimate and aimed at expanding U.S. control in the Middle East.

Due to Iraq's constant support for the Palestinian struggle, tremendous sympathy was lavished upon Sadam Hussein in the Palestinian street, which, much like the Arab and Muslim streets all over the world, demonstrates solidarity with the Iraqis in light of the coalition's offensive. Moreover, it was recently reported that Palestinian volunteers set out to assist Iraq, including activists of the Palestinian Islamic Jihad, who plan to perpetrate suicide missions against U.S. forces stationed in that country.

The Support of Senior Iraqi Officials for the Palestinian Struggle

Confiscated documents discovered during the Defense Shield Campaign reveal that the central member of the senior Iraqi leadership who issued Iraqi aid to Palestinian terror in the territories was Teh Yassin Ramadan, Sadam Hussein's vice president, a member of the Revolutionary Leadership Council" (Iraq's supreme body of leadership), and Sadam Hussein's right-hand man. Teh Yassin Ramadan, one of the veteran leaders of the Ba'ath Party, is defined in one of the confiscated documents as the entity responsible for the Palestinian issue in the all-Arab leadership of the Ba'ath Party.[167] Ramadan was one of the leaders of the "hawkish" line in Iraqi foreign policy, both towards the United States and the West, as well as towards Israel, and was known to be one of the most enthusiastic and sharp spokesmen for the Iraqi government.

The confiscated documents attest to Ramadan's link to financial issues and indicate that the "Palestine Bureau" which he headed "specialized" in the encouragement of Palestinian terror through the deliberate use of financial leverage, such as turning the "Arab Liberation Front" (under Iraq patronage) to the Iraqi regime's main "payment contractor" in the territories of the Palestinian Authority. At the same time, Ramadan was also involved in issuing instructions pertaining to military activity. In a letter in his handwriting there appeared code sentences referring to "military action" in Gaza and in the West Bank, and to requests for funds (from Iraq) for combat means. Thus, it is reasonable to conclude that Iraqi policy and Iraqi activity in the territories were directed by the highest echelon in the Iraqi regime. It appears that Sadam Hussein was personally involved in the overall direction and supervision of this policy, which was under the command of his deputy.

In Ramallah, the most prominent figure to handle the activities in the territories was Rakhad Mahmud Salame Salem (Abu Mahmud), an Iraqi citizen who was secretary of the Arab Liberation Front in the territories, and secretary of the Palestinian organization's leadership in the Ba'ath Party. Rakhad Salem was born in Kabri (near Acre) in 1944 and is a teacher by profession. He has been a member of the Iraqi Ba'ath Party since the 1960s. Until the war in Lebanon he served as the commander of the military arm of the Arab Liberation Front in Lebanon and also served as deputy secretary general and secretary general of the organization. In 1966, Rakhad Salem moved to the West Bank and since then has resided in Bir Zeit near Ramallah. He is a member of the Islamic and National Forces in the West Bank and coordinates the activities of the Organization for the Support of Iraq. He is currently under arrest in Israel for his involvement in terrorist activity.

Terror Activity of Palestinian Organizations under Iraqi Sponsorship

From the beginning of 2001, the Iraqis encouraged the unconcealed dispatch of combat means to the Palestinian Authority. In an Iraqi proposal for a resolution placed before the Arab League in Cairo (April 2), the Iraqis included a clear clause referring to "support for the Palestinian Intifada in the form of all sorts of weapons, headed by anti-tank weapons via Egypt, Jordan, Syria, and Lebanon." This proposal followed Sadam Hussein's declaration that "if the Palestinians had anti-tank missiles they would succeed in destroying the Israeli tanks and prevent them from occupying Palestinian cities...if the Arabs wanted it, and this is a simple matter, one need only turn a blind eye to the arrival of this type of weapon."[168] We have no information regarding the measure of success that Iraq experienced in dispatching consignments of combat means to the Palestinians in the areas of Judea and Samaria.

The Arab Liberation Front and the Ba'ath Party in the territories served mainly as Iraq's "payment contractors" in the framework of the policy to encourage terror. However, the Iraqis also recruited the Arab Liberation Front for terrorist activity and it was against this background that a terrorist cell with four members was arrested—the terrorists had been trained in Iraq and had returned to the territories in order to perpetrate attacks against Israelis. The terrorists were recruited in Judea and Samaria by the Arab Liberation Front, received financial remuneration, and traveled via the Allenby Bridge to Jordan and from there in a taxi to Baghdad.

The Iraqi regime also used another sponsor organization, the Palestinian Liberation Front, headed by Muhammad Zidan (Abu al-Abas), as an operational tool to perpetrate terror activity against Israel. In 1986, this organization perpetrated the terror attack aboard the *Achille Lauro* ship, in which an American citizen was killed. The Palestinian Liberation Front is operated by the Iraqis in the West Bank. (Muhammad Zidan was arrested in April 2003 by U.S. forces in Iraq during an attempt to flee to Syria.)

Members of the organization's cells arrested in the territories confessed that they had been sent to Iraq to undergo military training courses, during which they were instructed by a senior leader of the organization (who was arrested in Italy during the *Achille Lauro* affair) to perpetrate attacks against both Israeli military and civilian targets. These training sessions were conducted in coordination with the Iraqi authorities and with the direct support of the Iraqi administration; Abu al-Abas, secretary general of the Front, was also involved (he visited one of the cells at the end of the training course).

Members of one of the organization's cells kidnapped and murdered Yuri Gushchin, a nineteen-year-old student from Pisgat Ze'ev (a neighborhood of Jerusalem) and planted an explosive device at the "Checkpost," a crowded public location north of Haifa. Muhammad Faruk Abu Roob, a junior officer in the Palestinian intelligence organization, set out for Iraq, underwent training at the "Alkuds" camp of Abu al-Abas's organization, and returned to the territories where he was apprehended by the Israeli security forces. During his interrogation, he recounted that Abu al-Abas had instructed him to conduct a "mega attack" by poisoning the water in the national water carrier.[169] The mission proved to be unworkable, but Abu Roob recruited several additional members for his terror cell and planned to carry out other attacks, however, he was arrested before he had the opportunity to perpetrate them.[170] These examples attest to the efforts made by Iraq to encourage and increase Palestinian terror activity against Israel.

The propaganda level. Iraq supported the Palestinians via propaganda; the Iraqi propaganda included anti-Semitic motifs and praise for suicide attacks—Sadam Hussein declared his intention to establish a monument in memory of the female terrorist who perpetrated an attack in Jerusalem. Iraq attacked the Arab states that made no effort to protect the Palestinians (while the besieged Iraq was willing to lead the fighting Arab camp), and called upon the Arab masses to place pressure on their leaders.

The economic level. Iraq viewed the economic aid that it provided to the Palestinian Authority and the Palestinian population as important leverage to enhance its influence and further its goals in the Palestinian and Arab arenas. It appears that the economic and other support provided by Iraq did indeed boost its status in the Arab street and it is portrayed as the only Arab country to stand shoulder-to-shoulder with the Palestinians and come to their aid in their darkest hour.

The economic ties between Iraq and the Palestinians existed on two levels:

- The formal level opposite the Palestinian Authority and its representatives.
- Direct contact with the Palestinian population (mainly families of the shahids).

Iraq demonstrated its willingness to tighten commercial ties with the Authority by establishing a permanent fair for the sale of Palestinian products in Baghdad. It also agreed to provide direct assistance by covering the debts of Palestinian hospitals to their Jordanian counterparts, or by promising to send the Authority radio and television equipment after the destruction of the Palestinian broadcasting authority by the IDF.

Documents confiscated from the Mukatah (Arafat's headquarters in Ramallah) indicate that Fuad Shubkhi (former director of the General Security Administration) established an oil brokerage company called Eagle Petroleum Ltd. in Cyprus. It would appear that his intention was to sell and perhaps even smuggle Iraqi oil. The brokerage in deals within the framework of the "oil in exchange for food" program usually yielded commissions of about one dollar per oil barrel. Thus, an average oil deal that covers hundreds of thousands and up to millions of oil barrels could well yield millions of dollars for entities in the Palestinian Authority.

Iraq also transferred direct aid to the Palestinian population with the aim of incorporating its messages within the Arab world, thus proving that it was living up to its principles.

The humanitarian level. Medical aid was provided to the Intifada casualties, either by transferring them to Iraq or by dispatching medical teams to Jordanian hospitals. Iraq also enabled Palestinians from the territories to enroll for studies in Iraqi academic institutions at the expense of the Iraqi government. Iraq dispatched humanitarian aid (food, medical equipment, medicine, etc.) to the Palestinian Authority.

The Palestinian Authority regarded the Iraqi channel as a vital source of financial aid, and its representatives, including Azzam Al Ahmad, who was responsible for the ties with Iraq, visited Iraq several times between 2000 and 2003 in order to promote the issue of monetary aid.

Confiscated documents also indicated that the Iraqi policy in the areas of Judea and Samaria was carried out via the Palestine Bureau under the all-Arab leadership of the Iraqi Ba'ath Party. These documents exposed lengthy correspondences between the leadership of the Arab Liberation Front and the Ba'ath Party in Ramallah (mainly Rakhad Salem) and an individual named Abu Hassan, none other than Teh Yassin Ramadan, director of the Palestinian Bureau under the all-Arab leadership of the Ba'ath Party in Iraq.

The three bodies through which the Iraqi regime operated in the territories were The Arab Liberation Front, The Palestinian Liberation Front (terror organizations that operated under Iraqi patronage), and the Palestinian branch of the Iraqi Ba'ath Party. These three entities served as "influential agents" for the Iraqi regime in the territories, acting according to the latter's guidelines and enjoying generous Iraqi financing.

In the framework of the policy supporting violence and terror in the territories, the Iraqi regime made extensive use of financial leverage. The Iraqis attributed particular importance to aid for the families of the Intifada martyrs, particularly the shahids' families. In addition, the Iraqis supported the injured and handicapped who were granted between $500 and $5,000, according to the level of the injury. The confiscated documents revealed that in order to encourage the phenomenon of suicide attacks, Iraq clearly differentiated between the categories—which was not customary among other Arab nations that transferred funds to the families of the shahids—to distinguish between the financial grant transferred to the family of a "regular" martyr and that bestowed upon a martyr who died during a suicide mission.

Confiscated documents in Israel's hands indicate that the Iraqi policy in the matter of support for shahids' families underwent three developments in the course of the Intifada:

- From the beginning of the Intifada until August 2001 there was no clear policy distinguishing between "regular" martyrs and suicide martyrs, and each family received $10,000.
- According to a confiscated document, in August 2001, Sadam Hussein decided to increase the monetary grants for the families of suicide terrorists (*awal al-istshadin*) from $10,000 to $15,000. This decision was publicly announced in the Palestinian media. The grant for a regular martyr remained $10,000, and the decision thus created a gap of $5,000.
- After a visit to Iraq (March 11, 2002) by Farouk Kadumi, head of the PLO's political department, this gap increased and the sum allocated to each family of a suicide terrorist was upped to $25,000 (along with a personally worded certificate of esteem). The amount granted to the family of a regular martyr remained $10,000, and the discrepancy between the latter and the reward allocated to the family of a shahid widened significantly to $15,000. (See appendix.)

According to another confiscated document sometimes there is internal differentiation within the category of suicide attackers between those who succeeded in their mission and those who failed. A document sent to Rakhad Salem, secretary of the Arab Liberation Front and the Ba'ath, (June 14, 2002), by a member of the Arab Liberation Front in Bethlehem stated:

Please distribute the grant of the commander Sadam Hussein to the families of the martyrs specified in the table below. These martyrs fell during the recent skirmishes in Bethlehem and they are divided into three categories:

- Category A—Suicide attackers (*istshahidin*) who successfully accomplished their missions.
- Category B—Suicide attackers who failed to carry out their mission.
- Category C—Martyrs shot by the Zionists.

A table was attached to the letter that divided the martyrs into the three categories: four martyrs in the first category; eight in the second; and forty-two in the third.

In the bureaucratic correspondence of the Arab Liberation Front in the territories, a document was found that discussed the issue of "who is a suicide attacker?" This preoccupation is not simply theoretical. The precise definition of the distinctions between a regular martyr or a martyr who carried out a shooting attack during which he was killed, and a suicide attacker who wore the explosive device on his body was extremely important, because it served as a basis for the transfer of a larger amount of money to the families of shahids, as well as the wording of the certificate. This issue arose in the beginning of May 2002 when the representative of the Arab Liberation Front in Jenin claimed that the two terrorists who perpetrated suicide attacks in Afula on November 27, 2001 were not suicide attackers because they fired machine guns (an action that leaves a chance of survival) rather than wear belt bombs (a suicide attack that allows no chance of survival). Abu Mahmud, secretary of the Arab Liberation Front and the Ba'ath in the territories, was asked to consider the matter.

After the Defense Shield campaign, the Iraq regime decided to facilitate its aid for the territories. Priority and preference were to be given to two projects:

- The allocation of support to the families of martyrs who fell during the Intifada, with priority to the families of terrorists who perpetrated suicide attacks. The support was awarded to families in the West Bank and Gaza with preference for Jenin. According to the confiscated documents, the Iraqis clearly differentiated between martyrs who fell during the Intifada and who did not necessarily perpetrate an intentional suicide attack, and those who perpetrated intentional suicide attacks (*al-istshadin*), and who should be encouraged according to the Iraqi perception.
- Reconstruction of houses demolished by the IDF in the Jenin refugee camp during the Defense Shield campaign as a means to boost the Palestinians' sense of purpose. It would appear that the tough fighting that took place in the camp, the reputation that the camp had acquired as "the capital of the suicide attackers," and the communication-related and political attention that it attracted, all granted this project special significance in the Iraqi view. The reconstruction of homes demolished in Rafiah in the Gaza Strip and at other places was given lower priority.

Terror against the Background of the American Offensive in Iraq

Following the launching of the American-led coalition attack in Iraq in 2003, Sadam Hussein's regime waged a defensive war of survival on two levels:

1. The intensive conventional combat level through the regular army and the Republican Guard.
2. The combat level of terror and guerrilla warfare that developed at the same time as the main combat channel and which continued after the first type had ended.

Several factors are available to the Iraqis in the area of guerrilla and terror warfare:

- Military forces left behind the lines of the coalition forces.
- Semi-military forces like the Ba'ath Party's militia or the fedayeen forces of Kusai, Sadam Hussein's son.
- Armed civilians who might act as individuals or as part of local organizations.
- Volunteers from the Muslim and Arab world.
- Various terror organizations:

- • Ansar al-Islam in the country's northern sector
- • Palestinian terror organizations

At this time, however, it appears that guerrilla and terror combat in the Iraqi arena is still in its initial stages of development, but even so it is possible to point out several conspicuous attacks that have been perpetrated since the launching of the offensive:

- • A suicide attack in Kurdistan
- • An attack launched against Division 101 in Kuwait
- • A suicide attack against an American roadblock north of Najef
- • An attempt to run over American soldiers in Kuwait.

A more detailed summary of these attacks follows.

The suicide attack in Kurdistan.[171] On March 22, 2003, the first suicide attack was perpetrated within the framework of the second Gulf War called Iraqi Freedom. Five people were killed in the explosion of a car bomb at a checkpoint near the city of Halabgeh in northern Iraq. The Kurds claimed that the Ansar al-Islam organization was responsible for the attack. The suicide attacker was riding in a taxi when he detonated the explosive device. Paul Moran, an Australian photographer representing ABC, was killed, and Eric Campbell, the correspondent who was with him, was slightly injured. The other fatalities included a civilian and three Kurd fighters. Nine people were injured and transferred for treatment to a hospital in the city of Sulmania.

The attack was apparently carried out by the Ansar al-Islam organization in retaliation for the previous night's U.S. bombings of its bases in the Kurd region, in which several of its people reportedly had been killed. Radical Muslims accused the Kurds of collaborating with the United States in order to eradicate the Islamic presence in northern Iraq and expand the influence of the Kurd National Party in the region.

The attack on the Command Headquarters of Division 101.[172] On March 22, 2003, two grenades were lobbed into the headquarters of Division 101 in Kuwait The attacker was a thirty-two-year-old U.S. Muslim soldier named Hassan Akhbar who perpetrated the attack as an expression of opposition to the U.S. offensive in Iraq. One American soldier was killed and twelve were injured in the attack. It is possible that the attacker's intention was to assassinate the division's commander who was in the vicinity at the time.

The attack against an American Force in Western Iraq.[173] On March 27, 2003, two Iraqi women detonated themselves near an American force in western Iraq. Three American soldiers and the two attackers were killed in the incident.

The attack at the American roadblock near Najef. On March 29, 2003, a car bomb driven by a suicide terrorist exploded at an American checkpoint some 30 kilometers north of Najef on the main road leading to Baghdad. According to the commander of the American forces in the area, a taxi drove up to the checkpoint, the driver gave the soldiers a friendly wave and yelled out in English that he was coming to pick up an injured person. Four soldiers approached the taxi to check it out. The driver opened the trunk and detonated a large explosive device lying there. The four soldiers and the taxi driver were killed in the incident.[174]

Iraqi television reported that the suicide attacker was Ali Noamni, an officer in the Iraqi army, and that Sadam Hussein decided to award him two medals and promote him posthumously.[175]

In a press conference held on March 29 with Iraqi vice president Teh Yassin Ramadan, Hussein stated:[176]

> The United States will bring about a situation whereby the whole world will fill up with martyrs against it. We will pursue the enemy in its own land.

In response to a question posed by a British correspondent whether suicide attacks would from that time on become part of the Iraqi policy, Hussein replied:[177]

> We do not call this a suicide attack. This is not the action of a person who is sick of his life, but rather of an individual who sheds his own blood so that others will survive.

The attempt to run down American soldiers in Kuwait.[178] On March 30, 2003, a truck intentionally drove into a group of U.S. soldiers standing outside of a shop near the Udairi base in Kuwait. Fifteen American soldiers were injured in the attack.

The termination of Iraqi suicide terrorists by U.S. forces.[179] On April 6, 2003, American soldiers killed six Iraqis who were planning to carry out a suicide attack.

An attack at the American roadblock north of Baghdad.[180] On April 10, 2003, at 7:35 p.m., a suicide terrorist detonated himself at a U.S. marine checkpoint north of Baghdad. Four marines were injured and the terrorist perished in the incident.

Detection of a stockpile of belt bombs in Baghdad. On April 12, 2003, a marines force searching a school in Baghdad discovered forty belt bombs primed for use. The belt bombs discovered in a classroom were made of leather and contained standard explosive blocks. An investigation of the incident revealed that a fedayeen force that had arrived on the spot several days previously had planted the belt bombs and other combat materials and had intended to use them during the fighting.

Suicide Attacks in Iraq following the conclusion of Operation Iraqi Freedom

Since President Bush announced the cessation of the main military operation in Iraq (May 1, 2003), more than 200 American soldiers have been killed as a result of violent Iraqi resistance, or in operations against these same resistance elements.

Four main groups of targets may be discerned:

• American and British soldiers stationed in Iraq
• The offices and representatives of humanitarian organizations (who are seen as American collaborators in their efforts to rebuild Iraq)
• Iraqi officials (representatives of the governing council, the provisional government, and the constitutional committee, who are also seen as coalition collaborators)
• Iraqi security forces

"The resistance" uses a variety of methods and means to perpetrate these attacks, such as road bombs, ambushes, the launching of rockets and mortars, etc. Suicide attacks are a central element of the resistance's modus operandi, and thus far the bloodiest. Following is a list of the main suicide attacks carried out on Iraqi soil during the period in question.

1. On August 7, 2003, a car rigged with explosives driven by a suicide bomber blew up near the Jordanian embassy in Baghdad; eleven people were killed.
2. On August 19, 2003, a car rigged with explosives driven by a suicide bomber blew up near the United Nations Baghdadi headquarters. On August 22, this scenario was repeated; twenty-four people were killed in the attacks, including the secretary general's emissary Sergio Vieira de Mello.
3. On August 30, 2003, a suicide attack took place in Imam Ali's mosque in Nagef. Ninety-five people were killed in the attack and hundreds were injured. Among the dead was the Shi'ite leader Ayatollah Boqir al hakim, who was the target of the attack.
4. On September 22, 2003, a suicide attack outside the UN compound in Baghdad killed the driver and a policeman, and wounded eleven people. The blast occurred at the entrance to a parking lot at the Canal Hotel, which is located next to the UN compound. The Canal Hotel was targeted previously by a car bomb in August that included among its victims the UN's top envoy Sergio Vieira de Mello.
5. On October 4, 2003, a car rigged with explosives driven by a suicide bomber blew up near the police headquarters in the Medinat al-Sadi neighborhood in Baghdad; nine policemen were killed.
6. On October 14, 2003, a car bomb exploded outside the Turkish embassy, killing the suicide bomber and injuring at least two embassy staff members.

7. On October 27, 2003, a series of suicide car bombings struck the Red Cross headquarters and three police stations in Baghdad, killing at least thirty-four people and wounding more than 224. The bombings, which took place within a period of forty-five minutes, appeared to be well coordinated and showed a greater degree of sophistication than any yet carried out in the Iraqi capital.

8. On November 12, 2003, a car rigged with explosives driven by a suicide bomber blew up at an Italian military base in Nasariyah; twenty-seven people were killed, among them eighteen Italian security personnel.

9. On November 22, 2003, two suicide attacks took place against police stations in the townships of Haquba and Khan Bani Sa'ad, north of Baghdad. The modus operandi in both cases was a car rigged with explosives driven by suicide bombers who blew themselves up half an hour apart; thirteen people were killed and dozens injured.

Summary

During the offensive of the coalition forces in Iraq and mainly after its successful completion, guerrilla warfare and terror have gradually been developing against the American, British, and international forces in Iraq. To date, it is possible to mention several prominent attacks, which have already taken a heavy toll in comparison to the casualties sustained by the coalition forces in intensive conventional fighting. Many and varied powerbrokers are active in the Iraqi arena that are gradually joining the guerrilla and terror combat. The long logistic supply lines and the densely populated areas in southern and central Iraq, as well as the rough mountainous terrain in its northern sector turn these areas into relatively convenient arenas for terror and guerrilla activities.

Moreover, even after subjugation in the main campaign had been achieved and Sadam Hussein's regular army had been eliminated (including the Republican Guard) and Sadam captured, this did not suffice to bring about the end of the guerrilla and terror warfare, which will require considerable specialized input by the coalition forces, because for most of the radical Islamic movements Iraq has turned into a theater of Jihad (holy war). Attacks against the coalition forces or targets identified with them occur not only in the former fighting arena in Iraq but also in the periphery, in neighboring countries, and worldwide, as has been witnessed in Saudi Arabia, Turkey, and Morocco.

The State of Israel and Jewish targets worldwide constitute, at any given time, objectives for Islamic terror organizations, and current timing may boost the motivation of these organizations to intensify the attacks against Israel, as demonstrated in Morocco and Turkey. It is too early to assess the future of the post-war reality in Iraq but it is already clear that in for foreseeable future Iraqi aid to the Palestinian armed struggle has ceased, thus significantly decreasing the aid to families of Palestinian suicide attackers, the PA, and Iraqi-affiliated organizations.

Syria and Its Involvement in Suicide Terror[181]

Syria is one of the countries that utilizes terror as a major tool to promote its strategic goals. In addition, Syria cooperates closely with Iran, which is one of the seven-member "club" defined by the U.S. State Department as countries that support terror, and both Syria and Iran have been denounced because of their efforts to acquire weapons of mass destruction. Syria constitutes an exception among the countries that support terror, because in the past it joined the political process and is currently a member of the Security Council.

Syria has maintained a consistent strategy of encouraging the Intifada and supporting terror activities perpetrated in Israel. The goal of its policy is to enable the dominance of the radical Iranian-Syrian axis in the Middle East, promote the national interests of each of the axis members, and significantly weaken the State of Israel. These goals, among others, are to be achieved by inflaming and escalating the Intifada, undermining attempts to achieve a ceasefire, and expanding the dimensions of the conflict deep inside Israel. The declared aim is to create rifts and schisms in Israeli society, damage the Israeli economy, and neutralize any chance of an Israeli-Palestinian agreement or renewed momentum of the political process.

The method for realizing this strategy is by encouraging and instigating terror in Israel and the territories via the Palestinian and Lebanese terror organizations, radical Islamic organizations. and leftwing movements under Syrian or Iranian patronage. These organizations, which participate in or support Palestinian terror, can be divided into three categories:

1. Organizations with a radical Islamic character: The Hamas, and the Islamic Jihad in Palestine.
2. Leftwing Palestinian organizations: The Popular Front—the General Command (Jibril), the Popular Front/Habash, the Democratic Popular Front/Hawatma, the Palestinian Liberation Front, Fatah/Abu Musa, and the radical faction in the National Struggle Front.
3. Terror organizations operating from Lebanon: The Hizballah (a Lebanese terror organization) and the "13th of the Black September Brigades," a terrorist faction that split off from the Fatah and is headed by Munir al-Makdakh.

Syria and Iran cooperate closely on all matters related to the encouragement, collaboration, and activation of terror against Israel. Iran provides the radical Islamic ideology, supplies the terror organizations with vast sums of money, dispatches combat means directly (as expressed in the affair of the *Karin A* ship) and, indirectly, places at the disposal of the Intifada Palestinian Islamic organizations and the Lebanese Hizballah, which operate under its patronage.

Syria allows the use of its territory as a central operational base vis-à-vis the territories, places the area of Lebanon at the disposal of the support system for the territories (transferring combat weapons and funds, training), enables the Hizballah to exert pressure on Israel along the Israeli-Lebanese border to aid the Intifada, places leftwing Palestinian organizations under its patronage at the disposal of the struggle, aids terror organizations in the area of training, enables Iran to transfer funding and combat means to the territories, and grants the terror activities propaganda-oriented and political support in the inter-Arab and international arenas.

Characteristics of Iranian and Syrian Aid Granted to the Palestinians in Military, Operational, and Monetary Areas

Since the beginning of the Intifada to date, Syria has perpetually orchestrated ongoing terror and violent acts in the territories, under Syrian-Iranian supervision, and via the organizations under their sponsorship. The political and operational leaders of the three leading organizations—the Islamic Jihad, the Hamas, and Jibril's Front—are located in Damascus. In addition, Syria also houses an extensive infrastructure of these organizations and others, including headquarters, offices, training camps, and warehouses for combat means and equipment.

This orchestration is expressed both in the transfer of instructions to the various organizations active in the territories and in the intensive activity aimed at improving the organizations' capabilities in the territories: Transferring funds to various organizations and areas, running training operations in Syria and Lebanon, supervision over the appointment of activists in the field, encouraging operational cooperation between the various organizations, transferring qualitative combat means to the territories, both from Lebanon via Jibril's Front (such as the *Santorini* boat), and also directly from Iran (such as the *Karin A* boat).

Salient expressions of this policy can be found in the intelligence reports of the Palestinian security apparatus that were submitted to Arafat for perusal. The intelligence report (December 10, 2000) submitted by Amin al-Hindi, director of general intelligence, discusses the transfer of large amounts of money to the territories by Iran ($400,000 for the Az a-Din al-Kassam Brigades, $700,000 for the Islamic opposition organizations in the authority). According to the document, these funds were designated for "support of the Hamas' military branch within and for the encouragement of suicide activities." According to the document, the Hamas leadership in Syria maintains contact with activists of the Az a-Din al-Kassam Brigades in all matters related to military attacks against Israeli targets. An intelligence report (December 31, 2001) submitted by Jibril al-Rajub, the head of another Palestinian security service, discussed intensive meetings in Damascus attended by Hamas,

Islamic Jihad, and Hizballah activists "in order to increase the joint activities inside, with the aid of Iranian funds." This, "following the transfer of an Iranian message to the Hamas and Islamic Jihad leaders according to which calm is not to be allowed during the present time." "What is required at this time," states the document, "is to perpetrate suicide attacks against Israeli targets in Gaza, the West Bank and inside Israel."

An illustration of the nature of the ongoing orchestration emanating from Damascus from the point of view of the terrorists who are active in the field is revealed in the interrogation of Islamic Jihad operational senior leaders in the Jenin and Hebron areas, who were captured in the Defense Shield campaign.

Examples of Syrian Involvement in Suicide Terror

Orchestration of the activities in the Jenin area. Ali al-Sadi (Tsipori) and Thabat Mardawi are two senior figures in the Islamic Jihad's military-operational infrastructure in the Jenin area, who maintained ongoing contact with the organization's leadership in Damascus and who were arrested in the Defense Shield campaign. In interrogations they shed light on the orchestration of the organization's operational activity by its Syria-based leadership (with full knowledge and support of Bashar Asad's regime).

Following are the main characterizations of these two senior figures, each of whom is responsible for the killing and injury of many dozens of Israeli citizens:

- Ali Saliman Said al-Sadi (Tsipori), forty years old, is from the Jenin refugee camp. He is one of the most senior members of the Islamic Jihad's operational network in the city. He was captured during the Defense Shield campaign. During his interrogation he confessed to involvement in a large number of attacks inside Israeli territory: Detonating a car bomb in Hadera (May 25, 2001), detonating an explosive device in a trashcan in Hadera (June 20, 2001), an attempted suicide attack in Binyamina (July 6, 2001), an attempted suicide attack in Haifa (July 22, 2001), an attempted suicide attack on a bus in Tel Teomin near Bet Shean (August 2, 2001), a suicide attack at the Wall Street restaurant in Kiryat Motzkin (August 22, 2001), an attempted suicide attack in Umm el Fahem (August 16, 2001), a suicide attack at the entrance to Kibbutz Shluhot (October 7, 2001), a suicide attack at the Checkpost intersection near Haifa (October 9, 2001).
- Thabat Azmi Saliman Mardawi, twenty-six years old, originally from Ma'arba (near Jenin), is one of the senior leaders of the Islamic Jihad's operational network in Jenin. He was arrested during the Defense Shield campaign. In his interrogation, he confessed to a large number of attacks on Israeli territory: Detonating a car bomb in Haifa's central bus station (May 25, 2001), an attempted suicide attack in Afula (July 11, 2001), a suicide attack in Binyamina (July 16, 2001), an attempted suicide attack on a bus at Tel Teomim near Bet Shean (August 2, 2001), a suicide attack at

the Wall Street restaurant in Kiryat Motzkin (August 22, 2001), shooting at a bus south of the Adam Bridge (September 9, 2001), a shooting attack from a moving vehicle on an Israeli car in the northern sector of the Jordan Valley (September 24, 2001), a suicide attack at the entrance to Kibbutz Shluhot (October 7, 2001), a suicide attack on a bus traveling from Tel Aviv to Nazareth (March 20, 2002).

These two senior terrorists, who were responsible for the perpetration of many murderous attacks in Israel, confessed that they had maintained constant contact with Dr. Ramadan Shalah, secretary general of the Islamic Jihad in Damascus. They were also in touch with his aides, members of the Jihad Headquarters. The two disclosed that they would call the Islamic Jihad's headquarters in Damascus regularly in order to discuss a wide range of subjects such as:

- Clarification of the political positions of the organization's leadership in Damascus (regarding the organization's suicide attack policy).
- The claiming of responsibility vis-à-vis the headquarters regarding attacks perpetrated by members of the organization.
- Requests for funds.
- Receipt of training regarding the production of combat means.

Contact with the Islamic Jihad headquarters in Damascus was made over the phone using code names, in order to prevent the exposure of those taking part in the conversation (Thabat Mardawi called himself "Yosef"). The latter also disclosed that for a year he sent email messages and received responses within a day. He and Ali "Tsipori" received instructions on the production of explosive devices and diagrams via email.

Ali Tsipori disclosed in his interrogation that during the month of Ramadan (which began on November 16 and ended on December 16, 2001), he had decided to perpetrate a joint attack of the Islamic Jihad and the Fatah. He claimed that, as a senior member of the organization, he had authorization from the leadership in Syria to reach an agreement with the Fatah regarding the perpetration of joint attacks. His interrogation further revealed that on the ongoing tactical level, the leadership in Syria had allowed operational agents in the field leeway in all matters related to the choice of targets and the modus operandi.

Contact between senior activists in the Jenin area and the headquarters in Damascus was also maintained during the Defense Shield campaign. Ali Tsipori divulged that during the fighting he spoke to Dr. Ramadan, reported to him that "everything was fine," and that it was decided not to withdraw.

Because of the outstanding political-informational significance involved in the perpetration of attacks or the decision to temporarily stop them, the leadership in Damascus would transmit a "red light" or "green light" to its agents in the field regarding the perpetration of attacks. An example of this is the period following the September 11 attacks in the United States. Thabat Mardawi disclosed that following the attacks in the United States, instructions were received from Dr. Ramadan Shalakh (on a temporary and restricted basis) not to perpetrate attacks in Israel, so that there would be no analogy between Al-Qaida and the Islamic Jihad. Mardawi added that after the termination of Raad Karmi (a senior member of the Martyrs of the Al-Aksa Brigades in Tulkarem), the organization's leaders decided to renew the attacks in Israeli territory.

It is possible that the Syrian regime (after coordination with Iran), stood behind this command, because it sometimes imposed temporary restrictions on the terror organizations acting under its sponsorship when it was under pressure or if international political circumstances were not amenable.

The Popular Front (Jibril). Aside from the ongoing orchestration via emissaries, there were also cases in which instructions to act in the territories and Israel were issued by the organization's offices in Damascus, following training there. An example can be found in the case of two terrorists from Jibril's organization who were taken into custody in the summer of 2001, Rami Fauzi Sa'id Katuni and Samach Mahmud Salim Jibril. The two were recruited in the Nablus area, trained in Syria, and were sent back to the territories after undergoing briefings in Syria by the Front's activists to perpetrate a series of attacks including a suicide attack at the Azrieli Towers in Tel Aviv.

Following are the main issues that arose in the interrogation of the pair, which were also expressed in the charge sheets filed against them by the IDF military prosecution. In the summer of 1991, these two terrorists were dispatched from the refugee camp Ein Beit Alma near Nablus to Syria to undergo military training. The two set out on their mission on July 10 and traveled to Syria via Amman. In Damascus, the two were brought to the offices of Jibril's Popular Front where they met Jihad Ahmad Jibril, son of the leader of the Front, Ahmad Jibril (Jihad Jibril was killed in an explosion in his car on May 20 2002). Jihad Jibril dispatched them to a military training camp called "September 17," a forty-five-minute drive from Damascus.

At the "September 17" camp they underwent training in light weapons, sabotage, and the preparation of improvised explosives and detonators, constructing a delay mechanism, and the production of belt bombs and their activation in suicide attacks for mass destruction. Upon the completion of their training they returned to the offices of the Front in Damascus.

At the offices, the two were informed of their missions upon their return to the territories. The two disclosed a list of missions that they were to perpetrate: launching mortars, planting explosive devices, shooting at a military patrol, attacking IDF APCs, and suicide attacks via a car bomb at the Azrieli Towers in Tel Aviv. They asked the Front's operator in Damascus to assist them in the perpetration of the attack at the Azrieli Towers.

The Front's operator replied that the two would receive assistance from Israeli Arabs, and that the Front's representative in Nablus would supply the

Table 3.1
A Collection of Syrian Statements in Support of Suicide Terror
(since the beginning of 2001)

Speaker	Source	Statement
Vice President of Syria Abd Al Khalim Khaddam[185]	Al Ahram, Egypt, November 16, 2001.	"We have never been able to beat Israel in amassing arms and in international aid, and the importance of the opposition is the use of weapons which Israel does not possess—the weapon of the aspiration to express resistance and achieve a martyr's death. A form of power, because it cannot contend with this weapon."
Foreign Minister Al Sharah	*Al-Rai al-Am*, Kuwait, December 25, 2001	"It is possible to balance (the implication is Israel's military-technological capabilities) by focusing on the enemy's vulnerabilities…if a person chooses to detonate himself no power can prevent him from doing so…Syria gave everything to the Intifada."
Propaganda	Damascus Radio, January 1, 2002	"The entire world knows that Syria, its political leadership and its Arab nation which has struggled throughout history, turned the Syrian Arab land into a training camp, into a safe home and a stockpile of weapons for the Palestinian rebels."
	Damascus Radio, March 5, 2002	"The 'opposition' must continue and we must vary the kind of actions against the soldiers at their roadblocks and positions and against the scum from among the settlers in the settlements and on the roads. The Zionists will not be left with even one place where they can feel safe."

President Bashar Asad	FTV television, Lebanon, March 27, 2002	"Regarding a conqueror, no such definition exists as soldier and civilian. There is a discrimination between armed and unarmed, but in Israel they are all armed. In any case, the term we adopted, 'opposition to invasion,' is a legitimate right."
Propaganda	Damascus Radio, March 30, 2002	"Our unique heroes who commit suicide will not restrict themselves to territorial boundaries and no Zionist will be immune. The fire that killed the criminal Ze'evi arrived a few days ago at the home of the war criminal Sharon…and if he had not been far away from home, would have shattered him."
Propaganda	Damascus Radio, May 9, 2002	"The wonderful and special suicide attack undertaken by some members of the Palestinian people in Rishon Lezion, is a practical declaration before the entire world regarding the way to liberate the Palestinian Arab land from the Israeli colonialism."
President Bashar Asad	*Al-Mejad*, Jordan, May 13, 2002	"Syria will continue to embrace the liberation movement and the 'Palestinian opposition,' even if this will entail sacrifices or cause pressure to be imposed upon it…as long as there is conquest, the 'opposition' will continue to exist and will be legitimate…. I do not want to suppress demonstrations in Syria that support Palestine, the Intifada and the 'opposition'; on the contrary, if I weren't the president of Syria I would not hesitate to participate in them."
President Bashar Asad	Sana, May 21, 2002	Arabs have only the path of opposition against Israel."

weapons and explosives required for these attacks. Arrangements for communications between the two terrorists and Damascus were made prior to their departure. Their arrest at the Allenby Bridge on August 7, 2001 prevented the realization of these plans.

The Hamas—Briefing activists in Damascus. In the second half of 2001, over twenty Hamas activists were arrested who had been recruited in the Arab countries, trained and briefed in Syria, and who had taken part in brutal terror attacks against Israeli civilians.

Interrogation of these Hamas activists revealed several significant factors:

- Most of those taken into custody were students who had been recruited into the Hamas ranks during their studies at universities in Syria, Yemen, Sudan, and other Arab countries. The students were recruited by activists from the Hamas headquarters in Damascus and were sent to undergo training in Syria and Lebanon.
- At the training camps the students practiced operating weapons as well as the preparation of explosive devices and belt bombs. They also received instruction in matters related to intelligence activity and attack techniques against civilian and military targets in addition to training in conducting kidnappings.
- At the end of the training, the recruited agents were sent back to the territories, where they were instructed to establish terror cells. This activity was part of the Hamas' efforts to rehabilitate its military branch, which had been impaired by the Israeli security services.
- After the exposure of this organizational activity, some of those arrested confessed to their involvement in two suicide attacks in Netanya in April and May 2001, in which eight Israeli civilians were killed and over 100 were wounded.
- Addressing the latest report of the U.S. State Department, in which Syria was defined as a state that supports terror, the Syrian Foreign Minister Sharah stated, "Syria has never financed terror."[182] Syria does indeed lack Iran's economic capabilities and generally does not provide direct funding for terror organizations, but it does allow Iran to use the official Syrian banking system for the transfer of funds to the territories. This enables the Syrian regime technically to supervise the transfer of funds to the territories.
- This flow of large sums of money significantly improves the operational capabilities of the organizations sponsored by Iran, and particularly those of the Islamic Jihad, which, in contrast to the Hamas and Fatah, does not have a grassroots within the Palestinian population. These large amounts of money directly and indirectly finance terror activity and constitute a motivating and encouraging factor for its perpetration by all of the terror organizations.

The funds transferred from Damascus served various purposes: the preparation of terror attacks in Israel, support for the families of the martyrs and prisoners, purchase of combat means as well as designated equipment required for attacks, such as IDF uniforms. In a confiscated document of the general intelligence in the Jenin area there are two examples of the receipt of large sums of money transferred from Dr. Ramadan Shalakh in Damascus to the organization's members in Jenin:

(1) A sum of $ 31,000 was supposed to be transmitted to Ali Tsipori, but never reached its destination. This sum was defined as "the remaining expenses" related to the suicide attack in Afula (November 27, 2001); (2) A sum of $127,000 was transferred for the support of the families of martyrs and prisoners. (This sum also did not reach its destination.)

Large sums of money transferred from Syria to Islamic Jihad terror activists in Jenin significantly boosted the organization's capabilities there and positioned it as a leading organization whose source is the Jenin area, which was known for its many suicide attacks (Jenin was called "the capital of the suicide terrorists"). According to a confiscated document of the general intelligence, this enabled activists of the Islamic Jihad to finance Fatah attacks (to the great frustration of the Fatah/Martrys of the Al-Aksa Brigades which suffered from a chronic lack of funds), assist the families of Fatah martyrs, bribe members of the Authority's security mechanisms, and recruit the Fatah/Martyrs of the Al-Aksa Brigades to take part in joint terror attacks within Israel (like the suicide attack in Afula on November 27, 2001).

Syria and the U.S. War against Iraq (2003)

In the months preceding the American-Iraqi war (Iraqi Freedom), Syria took Iraq's side and did its best to prevent the offensive of the U.S.-led coalition against Sadam Hussein's regime. After the beginning of the U.S. offensive, the Syrians allowed the passage of volunteers from all parts of the Arab world who set out to help Iraq fight the Americans. The United States also accused Syria of transferring combat means such as night-vision equipment to Iraq. At the final stages of the campaign there were news reports that Syria had provided refuge to many of the senior members of Sadam's regime who fled Iraq, many of whom were wanted by the United States.

In the light of these Syrian steps, the White House announced on April 14, 2003, that Syria was included in the "evil axis" of the most dangerous countries, together with Libya, Iran, and North Korea.[183]

At the end of a meeting with the Kuwaiti foreign minister, Secretary of State Colin Powell stated:

> We believe that Syria must reexamine its deeds and behavior, and I hope the administration in Syria will understand its obligations at this time—not only with regard to the provision of a haven for senior Iraqis but also in all matters related to the provision of sponsorship for terror organizations and their support.

U.S. Defense Secretary Donald Rumsfeld recently referred to the Syrian threat and accused that country of conducting experiments in chemical warfare for over a year: "I would say that we have seen experiments in chemical weapons in Syria in the last 12-15 months."

In an interview given to *Yediot Aharonot*, the Israeli prime minister stated that Israel is aware that President Assad had provided safe refuge to some of the senior leaders of Sadam's regime and that Iraqi equipment had been moved to Syria on the eve of the war in order to conceal it from the Americans or to arm the Hizballah. Prime Minster Sharon called for the United States to put pressure on Syria and listed a series of demands that he believed the United States should make of Assad:[184]

- Banish and dismantle the Palestinian terror organizations active in Damascus—the Hamas and Islamic Jihad.
- Banish the Iranian Revolutionary Guards from the Lebanon Valley, which is under complete Syrian control.
- Cease cooperation with Iran, including attempts to convey weapons to the Palestinian Authority and incite Israeli Arabs.
- Deploy the Lebanese army along the Israeli border and banish the Hizballah from that area.
- Dismantle the missile array positioned by the Hizballah on the Israeli border.

The spokeswoman of the Syrian Foreign Ministry denied these allegations against Syria, stating, "The only country in the Middle East that possesses weapons for mass destruction is Israel."

It would appear that the end of the American offensive in Iraq will enable it to deal with other countries that support terror such as Syria.

Thus, Syria has two choices: To meet the American demands and cease its support of terror, to cease the development and stockpiling of non-conventional combat means, and banish the remnants of Sadam's regime or to enter into a confrontation with the United States.

Saudi Arabia and Suicide Terror

The status of Saudi Arabia vis-à-vis the issue of Islamic terror is unique and particularly complex, because, on the one hand, Saudi Arabia is an ally of the United States and it opposes and combats Islamic terror posing a threat to its regime while, on the other hand, it supports and aids radical Islamic organizations in their activities at distant arenas.

The roots of the "Islamic dilemma" of the Saudi regime are to be found in the historical alliance between Muhammad Ibn Saud, founder of the Saudi dynasty, and Muhammad Ibn Abd al-Wahab. The Saudi dynasty won the religious legitimacy and in exchange promised to cooperate with the Wahabian dynasty in government and offered legitimacy to the religious school of thought that it represents. However, there is a fundamental contradiction between the pro-Western lifestyle and policy of the Saudi monarchy and the radical, puritanical worldview of the Wahabian school of thought.

The survival capabilities of the Saudi monarchy are based upon several central components:

- Religious (including Islamic) legitimization as "guardians of the holy sites." This legitimization is preserved through the support of the official religious establishment.
- Most of the essential services in the state are funded or subsidized by the government and generate a dependency of the population on the regime (in the areas of education, health, transportation, social services, etc.).
- An elite group of interested parties who help to preserve the regime.
- A secret police and internal security services whose job it is to take a ruthless stand against any subversive activity vis-à-vis the regime.
- The investment of huge sums of money in the Army and the National Guard in order to ensure their loyalty and effectiveness in preserving the regime.
- U.S. and Western aid and support.

Saudi Arabia is involved in the export of radicalism and Islamic terror on several levels:

- Saudi Arabia is the stronghold and nucleus of influence for the Wahabian movements that act to export the radical Islamic ideas from the Wahabian school of thought to Islamic focal points throughout the Muslim world (Chechnya, the Balkan, Afghanistan, the African continent, and more).
- Saudi Arabia acts to disseminate radical Islam via charities and relief organizations that serve radical Islamic organizations and entities with the full knowledge of the authorities.
- Saudi Arabia openly aids the Palestinian Islamic terror organizations, mainly the Hamas, in their struggle against Israel.
- Saudi Arabia was one of only three countries in the world to recognize the Taliban regime in Afghanistan, and even offered it aid up to September 11, 2001.
- Saudi Arabia enables "private" entities with capital to aid and support radical Islamic entities. The support or "adoption" of these entities is sometimes enacted as part of internal power struggles within the Saudi monarchy.
- The Saudi regime welcomed the departure of Saudi volunteers to participate in the Jihad in Afghanistan, including Osama Bin-Laden. Even after the inherent risk posed by the Afghan "alumni" against the Saudi regime has become evident, Saudi authorities still enable Saudi volunteers to set out for points of friction vis-à-vis Muslim populations in distress, such as the Balkan and Chechnya.

Upon his return to Saudi Arabia after the Jihad in Afghanistan, Osama Bin-Laden was greeted with great enthusiasm by the Islamic population, and even on the part of the government. However, the growing criticism that he expressed against the Saudi stance regarding the Gulf War ultimately brought about his expulsion from Saudi Arabia and the revoking of his Saudi passport. Bin-Laden's banishment from Saudi Arabia did not prevent widespread solidarity of radical circles with him and his worldview, and many joined the ranks of Al-Qaida and terror infrastructures that he founded all over the world. Thus, it is no coincidence that fifteen of the suicide attack perpetrators on September 11, 2001, were Saudi citizens.

The Saudi monarchy faces threats posed by the opposition and motivated by a combination of social, economic, ideological, and religious causes. Over the years, the extravagant and wasteful lifestyle of the Saudi monarchy, the inequality in the distribution of the country's resources and riches, and the "Non-Islamic" behavior of the country's leadership have generated wide cadres of opposition elements within Islamic circles that aspire to topple the regime and replace it with a "real" religious Islamic state in Saudi Arabia.

External factors also pose a threat to the regime, for instance Iran's subversion and its attempt to export the Khomeinist revolution to Saudi Arabia, and Sadam Hussein's activity against the Saudi regime. The threats that the Saudi regime faces on the one hand, and its power bases that rely on Western support as well as the power brokers close to the regime on the other hand, force the regime to adopt a cautious and complicated policy regarding the manner of handling radical Islam and terror.

In the course of the Defense Shield campaign, confiscated Saudi and Palestinian documents were found that dealt with the systematic and ongoing transfer of large amounts of money to the territories by Saudi institutions and organizations for the purpose of "supporting the Intifada." These funds are allocated for various goals: Supporting the families of the victims of violent incidents, including the families of suicide terrorists killed during an attack; support for families of the terrorists incarcerated in prison; medical aid for wounded terrorists; and various projects, often of a political nature, such as renovating the Machpelah Cave and nearby houses in Hebron, or the repair of housing in the Old City of Jerusalem.[186]

Purportedly, this Saudi aid is religious and humanitarian in its nature, as Saudi spokesmen claim in the United States. However, confiscated documents reveal another aspect of the Saudi aid: The documents clearly indicate that these funds also served to support terror organizations and fanned the flames of the violence raging in the territories since September 2000. In this framework, the Saudis transferred money to the Hamas (which is included in the U.S. list of terror organizations), to organizations and entities affiliated with it, to additional radical Islamic entities in the territories, and to the families of suicide terrorists who perpetrated murderous attacks among civilian populations in Israel.[187]

Among the Saudi institutions and organizations that are involved in the transfer of money to assist the Intifada, a particularly prominent name is that of "The Saudi Committee for the Aid of the Al-Aksa Intifada," headed by the

Saudi minister of the interior, the Emir Naif Ibn Abd al-Aziz. According to confiscated documents, this committee transferred large sums of money to the families of Palestinians who died in violent incidents, including prominent individuals that planned and directed murderous attacks in Israel or perpetrated suicide attacks that caused hundreds of fatalities and casualties. The confiscated material indicates that the Saudi committee knew which families received the funds and in some cases they were also familiar with the circumstances of the suicide attackers' deaths. This knowledge was based on data received from Islamic entities in the territories, including the "charity committee" of Tulkarem, which is identified with the Hamas (where Saudi documents were found, including tables from the Saudi committee specifying the sequence of money transfers to families of the Intifada martyrs).[188]

The transfer of large sums of money, without effective supervision, to the terror organizations, to individuals and entities affiliated with them, and to the terrorists' families has three main implications:

1. Encouraging terror activity: Terror activities, including suicide terror, elicit large rewards for the martyr's family from several Arab countries that are essentially "competing" among themselves. Among these countries the most prominent are Iraq (first place) and Saudi Arabia (second place). The family of an Intifada martyr receives one-time aid from Arab countries and the PA that is equivalent to about six years of work. In addition to the one-time assistance, the Saudis also grant the martyrs' families ongoing support. On top of this, they help the families of prisoners and the injured (for example, in the confiscated papers there appeared a list of 500 prisoners that carried the logo of the "Saudi Committee for the Support of the Al-Aksa Intifada.") Thus, a terrorist about to perpetrate an attack knows that his family will receive large sums of money after his death, or even if he is injured or arrested. This fact undoubtedly contributes to the increased motivation of the terrorists dispatched to carry out a terror attack, and encourages the phenomenon of suicide.

2. The reinforcement of the Hamas attack mechanism. It is reasonable to assume that part of the sums of money transferred to the Hamas or to entities connected to it also "trickled down" to the organization's military-operational mechanism (the Brigades of Az a-Din al-Kassam) and served to finance military action and terror attacks. It is to be noted in this connection that during the Defense Shield campaign considerable material of the Hamas and its operational branch, the Az a-Din al-Kassam Brigades, was found on the premises of the "Charity Committee" in Tulkarem, which is in contact with the Saudi committee. Among other documents, there was incitement material vis-à-vis Jihad and terror, and encouragement of suicide attacks, as well as photographs of suicide attackers (for example an announcement published by the Az a-Din al-Kassam Brigades in which the organization claimed responsibility for

the murder of civilians at the Park Hotel in Netanya on Seder night), or a section from the will of Doctor Abdallah Azzam, Osama Bin-Laden's spiritual mentor and good friend, which advocates the Jihad whose aim is to eradicate "all of the idol worshippers, the infidels and the wicked."

3. Boosting the status of the Hamas within the population while weakening that of the PA. Financial aid transferred by the Saudi committee and Islamic institutions worldwide (including those affiliated with radical Islam) was in many cases funneled to institutions and individuals identified with the Hamas (including the charity committee in Tulkarem). The Palestinian population identified the financial aid they received with the Hamas and its widespread network of welfare institutions. This fact intensified popular support for the Hamas, weakened the PA and generated an economic-social infrastructure upon which the operational suicide network was based.

Documents confiscated by the IDF indicate that the PA and its leader, Yasser Arafat, were fully aware of these negative implications, and were particularly perturbed by the strengthened status of the Hamas in contrast to the PA. Attempts made by the PA during the first few months of the Intifada to persuade the Saudis to channel the aid through the Authority fell on deaf ears. The Saudis, for reasons of their own, preferred to transfer the money to Islamic entities, mainly those affiliated with the Hamas. At the same time, the PA's security services did not take resolute steps to supervise the transfer of funds to the "charity committees" and other entities affiliated with the Hamas and the radical Islam. This was due to the fear of public criticism and also because of budget constrictions that prevented the PA from providing suitable alternatives to the large amounts of money channeled to the Hamas and other affiliated entities.

Saudi Arabia has paid out at least $33 million to the families of Palestinian martyrs who fell in the fighting against Israel, including suicide attackers.[189] The Saudis do not differentiate between the various Palestinian martyrs (in contrast to the Iraq's preferential treatment for the families of suicide attackers), and offer each family $5,300. In addition, Saudi Arabia grants medical aid and hospitalization for the injured Palestinians in Saudi hospitals, and offers the families of the injured victims $4,000.[190] The Saudi Arabian Embassy in Washington has disclosed that the Saudi minister of the interior, the Emir Naif Ibn Abd al-Aziz, administers the fund for financing compensation for the Al-Aksa Intifada victims.[191] The embassy also announced that in December 2001, Saudi Arabia decided to allocate an additional $50 million for the aid of the martyrs' families and the injured Palestinians.[192]

During Prime Minister Ariel Sharon's visit to Washington at the end of the Defense Shield campaign, Israel displayed confiscated documents that were discovered during the campaign and pertained to the Saudi aid granted to the families of Palestinian suicide terrorists before the United States and the international media. Israel appealed to the United States to act in Saudi Arabia to put an end to this activity, which encourages suicide terror.[193]

The Saudi regime takes all of the necessary actions vis-à-vis entities that constitute a threat to the regime's stability, including the execution of terrorists. Nevertheless, at the same time, it enables radical entities from Saudi Arabia to act outside of its boundaries almost without disruption, thus creating a "modus vivendi" with these elements.

The United States and the West must also treat the government in Saudi Arabia with "kid gloves." This policy must trigger resolute action by the Saudi authorities against Islamic terror entities, but the amount of pressure to be applied on the Saudi regime must be at the correct level, in order to avoid causing its collapse and the risk of the establishment of a radical Islamic regime in this country.

The series of suicide attacks that took place in Riyadh at the end of the war in Iraq serves as fresh evidence of the danger inherent to Saudi Arabia's ambivalent policy. These attacks, which were directed against Western targets on Saudi territory but also against the Saudi regime, forced the Saudi authorities to launch an aggressive campaign to eradicate terror infrastructures that had taken root in their country.

Based on confiscated documents, the following are several examples of Saudi Arabian involvement in the Intifada:

26.11.2001
The Palestine Liberation Organization
The National Authority
The President's Office

Attn: The brother the President the Commander the Symbol Abu-Amar, may God protect him.

With the blessings of the homeland.
1. Last Friday, the Saudi Committee for Support of the al-Kuds Intifada published a list in the al-Kuds newspaper containing over one thousand civilians from among those wounded in the Intifada in the areas of Ramallah, Hebron, and Nablus. The ad calls for them to come to the branches of the Arab Bank and claim their allowance, which has not been distributed for several months.
2. The activities of this committee are supervised by Sheikh Ahmed al-Kard (a senior Hamas activist from Khan Unis in the Gaza Strip. A member of the radical Islamic Party active in the Gaza Strip and affiliated with Hamas ideology), head of the "Al-Zalakh" Islamic Association (a large association in Gaza which is affiliated with the Hamas). In addition he heads the supreme central committee for emergency aid although nobody appointed him as such). This committee has assumed supervision over the payment and handling of all monetary aid arriving from the Gulf, from the Islamic countries and from the "coalition of charity" (Aatlap al-khir, an entity that assists the "charity committees," which includes a worldwide network of Islamic and pro-Palestinian organizations. It is headed by Sheikh Yosef Kardawi, a radical Islamic cleric). This serves their sectarian inclinations.

3. The publication of these ads constitutes a grave security situation. Because its primary meaning is the adding of the names of the wounded to the black lists. In addition, the meaning of the publication is that there is a failure in the preparation of the lists (by the PA). This matter is harmful for our people vis-à-vis those who transfer the funds and the aid entities.

4. The absurd aspect is that al-Kard arrogantly appeared on the screen of the Palestinian satellite television on the "Do Good" program aired yesterday, because he is deemed to be one of the most prominent philanthropists in Palestine.

For your perusal.

[The end is missing.]

At the top of the fax, the following remarks appear in Arafat's handwriting:

Dr. Sha'at (Nabil Sha'at)
Al-Tarifi (Jamil Tarifi, the Minister for Civil Affairs)
Dr. Tsa'ab Arikat
Nabil (Abu-Radina, Arafat's spokesperson)
Al-Tamimi (apparently Abu al-Sa'id al-Tamimi, Under Secretary for Internal Affairs)
Al-Magaida
Al-Jebali
Haj Ismail
Amin (al-Hindi)
Jibril Rajub
Al-Dahlan
Al-Tirawi

A printed article from the Al-Hayat al-Jadida *newspaper:*
In the name of Allah the merciful and the compassionate:

1. The Association of the Center for Social and Psychological Research of the Wounded Palestinians, telephone number 2966657—2986863—Ramallah, announces that in cooperation and coordination with the general secretariat of the Saudi Committee for the Support of the Al-Aksa Intifada, the Kingdom of Saudi Arabia—Riad, and according to the instructions of the Emir Naif Ibn Abd al-Aziz, The Minister of the Interior and the general supervisor of the committee, the families of martyrs whose names appear above should go to the Arab Bank closest to their home in order to claim the tenth payment from the Saudi committee. The amount is 5216.06 (?) American dollars per family. Claims can be made from the morning of Wednesday 20.2.2002.

2. For your information, the recipients in this cycle of payments are 200 martyrs' families with a total sum of… (the amount is not clear) according to the lists hereby attached.

Handwritten comments.

3. *Our dear ones, "The Saudi Committee for the Support of the Al-Aksa Intifada," may God preserve them, for your perusal: This item was published in the newspaper Al-Hayat al-Jadida in Ramallah, Palestine, issue no. 2236 dated Hajri 6 of Dualhajja 1422 (which is parallel to the date of 18.2.2001).*

Your brothers,
Haj Azam Alkhachar/Akba
Chairman of the Executive Committee

The dear brother Abu al-Az, may God preserve him
Report from the land
Blessings Tulkarem
Attached are the names of the families of the martyrs in Tulkarem ...(not clear).

Iran and Suicide Terror[194]

In a speech delivered in February 2002, President George Bush defined Iran as one of the countries in the "axis of evil" that supports terror and is occupied in the attempt to create weapons for mass destruction. Since the early 1980s, Iran has appeared on the U.S. State Department's list of countries that support terror. Since the Islamic revolution in 1979, Iran was indeed one of the most prominent countries to use terror for the promotion of their objectives in the international arena.

A comprehensive analysis of terror activities perpetrated during the reviewed period of twenty years from 1979 to 2000 (an analysis based on research institutes and publications in the media), indicates that 260 attacks were perpetrated abroad by Iranian entities or organizations under Shiite or Palestinian sponsorship (on an average, a little over one attack per month over a twenty-year period). The Iranian terrorist activity is performed in a sophisticated manner, with Iran making every effort not to leave "fingerprints" behind that may serve to identify the country as the backer of terror attacks. Moreover, in its public declarations, the Iranian leadership expresses its reservations regarding terror activity and condemns it, and this is also true of its sponsored organizations such as the Hizballah. Iran's attempt to conceal the terror activity in which it is involved enables it to tap the maximum benefit from this activity: On the one hand, this bars the terror victim from paying Iran back for its activity, while on the other hand the country sets itself up as an intermediary trying to bridge the gap between the victim and the terror organization, and through its active participation in negotiations and discussion processes achieves its goals.

Most of the information that exposed Iran's involvement in terror activities came to light when perpetrators of acts of terror were apprehended and brought to trial, as well as following the perpetration of acts of terror where the claiming of responsibility by the responsible organizations included declarations and/or demands that clearly reflected Iranian interests.

There is a close link between acts of terror and Iran's foreign policy; the consistent and systematic use of terror in order to force Iranian wishes on other countries when the goal was not achieved via accepted diplomatic means is a prominent factor. Salient examples of this policy are Kuwait and France, which constituted central targets for Iranian/Shiite terror activities, mainly due to their stance regarding the issue of the war between Iran and Iraq, and their support of Iraq.

In most cases, the weapon of terror was wielded in order to achieve a wide range of Iranian goals vis-à-vis the victim. For example, Iran's demands of France were the removal of its forces from Lebanon, ceasing its support of the Iraqi army, shifting its position vis-à-vis the Arab-Israeli conflict, the return of Iranian funds frozen in France, the banishment of exiles and Iranian opposition organizations from France, and the release of Shiite terrorists arrested in France. These goals were achieved one after the other, through a "series" of various sorts of terror attacks (car bombs, kidnapping of hostages, sabotage, and more), which ultimately brought about repeated French surrender to Iranian demands.

In most cases, the timing of the terror attacks was planned with great care, and was aimed at serving political processes in the course of negotiations with the victim, or sometimes served as a catalyst for the launching of this type of negotiation. Although one might theoretically portray the Iranian terror policy as a rational and sober method to achieve Iranian goals, it is important to point out several other phenomena that have significant impact on the formulation of Iranian policy.

1. The use of terror in the international arena constitutes a focal point for controversy in the higher echelons of the Iranian regime, between the circles that are often called "moderate" and those considered "radical," and which support the uncompromising struggle against the enemies of the revolution. Thus, the scope of the use of terror and its objectives to a large degree reflect the internal power struggles inside Iran.
2. Iran has often conducted an ambivalent foreign policy, where the moderates aspire to negotiate and reach compromise, while, at the same time, radical entities continue to be involved in acts of terror (sometimes with the aim of "torpedoing" the steps initiated by the moderates).
3. Iran's ambivalent policy has provided it with flexibility in its political course and has made it difficult for its adversaries to formulate a forceful policy that will provide an adequate response to Iranian terror, on the assumption that the moderate elements in the Iranian regime must be encouraged vis-à-vis the extremists, from the aspect of "the lesser of two evils."

One may observe several examples in which there is evidence of Iranian readiness to sacrifice political interests on the altar of ideology. A salient example of this issue is the affair involving Salman Rushdie. When condemning the British writer to death, Khomeini sentenced Iran to a confrontation with the Western democracies, as this issue focused on the controversy between Islamic values and principles, on the one hand, and democratic Western cultural values on the other.

This affair sheds light on the character of the Iranian leadership: Primarily, there was complete agreement between the moderates and the radical elements that Rushdie must die. Secondly, even after the death of Khomeini, under the leadership of Rafsanjani and Khatami, it was made perfectly clear that the sentence was still valid (although Iran would not act to implement it).

Thus, it is possible to state that there are some ideological and religious basic principles regarding which there is a consensus within the Iranian regime, while in less fundamental areas, the Iranian policy is pragmatic and motivated primarily by cost/benefit considerations.

The dilemma regarding the issue of Iranian leadership (moderates versus extremists) stems primarily from the observation angle and judgment according to Western norms and values. A close examination of the deeds and declarations of the Iranian leaders, both moderate and extremists, leads us to the conclusion that in reality the more accurate differentiation would be between radical and more radical leadership. As long as Khomeini's theories serve as a source for legitimization and as a guide for Iranian leadership, the differences between the radical elements and the moderate ones will be expressed in varying approaches to achieving goals, but not in their fundamental essence.

In the matter of Iran's control over sponsored Shiite and Palestinian organizations, it is to be noted that during the entire period under review Iran demonstrated control and influence over the sponsored organizations. However, this statement must be qualified as well, because the control and influence over sponsored organizations is sometimes in the hands of entities that do not stand at the head of Iran's official leadership. Thus, one might say that the internal power struggles in Iran have considerable impact upon the sponsored organizations that obey the orders of various entities within the Iranian government.

Also worthy of notice is the fact that the sponsored organizations have their own goals and needs, which at times do not fully comply with the interests of the "patron" state. In this regard, one sees that in most terror attacks Shiite and Palestinian terror organizations raised demands that included the release of incarcerated terrorists in various countries as well as ransom money (demands that serve the organizations' interests first of all). The arrest of Shiite terrorists in various countries all over the world sometimes turned countries that were not initially defined as targets for terror attacks into terror victims (such as Switzerland and Germany). Attacks against these countries did not usually serve Iranian interests and were only initiated to liberate the imprisoned terror victims.

Iran was the first country to introduce the method of suicide terror into the combat arsenal of the Middle Eastern arena (see extensive discussion in chapter 2). Its approach to this issue has not budged since the 1980s and it currently encourages Palestinians to use the weapon of suicide terror as a strategic means to fight Israel. Iran and Syria are deeply entrenched in terror, and they finance and operate many of the Palestinian terror organizations.

Iranian Involvement in the Al-Aksa Intifada[195]

Iran, labeled by the U.S. State Department as a country that supports terror, has adopted a consistent strategy of encouraging and fanning the flames of the Palestinian Intifada by providing political and informational support and practical aid for the perpetration of terror activities in Israel. This strategy is meant to achieve several objectives; the weakening of Israel due to the creation of rifts and estrangement within its society, as well as dealing a blow to its economy; the reinforcement of radical Islamic forces within the Palestinian Authority; torpedoing any chance of an Israeli-Palestinian agreement as well as preventing the renewal of the political process. All this is part of the use that Iran makes of the "terror weapon" as a tool to promote its national interests.

This Iranian strategy fits in well with the use that Yasser Arafat makes of violence and the terror weapon as leverage for the promotion of his strategic goals, particularly since September 2000. This is why to date there has been no serious controversy between Iran and the radical Islamic opposition that enjoys its support, on the one hand, and the Palestinian Authority on the other. On the contrary, during the Intifadat Al-Aksa the Iranians have given the PA direct aid (the Karin A affair), as well as indirect aid to the Fatah and the Martyrs of the Al-Aksa Brigades, which are under Arafat's control (via Munir al-Makdakh, a former Fatah member based in Lebanon).

From time to time, Iran denies the military-operational character of the aid that it grants to organizations defined by the United States and the international community as terror organizations, and presents it as political, informational, and humanitarian aid. Nevertheless, findings that emerged from the interrogations of senior terrorists who were taken captive by the IDF during the Defense Shield campaign, along with documents confiscated from the PA during the campaign and information accumulated in the course of the Intifada, unequivocally prove the deceitful nature of the Iranian denials.

The way that the Iranian terror strategy is implemented is through the encouragement and support of terror in Israel and the territories via Palestinian and Lebanese as well as radical Islamic terror organizations and left-wing organizations sponsored by Syria or Iran.

In addition to this Iranian and Syrian support during the Intifada, indirect Iranian aid has also been granted to the Fatah and the Martyrs of the Al-Aksa Brigades, due to their willingness to contribute to the circle of violence and terror.

Out of these organizations, three organizations serving as central "performance contractors" in the service of Syria and Iran are highly visible:

- The Palestinian Islamic Jihad
- The Hamas and its military branch, "the Brigades of Az a-Din al-Kassam"
- The Popular Front for the Liberation of Palestine/the General Command (the organization of Ahmad Jibril)

While these three organizations have been defined by the United States as terror organizations, the Palestinian Islamic Jihad and the Brigades of Az a-Din al-Kassam are also defined as terror organizations by the European Union.

From a range of sources, it appears that Iranian aid granted to Palestinian terror in the territories is diverse and is expressed in five areas:

- Political and propaganda support—The Iranian media systematically encourage the continued Intifada and glorify the violent acts and suicide attacks. At inter-Arab and international forums, Iran emphasizes the supposed legitimacy of the Palestinian terror ("national resistance"). It hosts conferences aimed at the continued support of terror, opposes agreements and arrangements that would put an end to terror, and criticizes the United States and Arab regimes (Egypt, Jordan, and Saudi Arabia) that are making an effort to terminate the terror and open up discussion and negotiation channels.
- The direction of terror—The Iranians are regularly active in preventing the situation in the territories from abating and encourage increased terror. Iran achieves this goal through the Palestinian organizations that it sponsors, mainly the Islamic Jihad, the Hamas, and the Popular Front/Jibril. This direction includes coordination and briefings for the perpetration of terror attacks (using telephones, the Internet, and summoning activists), and assistance in the preparation of mega terror attacks (the intent to detonate the Azrieli Towers, for example). In addition to the instruction to escalate and increase suicide terror attacks, sometimes orders are issued to temporarily cease the terror attacks when Iran has a vested interest (for example, following the September 11 attacks in the United States).
- Use of financial leverage—Financial leverage serves as a highly important instrument for the establishment of terror infrastructures and the motivation of terror activity. Findings of the interrogations of those arrested during the Defense Shield campaign indicate the existence of an established and systematic system for the transfer of large sums of money used by the Iranians, through the organizations that it sponsors, which utilize the banking system in Syria and the territories (the use of the "Arab bank" stands out as a central channel for transferring money to terror organizations). The questioning of prisoners has exposed the transfer of funds on a wide scale to the Islamic Jihad, the Hamas, and indirectly to the Fatah and the Martyrs of the Al-Aksa Brigades (in addition to the funds that the Fatah receives from the PA). These funds encouraged and fanned the murderous terror attacks in the territories and Israel, whose implementation was a precondition for the transfer of financial support for the terror activists in the field.
- Training and drills—Syria enables the terror organizations that it sponsors and which are sponsored by Iran to maintain a training infrastructure in its territory and in Lebanon. The interrogation of terror activists from the Hamas, the Islamic Jihad, and the Popular Front (Jibril) indicates that Syria maintains a widespread training infrastructure for terror activists at bases

of Jibril's Front and the Syrian army. Sometimes this training is pursued in the course of academic studies in Syria or other Arab states. This training includes designated professional instruction in constructing explosive devices, building electrical circuits and creating bomb belts. Professional instruction vis-à-vis these subjects was disseminated among terror activists in the territories via the Internet, and possibly also through videocassettes (a professional videocassette discovered in Nablus during the Defense Shield campaign included detailed instructions issued by an Az a-Din al-Kasam instructor regarding the preparation of explosive devices, including how to detonate buses and their inherent "vulnerabilities").

• The transfer of qualitative weaponry to the territories—Iran makes an effort to assist the Intifada by transferring qualitative weaponry to the territories, directly from its soil (the Karin A affair) and indirectly via Lebanon, through the PFLP-GC (Front/Jibril) and the Hizballah (the Santorini affair). The interrogation of the crewmembers of these ships revealed the role of Iran, the involvement of the Front/Jibril and the Hizballah, and Syria's connection with the smuggling incidents. There is no doubt that if this sophisticated weaponry had reached the territories, particularly the Katyushas and the Strella SA-7 anti-aircraft missiles, it would have significantly improved the capabilities of the terrorist organizations to strike at Israeli population centers (including large cities) as well as military and civilian air traffic, thus creating "a terror balance" reminiscent of Lebanon.

Despite the fact that Iran appears on the U.S. State Department list' of seven countries that support terror, and the Bush administration includes it as one of the three countries in the "axis of evil," there has been no essential change in the nature of Iran's support of terror, even after the incidents of September 11 and the American campaign against terror. On the contrary, Iran appears to have intensified its support of Middle Eastern and international terror organizations since then.

The Iranian regime not only assists Shiite organizations in Lebanon and Palestinian organizations in their conflict with Israel, it also allows use of its territory as the main transit site for the transfer of Bin-Laden's activists from Pakistan and Afghanistan to various areas of the world. The Iranians also offer their soil, in the vicinity of their common border with Afghanistan, as a haven for Al-Qaida activists fleeing the American offensives.

It appears that Iranian terror is basically motivated by rational considerations (in addition to ideological and other considerations that should not be dismissed). Therefore, in most instances the use of terror is based on cost/benefit calculations. The decision to activate terror is the direct result of these calculations and stems from considerations of those backing the terror vis-à-vis the risks and the ability to achieve results in relationship to the victim.

To summarize, it can be said that in the overall balance, Iran may reach the conclusion (the correct one from its own point of view) that terror pays off.

The Iranian balance in this regard testifies to a high degree of success in achieving political objectives in comparison to the relatively low price that it has been required to pay, at least up until now. Therefore, it is reasonable to assume that Iran will continue using terror in order to promote its goals in the international arena, and to support Islamic terror organizations and the Palestinian struggle against Israel while encouraging them to continue the perpetration of terror attacks.

To date, the invasion of Iraq by the American-led coalition and the presence of U.S. forces along its borders (in Afghanistan and Iraq) have not inspired Iran to change its approach to terror vis-à-vis the Arab-Israeli conflict, although at least in the Lebanese arena it appears that Iran, together with Syria, is acting to restrain the Hizballah. It would appear that with the end of the U.S. campaign in Iraq, the issue of how to handle Iran has become highly important.

The United States resolutely demands that Iran refrain from supporting terror and cease its attempts to attain nuclear capabilities. Iran denies any involvement in terror or attempts to obtain the capabilities to create nuclear weapons. It does appear, however, that Iranian denials are inadequate and that Iran will have to consider carefully its future steps in the new global and regional reality.

Based on confiscated documents, the following are several examples of Iranian involvement in the Intifada.

> The National Palestinian Authority
> The Preventive Security Headquarters
> The General Headquarters
> Date: 31.10.2001
> Reference: 2001/10/1200

To the Brother the President Abu-Amar (Yasser Arafat) may God bless him.
Greetings of the Homeland.
Re: The opposition parties acting energetically to intensify the joint activity

According to the information at our disposal it appears that intensive meetings have been taking place in Damascus between leaders of the Hamas, the Islamic Jihad, the Popular Front and the Hizballah in order to boost the joint activity "inside" with financial assistance from Iran. This, following the receipt of an Iranian message by the leadership of the Hamas and the Islamic Jihad according to which there must be no lull in the situation at the current time. The financial aid will be transferred by the Hizballah in order to escalate the situation in the next few days. What the opposition parties are now required to do is to perpetrate suicide attacks against Israeli targets in Gaza, the West Bank and Israel.

Kindly peruse.
> With the blessings of the Revolution,
> Your brothers
> Jibril al-Rajub

Handwritten remarks by Arafat:
At the head of the page:

> Personal
> Distribution list:
> Al-Majaida
> Al-Haj Ismail
> Amin
> Al-Dahlan

PLO
The National Palestinian Authority
The President's Office

10.12.2000
To the President, the General Commander (Yasser Arafat), may God protect him.
Greetings,

Attached please find reports from the brother al-Hindi (Head of General Intelligence) which were received from the Lebanese arena, for the Hamas Organization (Az a-Din) al-Kassam. Here follows their content:

1.   The Az a-Din al-Kassam have only received $400,000 since the outbreak of the Intafada to date. The Brigades are ready to carry out attacks against Israeli targets, but the funds sent by Mussa Abu Marzuk (a member of the Hamas' political bureau) did not reach their destination.
2.   The Hamas organization in Syria issued instructions to the Brigades of Az a-Din al-Kassam "inside" according to which they must immediately send a financial report and an assessment regarding the military units "inside." The Hamas leadership in Syria has given "a green light" to the headquarters of the military branch to conduct military offensives against Israeli military goals without obligation to any resolution of the Hamas' military branch "inside." In addition, the Brigades have been asked to keep a distance from the Hamas leaders who are coordinated with the PA.
3.   Ismail Abu Shanab [one of the leaders of the Hamas in the Gaza Strip] and Ismail Henya [one of the senior Hamas leaders in the Gaza Strip and the director of Sheikh Yassin's bureau] are in contact with Musa Abu Marzuk [a member of the Hamas' political bureau. At the time that this document was written he was living in Syria]. In addition, Sheikh Jamal Salim [one of the leaders of the Hamas in Nablus who died in IDF thwarting activities in July 2001] is in touch with Imad al-Almi [head of the Hamas' "internal" committee and the Hamas representative in Syria]. There is a real crisis in the Hamas due to lack of coordination and previous organizational disputes.
4.   The Islamic religious clerics, Al-Jama'a al-Islamiya, Afif Nabulsi and the Hamas have agreed that this year's charitable donations [al-Zakkat] will be given to the Palestinian people and that the Hamas organization will distribute it "inside" far away from the Palestinian Authority.
5.   The gathered funds will not be sent to the Authority's areas but will rather be deposited in the accounts of Osama (Abu) Hamdan [the Hamas representative in Lebanon] and Haled Mashal [the head of the Hamas' political bureau who lives outside of the territories]. In addition, out of this sum a certain amount will be allocated for the support of the Hamas' military branch "inside."

6. The Iranian check for $700,000 reached the Palestinian opposition factions. This amount was included in the factions' general budget. Iran has consented to allocate sums of money for the martyrs of the Al-Aksa Intifada affiliated with these factions, who will die a martyr's death [*tastshahjdun*] during the perpetration of the military attacks that they enact against Israel.

Comments appear on the document:

Stamp:
       The General Department of Police
       The Bethlehem District Police
       The administration and organization
       Date 12.12.2000
       Reference mr-2140
Handwritten, black magic marker:
Important!

This should be distributed to all police stations, administrative bureaus and departments.

Appendix

Here follows the translation of a document related to grants provided to the families of martyrs:

Attn: Abu Mahmud (secretary of the Arab Liberation Front)

Dear Sir,
Attached please find a letter that I received in Jenin, for your perusal and handling.
Sincerely,
Abu-Liss

Dear Friend,
In the framework of the grants that Iraq provides for the families of all of the martyrs, it was decided to pay an amount of $25,000 for these families. In practical terms, this allocation was granted among the related parties in the Jenin district, but a problem has arisen regarding the family of the martyr Abd-Alkarim Abu-Nasa. This family is connected to the Arab Liberation Front.

On 27/11/01 Abd-Alkarim Abu-Nasa and Mutsafa Abu-Sariya perpetrated suicide attacks in Afula. They used machine guns in the attack. The two were killed and all of the relevant details indicate the fact that this was clearly a suicide attack.

The representative of the Arab Liberation Front in Jenin claims that this action cannot be recognized as a suicide attack because its perpetrators were not wearing bomb belts.

The families of these martyrs refuted this claim and they insist that it was a suicide attack, and request that this will be recognized as such, both from the point of view of esteem and from the point of view financial benefits to which they are entitled.

Notes

1. The description of the attack is based on Nahman Tal, *Confrontation at Home, Egyptian and Jordan Handling of the Radical Islam,* Papyrus Publishing, Tel Aviv University, 1999, p. 67.

2.   *Roz al-Yusuf,* Cairo, August 23, 1993.
3.   *October,* Cairo, August 22, 1993.
4.   Reuters, Cairo, October 16, 1995.
5.   *Domovina Net—Tuzla Night Owl* 1, 43 (May 19, 1986).
6.   Ibid.
7.   Shaul Shay and Yoram Schweitzer, *The Terror of the Afghan Alumni*, The International Policy Institute for Counter-Terror, The Interdisciplinary Center, Herzliya, September 2000.
8.   The attack was actually carried out by the Egyptian Islamic Jihad.
9.   Nahman Tal, *Confrontation at Home, Egyptian and Jordan Handling of the Radical Islam,* Papyrus Publishing, Tel Aviv University, 1999, p. 77.
10. Shaul Shay and Yoram Schweitzer, *The Terror of the Afghan Alumni.*
11. Nahman Tal, *Confrontation at Home, Egyptian and Jordan Handling of the Radical Islam*, p. 77.
12. Shaul Shay and Yoram Schweitzer, *The Terror of the Afghan Alumni.*
13. *Al-Ahram*, (Cairo), August 30, 1992.
14. The French News Agency from Algeria, December 8, 1991.
15. Shaul Shay and Yoram Schweitzer, *The Terror of the Afghan Alumni.*
16. Ibid.
17. AFP, July 28, 1995.
18. *Liberacion*, Paris, August 8, 1985.
19. *Washington Post*, May 23, 2002.
20. This section is based on *Lashkar e-Toiba, Terror Organizations Profile*, The International Policy Institute for Counter-Terror, The Interdisciplinary Center, Herzliya: www.ict.org.il, *Terrorism Groups: An Overview*, SATP, 2001 (Internet site of SATP).
21. LET = Lashkar e-Toiba.
22. *Jeish-e-Mohammad, Terror Organizations Profile*, The International Policy Institute for Counter-Terror, The Interdisciplinary Center, Herzliya: www.ict.org.il, *Terrorism Groups: An Overview*, SATP, 2001 (Internet site of SATP).
23. Yoram Schweitzer and Shaul Shay, *The Globalization of Terror*.
24. Pakistan News Service, www.pakenews.com, May 9, 2002.
25. Reuters, May 9, 2002.
26. *Dawn*, May 9, 2002.
27. Pakistan News Service, www.pakenews.com, May 9, 2002.
28. Ibid.
29. A.P., "FBI probes Karachi Bomb Attack," June 15, 2002; CBC, "Suicide Attack outside U.S. Consulate in Pakistan," June 14, 2002; Reuters, "Bomb outside U.S. Consulate in Karachi, Kills 11," June 14, 2002.
30. *The Times of India*, "Karachi Blast, Little Known Group Claims Responsibility," June 15, 2002.
31. Reuters, AP, and Pakistan News Service.
32. The GSPC cooperates operationally with Al-Qaida.
33. *Dawn*, November 26, 2001
34. Yossi Melman, "Four German Soldiers from the International Forces Were Killed in an Attack in Afghanistan," *Ha'aretz*, Tel Aviv, June 8, 2003.
35. Dogu Ergil, *Suicide Terrorism in Turkey: The Workers' Party of Kurdistan, in Countering Suicide Terrorism*, The International Policy Institute for Counter-Terror, The Interdisciplinary Center, Herzliya, 2001, pp. 105-128.
36. The information is based on the database of http://www.ict.org.il.
37. Ibid.

38. Ibid.
39. Arabic News.Com. June 7, 1999.
40. Dogu Ergil, *Suicide Terrorism in Turkey*, pp. 105-128.
41. Azam.Com, November 20, 1999.
42. *Maariv*, February 2, 2001.
43. Ibid.
44. The KGB's successor, the FSB—Federal Security Bureau.
45. *Guardian Unlimited*, September 19, 1999.
46. Ibid.
47. Ibid.
48. Ibid.
49. Ibid.
50. Reuven Paz, *Suicide Terrorist Operations in Chechnya—An Escalation in the Islamic Struggle*, ICT, http:/www.Ict.org.il.
51. http//www.ict.org.il, The International Policy Institute for Counter-Terror.
52. Ibid.
53. *Maariv*, Tel Aviv, October 24, 2002.
54. *Yediot Aharonot*, Tel Aviv, October 24, 2002.
55. *Yediot Aharonot*, Tel Aviv, October 28, 2002, quoting the French *La Journal De Dimanche*.
56. Ibid.
57. *Maariv*, Tel Aviv, October 27, 2002.
58. *Maariv*, Tel Aviv, October 27, 2002.
59. *Yediot Aharonot*, Tel Aviv, October 28, 2002.
60. This section is based on *Maariv*, Tel Aviv, May 14, 2003; *Intertass*, Moscow, May 14, 2003. Richard Balmforth, "At Least 30 Reported Killed in Chechnya Bomb Attack," Reuters, Moscow, May 14, 2003. *Ha'aretz*, Tel Aviv, May 15, 2003. *Yediot Aharonot*, Tel Aviv, May 16, 2003.
61. *Ha'aretz*, Tel Aviv, June 8, 2003.
62. Yuhov News, June 19, 2003.
63. Sarah Karush, "Female Suicide Bombers Kill 16 in Moscow," A.P., July 5, 2003.
64. *Maariv*, August 3, 2003.
65. Yukov News, December 9, 2003.
66. Based on reports to Reuters and A.P. from December 5, 2003.
67. This section is based on Yoram Shweitzer and Shaul Shay, *The Globalization of Terror: The Challenge of Al-Qaida and the Response of the International Community*, Transaction Publishers, New Brunswick, NJ, July 2003.
68. Yossef Bodanski, *Bin-Laden, the Man Who Declared War on America,* Forum, Roseville, CA, 1999, p. 263.
69. Ibid.
70. Ibid., p. 233.
71. Peter L. Begen, *Holy War Inside the Secret World of Osama Bin-Laden Inc.*, Weidenfield & Nicolson, London, 2001, p. 118.
72. Ibid., p. 119.
73. *Al-Halij*, United Arab Emirates, April 2, 2001.
74. *Newsweek*, March 19, 2001.
75. The French News Agency, Paris, October 17, 2000.
76. *Al-Zaman*, November 15, 2000.
77. *Al-Sharq al-Awsat*, London, November 13, 2000.
78. *Al-Sharq al-Awsat*, London, November 12, 2000.
79. This section is based on Yoram Shweitzer and Shaul Shay, *The Globalization of Terror: The Challenge of Al-Qaida and the Response of the International Community*.

80. *Yediot Aharonot*, Tel Aviv, December 14, 2001.
81. Ibid.
82. Al-Jazeera, October 7, 2001.
83. Abiensky Ze'ev, *Personal Terror, the Idea and Practice*, Hakibbutz Hameuhad Publishing, Tel Aviv, 1997, p. 30.
84. Al-Jazeera, December 27, 2001.
85. *New York Times*, New York, Internet, April 2, 2002.
86. *Yediot Aharonot*, Tel Aviv, December 14, 2001.
87. The data regarding the flights and suicide attackers are based on articles from *Time* magazine dated September 11, 2001, and *Newsweek*, September 24, 2001, pp.32-33, 52-53.
88. CNN, March 8, 2002.
89. *Time*, November 2001, p. 23.
90. *Yediot Aharonot*, Tel Aviv, December 14, 2001.
91. *New York Times*, Internet, April 16, 2002.
92. Walter Picuz, "Mueller Outlines Origin, Funding of September 11 Plot," *Washington Post*, Internet, June 6, 2002.
93. Nahum Guttman, "The Connection between the Airplane Hijackers Has Been Found: Letters of Guidance and Support in Arabic," *Ha'aretz*, September 30, 2001.
94. Ibid.
95. Al-Jazeera, April 17, 2002.
96. *Maariv*, Weekly Supplement, Tel Aviv, February 8, 2002, pp 28-29.
97. *Washington Post*, Internet, October 22, 2001.
98. Y. Schweitzer, "The Case of the Shoe Bomber," January 4, 2002, at www.ict.org.il.
99. *Al-Quds al-Arabi*, April 18, 2002.
100. *A-Sharq al-Awsat,* Internet, May 18, 2002
101. *Liberacion*, Internet April 18 2002, and Reuters from Berlin, April 18, 2002
102. Based on articles in *Ha'aretz*, October 7, 2002, *Yediot Aharonot*, October 7, 2002; *Maariv*, October 7, 2002; *Yemen Times*, October 7, 2002; *Yemen Observer*, October 8, 2002.
103. *Ha'aretz*, Tel Aviv, October 11, 2002.
104. Yukov News and CNN, August 5, 2003.
105. This section is based on articles in *Ha'aretz*, *Yediot Aharonot*, and *Maariv* during the dates November 29-December 5, 2002.
106. *Ha'aretz*, Tel Aviv, December 3, 2002.
107. *Yediot Aharonot*, December 2, 2002, quoting Defense Minister Shaul Mofaz.
108. *Ha'aretz*, Tel Aviv, December 3, 2002.
109. This section is based on (1) Daniel Sobelman, "Nine Terrorists Synchronized the Attack on the Residences of Foreign Citizens in the Capital of Riyadh," *Ha'aretz*, May 14, 2003; (2) Adnan Malik, "Saudi Arabia Acknowledges Security Gaps," AP Riyadh, May 14, 2003; (3) *Maariv*, Tel Aviv, May 14, 2003; (4) *Yediot Aharonot*, Tel Aviv, May 14, 2003; (5) Orli Azulay and Smadar Peri, "Bin-Laden Envisioned." *Yediot Aharonot*, May 14, 2003.
110. Yahoo News, CNN, AP, and Reuters.
111. This section is based on Ynet, Tel Aviv, May 17, 2003; CNN.com, May 17, 2003; *Washington Post*, May 17, 2003; Reuters, May 17, 2003; AP, May 17, 2003; *Yediot Aharonot*, Tel Aviv, May 18, 2003; *Maariv*, Tel Aviv, May 18, 2003; *Ha'aretz*, Tel Aviv, May 18, 2003; *Ha'aretz*, Tel Aviv, May 19, 2003.
112. *Yediot Aharonot*, November 16, 2003; *Maariv*, November 16, 2003.
113. *Maariv*, November 23, 2003; *Yediot Aharonot*, November 23, 2003.

114. *Yediot Aharonot*, December 26, 2003.
115. LTTE = The Liberation Tigers of Tamil Eelam.
116. Rohan Gunaratna, *Suicide Terrorism in Sri Lanka and India, in Countering Suicide Terrorism*, The International Policy Institute for Counter-Terror, The Interdisciplinary Center, Herzliya, 2001, p. 101.
117. Ibid., p. 103.
118. Ibid.
119. Yoram Schweitzer and Shaul Shay, *The Globalization of Terror*.
120. Rohan Gunaratna, "Suicide Terrorism: Global Threat," *Jane's Defense Intelligence Review*, October 20, 2000.
121. Rohan Gunaratna, *Suicide Terrorism in Sri Lanka and India*, p. 10.
122. U.S .Department of State, "Patterns of Global Terrorism, Overview of State Sponsored Terrorism," May 21, 2002.
123. Ariel Merari and Shlomi Elad, "Hostile Terrorist Activity, Palestinian Activity Overseas 1968-1986, Hakibbutz Hameuhad publication, The Jaffe Center for Strategic Studies, Tel Aviv University, 1986, pp. 110-111.
124. Shaul Shay, *Terror in the Service of the Imam*, Mifalot Publishing, The Interdisciplinary Center, Herzliya, 2001, pp. 110-111.
125. Ely Karmon, "The Iraqi Regime's Links to Terrorism," website of the ICT, The Interdisciplinary Center, Herzliya, August 30, 2002.
126. U.S. Government fact sheet, presented to the UN Security Council on June 27, 1993, "United States, Military Action against Iraqi Terrorism," June 26, 1993.
127. Ibid.
128. Ibid.
129. Ibid.
130. *Christian Science Monitor*, April 2, 2002.
131. It is to be noted that the above information has not been corroborated by other sources, so this report should not be regarded as a completely factual account.
132. Al-Jazeera, Qatar, February 11, 2003.
133. Ibid.
134. Al-Jazeera, February 12, 2003.
135. Yoram Schweitzer and Shaul Shay, *The Globalization of Terror*, pp. 204-205.
136. *The New Yorker*, February 4, 2003.
137. An interview with Mula Krikar, Alhayat, London, January 26, 2003.
138. *Maariv*, Tel Aviv, April 28, 2003.
139. Ibid.
140. Ibid.
141. Zvi Barel, "Little Afghanistan," *Ha'aretz*, February 14, 2002.
142. Ibid.
143. Ibid.
144. Ibid.
145. Ibid.
146. Ibid.
147. Ibid.
148. An interview with Mula Krikar, Al Hayat, London, January 26, 2003.
149. AP Agency from Iraq, March 31, 2003.
150. Ibid.
151. Ibid.
152. *The New Yorker*, February 4, 2003.
153. Ibid.
154. AP Agency in Iraq, March 31, 2003.

155. *Maariv*, Tel Aviv, February 6, 2003.
156. *Yediot Aharonot*, Tel Aviv, February 6, 2003.
157. Ibid.
158. Ibid.
159. Yoram Schweitzer and Shaul Shay, *The Globalization of Terror*, pp. 51-52.
160. Zvi Barel, "Little Afghanistan," *Ha'aretz*, February 14, 2002.
161. AP Agency from Washington, March 9, 2003.
162. *Washington Times*, March 4, 2003.
163. Ibid.
164. global security.org/wmd/world; and also IRNA, the Iranian Government's News Agency, April 20, 2001.
165. Shaul Shay, *Terror in the Service of the Imam*, pp. 155-158.
166. This section is based on the following sources: The Intelligence Department, Iraqi aid and encouragement of Palestinian terror in the territories, reference number 688/0055, September 2002; The Intelligence Department, reference number 688/0061, September 2002; The Intelligence Department, Iraq-Palestinian Authority ties, May 1, 2002. The Intelligence Department, Iraq and the conflict in the territories: terror, combat means and oil, September 2002.
167. Teh Yassin Ramadan, a Sunni Moslem, was born in 1939 in Mussol. Educated in a military academy, Ramadan is one of the veteran members of the Ba'ath Party, and before the latter took over the government he was arrested (in 1959) by the Kassem regime and ousted from the army. He continued with his forbidden activity in the party during the sixties as well and was arrested again in 1964. He participated in the Ba'ath Revolution in July 1968. Teh Yassin Ramadan was a member of the Revolutionary Leadership Council, the supreme body of leadership in Iraq. He founded the Iraqi "popular army" and was its commander for twenty years. In the eighties he also filled a series of crucial government and party roles including Minister of Industry, Minister of Finance, Minister of Housing, first deputy in the prime minister's office, deputy director of the president's bureau, deputy prime minister, and vice president since 1991.

    Ramadan played a central role in a small group, a "kitchen" cabinet, which has surrounded Sadam Hussein since the 1968 revolution. Ramadan's main area of responsibility in Iraqi politics was the financial aspect, and in this framework he was in charge of the promotion of Iraq's economic ties as a central part of its foreign policy (for example, he was responsible for the implementation of the retaliation and prioritization policy within the framework of the "oil in exchange for food" arrangement as well as free commerce regional agreements with countries in the area). Ramadan was also responsible for the oil sector—a vital, strategic area for Iraq.
168. Iraqi News Agency, January 8, 2001.
169. Smadar Peri, *Yediot Aharonot*, January 31, 2002.
170. Abu al Abas was arrested by the U.S. forces in Iraq during Operation Iraqi Freedom.
171. Ynet, March 22, 2003.
172. Ynet, March 23, 2003.
173. AP Agency, from Kuwait, March 30, 2003.
174. CNN.com, March 29, 2003.
175. *Ha'aretz*, Tel Aviv, March 30, 2003.
176. *Maariv*, Tel Aviv, March 30, 2003.
177. Ibid.
178. CNN.com, March 30, 2003.

179. *Maariv*, Tel Aviv, April 11, 2003.
180. CNN.com, April 12, 2003.
181. This section is based on a Military Intelligence document (based on interrogations of captured Palestinian terrorists, and confiscated documents of the Palestinian Authority), ref: 688/0050, September 2002.
182. AP, Syrian television, May 22, 2000.
183. *Yediot Aharonot*, Tel Aviv, April 15, 2003.
184. Ibid.
185. Ibid.
186. Intelligence Department document, reference 668/0037, May 5, 2002.
187. Ibid.
188. Ibid.
189. NewsMax.co, America's news page, April 9, 2002.
190. Ibid.
191. Ibid.
192. Ibid.
193. *Ha'aretz*, Tel Aviv, April 29, 2002.
194. This section is based on Shaul Shay, *Terror in the Service of the Imam.*
195. Based on a document of the Intelligence Department reference number 688/0050, September 2002.

4

Summary

Suicide Attacks Worldwide—Comparative Aspects

1. It is possible to number about fourteen active terror organizations that are currently involved in the perpetration of suicide attacks (the number would be greater if we added organizations that have conducted suicide terror attacks in the past but are no longer active in this area today). The most active organizations include Al-Qaida, Hizballah, Hamas, the Palestinian Islamic Jihad, Fatah, Lashkar e-Toiba, The Army of Muhammad, PKK, LTTE, and BKI.

2. Suicide attacks at various confrontation points in the world are perpetrated not only on an organizational basis, for example, in Chechnya, Afghanistan, and more.

3. Of the fourteen organizations perpetrating suicide attacks, twelve are Islamic, or are active vis-à-vis areas of conflict in Muslim countries. Of these twelve organizations, nine have a radical Islamic orientation, and three are secularly oriented.

4. Of the fourteen organizations mentioned above, five are directly active against Israel (Hizballah, Hamas, the Palestinian Islamic Jihad, Fatah, and the Popular Front), and three additional organizations constitute a threat and have already actively struck out at Jewish or Israeli targets located in various places worldwide (Al-Qaida, GIA, the Egyptian organizations).

5. The Arab-Israeli arena currently constitutes the main world focus for the perpetration of suicide attacks. Since the beginning of the Intifada Al-Aksa (October 2001-December 2003), some 123 suicide attacks have been executed and scores of others were thwarted.[1]

6. The Al-Qaida suicide attacks on September 11, 2001, took the highest toll of victims in history—about 3,000 fatalities (mega terror).

7. The "Tamil Tigers" in Sri Lanka is the organization to carry out the most suicide attacks in modern history: 168 attacks during the years 1987-2000.

8. Different approaches among the terror organizations vis-à-vis the issue of the use of suicide terror can be noted:

195

- Organizations that regard suicide terror as a strategic and central tool of their activities.
- Organizations that regard suicide terror as a tool to be used only in special circumstances.

The organizations that regard suicide terror as a strategic tool have developed mechanisms that promote this activity in the areas of recruitment, training, gathering of intelligence, planning, bomb-making laboratories, the logistic infrastructure of collaborators, etc. These organizations make intensive use of suicide attacks, usually while indiscriminately attacking civilian targets, in order to achieve their goals. Examples of these organizations are the Hamas, the Islamic Jihad, Fatah, GIA, and more.

Despite everything stated above, the recruitment of volunteers for suicide attacks is on an ad hoc basis and they do not have "suicide units." The only organization that has a regular suicide unit among its ranks from which perpetrators are dispatched is the Tamil Tigers.

Organizations that regard suicide terror as a unique and extraordinary tool make selective use of suicide terror in special circumstances such as:

- Difficult straits or a severe crisis in the organization's capability to cope with the adversary (for example, the PKK adopted the suicide attack pattern out of a sense of crisis).
- In exceptional circumstances in order to achieve a concrete goal. (For example, the Egyptian Al-Jama'a al-Islamiya perpetrated a suicide attack in Croatia in order to liberate a senior organization activist arrested in this country.)

Characteristic of these organizations are the sporadic nature of the suicide attacks, and the direct link between the use of this tool and a concrete occurrence, as well as the relatively limited period of time during which the organization uses the suicide terror.

9. All of the organizations dealing in suicide terror have the capability to produce explosive devices and train suicide attackers to carry out their mission. The know-how develops in each organization according to its experience and technological capabilities, but it is also possible to detect a phenomenon of knowledge transfer among organizations, and sometimes there is cooperation in the preparation and execution of the attacks. Here follow several examples of interorganizational cooperation related to attacks:

- Cooperation between the Hamas and the Palestinian Islamic Jihad.
- Cooperation between the Fatah, the Palestinian Islamic Jihad, and the Hamas.
- Cooperation between the Lashkar e-Toiba and the Army of Muhammad Organization (for example, in the attack against the Indian Parliament).

- The Global Jihad Front, headed by Al-Qaida, closely cooperates with fellow front organizations. This is also expressed in mutual assistance when perpetrating suicide attacks.

10. Most of the terror organizations make use of suicide attacks chiefly in each organization's main arena of confrontation:

- Palestinian and Shiite organizations in Israel.
- Pakistani organizations in the Kashmir Region and India.
- GIA in Algeria.
- PKK in Turkey.
- LTTE in Sri Lanka.

Nevertheless, there are organizations that perpetrate terror attacks in the international arena without geographical boundaries or a concrete arena: The most prominent organization in this category is Al-Qaida, which has perpetrated terror attacks at various locations in the world (Kenya, Tanzania, Yemen, the United States). The Egyptian organizations, the Islamic Jihad and the Al-Jama'a al-Islamiya, have refrained from perpetrating terror attacks in Egypt but carried out two attacks outside its boundaries: in Pakistan (against the Egyptian Embassy) and in Croatia (against the police headquarters).

Other organizations focus their main activities in the central arena of activity, but sometimes carry out suicide attacks in additional places:

- The Hizballah, whose main activities are in Lebanon, has also carried out attacks at other locations.
- The GIA planned a lone suicide attack in France. Recently the Jama'a al-Islamiya organization in Southeast Asia has started to launch suicide attacks. It perpetrated the suicide attacks on Bali, Indonesia, and was behind the thwarted attempt to carry out an attack in Singapore. This organization acts on a regional basis in Southeast Asia.

11. An examination of the motivation for carrying out suicide terror attacks in the various organizations indicates several categories:

- The religious-Islamic motive constitutes a primary component in most Islamic organizations.
- The nationalist motive constitutes a primary component among the secular organizations. However, at times the religious and nationalist motives are combined.
- In some cases, the dominant motive is the ethnic one, which is sometimes combined with the religious or national motive (as in the case of the Kurdish PKK or the Tamil Tigers in Sri Lanka).

12. The various terror organizations adopt different policies regarding the choice of targets for suicide attacks and their definition. Four main categories can be noted in this connection:

- An indiscriminate policy of attacks, mainly aimed at civilian targets (as in the case of the Palestinian organizations).
- A selective policy of attacks, which focuses on military or government targets and people identified with these entities (as in the case of the Tamil Tigers and the PKK).
- A policy of attacks that focuses on symbolic targets combined with mass casualties (as in the case of Al-Qaida).
- A policy of "mega terror": the perpetration of mass suicide attacks of strategic significance, possibly through the use of non-conventional means (as in the case of Al-Qaida).

13.   The modi operandi of the majority of terror organizations are similar: Attacks using belt bombs/explosive devices or a booby-trapped mode of transportation (on-land/aeronautical/maritime). The most frequent modi operandi to date have been the use of belt bombs and booby-trapped vehicles.

14. As to the ages of the suicide attackers, it is possible to generalize and state that the majority of the suicide attackers were unmarried men in their twenties. Nevertheless, it is impossible to arrive at a clear and accurate typology of the suicide terrorist.

15. Women have perpetrated suicide attacks mostly in the framework of secular organizations (Fatah, Tamil Tigers, Pro-Syrian organizations in Lebanon) and as a rule their relative part in the perpetration of suicide attacks is low profile, aside from the PKK, the majority of whose suicide attacks were perpetrated by women. Also, the number of female suicide attackers participating in suicide attacks in Chechnya has risen noticeably.

16. The number of suicide attacks in relationship to the overall number of attacks carried out by terror organizations is relatively low. Nevertheless, these attacks are perceived as qualitative and carry a far more prominent impact from the aspects of damage to human life and property, as well as their repercussions upon the media and public consciousness.

Terror Organizations That Deal with Suicide Terrorism Worldwide

- Al-Qaida (and additional organizations as well as independent terror cells that are a part of the Global Jihad Front).

IN THE ARENA OF CONFRONTATION AGAINST ISRAEL:
Radical Islamic Organizations:

- Hizballah
- Hamas
- The Palestinian Islamic Jihad
  Secular Palestinian Organizations:
- Fatah–Tanzim, the Martyrs of Al-Aksa Brigade
- The Popular Front for the Liberation of Palestine (PFLP)

During the eighties additional terror organizations perpetrated terror attacks against Israeli targets in Lebanon:

- Pro-Syrian terror organizations in Lebanon (four organizations).
- Amal (a Shi'ite secular organization)

In the Islamic confrontation arenas in various areas worldwide:
Radical Egyptian Organizations

- Al Jama'a al-Islamiya
- The Islamic Jihad (currently consolidated with Al-Qaida)
- The Armed Islamic Front in Algeria (GIA)
- The Al-Jama'a al-Islamiya of Southeast Asia (Indonesia, Malaysia, Singapore, Phillipines, Thailand)
- The Islamic Army of Aden and Abiyan (Yemen)
- The Islamic Jihad (Yemen)

Pakistani Terror Organizations Acting to Liberate the Kashmir Region

- Lashkar e-Toiba
- Jeish-e-Muhammad

Terror Activities Unaffiliated with an Organization in Afghanistan
Terror Activities Unaffiliated with an Organization by Chechen Separatists
The Kurdish Workers' Organization (PKK)
Organizations unconnected to Islam or to confrontations in Muslim states

- The Tamil Tigers Organization in Sri Lanka (LTTE)
- Several terror organizations in India including:
Sikh Terror Organizations

Operation Patterns for Dealing with Suicide Terrorism in Israel

Suicide terror is not an independent phenomenon that stands by itself but rather it constitutes a central part of the Palestinian-Israeli conflict and is perceived, both by the Palestinian and the Israeli sides, as a "strategic weapon."

The primary component when contending with suicide terror is the *intelligence component*. Although the suicide attack is supposedly the action of an individual, in actual fact the suicide attackers do not act in an empty vacuum and most of them are affiliated with established terror organizations (Hizballah, Hamas, Islamic Jihad, Fatah, etc.). In these organizations, an organized infrastructure is activated starting with the stage of the candidate's location and recruitment for the suicide attack until his dispatch and the claiming of responsibility for the attack. This widespread and complex organizational network enables an effective intelligence system to gather information that will serve to thwart the attack already in the various preparation stages (and, in fact, Israeli security services and the IDF thwarted scores of suicide attacks in the course of the Al-Aksa Intifada).

Effective intelligence constitutes the basis for the two main channels for contending with suicide attacks: (1) The defensive channel which issues warnings and prepares the security entities to prevent and thwart the attack; (2) The offensive channel (including activities to thwart the attack in order to stop the suicide attacker and/or his operators or to strike out at them) which conducts "focused thwarting" with the aim of striking out at the commanders of the terror organizations, those who dispatch the terrorists as well as other components of the organizational infrastructure, such as the "engineers" who prepare the explosive devices and operational activists who deal with the actual preparations and dispatch the suicide attackers.

The campaign against terror, in general, and suicide terror in particular, necessitates "systematic treatment," which includes an integration of defensive and offensive components. An effective fence and obstacles (such as the border fence surrounding the Gaza Strip) constitute the basis for effectual defensive preparedness that enables forces using those obstacles to thwart penetrations aimed at perpetrating attacks. (In the Gaza Strip almost 100 percent of all suicide attackers' attempts to enter Israeli territory in order to perpetrate attacks were prevented.)

Parallel to defensive action on the basis of an obstacle, offensive operational activity is also required in order to reach the terror infrastructures deep in Palestinian territory and strike out at them, forcing the terror activists to concentrate on their personal and organizational survival, a fact that reduces their ability to dispatch suicide terrorists to Israeli territory. The offensive against those who direct and operate the suicide attacks, through arrests and even terminations, constitutes a central component, when this activity is compounded by media coverage that intensifies the deterrent effect.

The Defense Shield campaign represents a successful example of significant damage inflicted on the terror infrastructures and reduction of the scope of attacks. Nevertheless, the terror infrastructures have constant renewal capabilities. Therefore, a one-time campaign cannot suffice, and the preservation of an ongoing offensive initiative is necessary in order to maintain the campaign's achievements, as implemented in the "Determined Path" campaign.

Aside from the military and security steps, informational action and psychological warfare is required to reduce the dimensions of the phenomenon. Primarily, action must be taken to de-legitimize terror and suicide attacks in the international order, and in Palestinian society. In this framework, action must be taken to deter the organizations from dispatching suicide attackers, including the religious clerics who encourage this activity. The deterrence activity must be consistent, prolonged, and ongoing for it to bear fruit.

The combined campaign against suicide terror necessitates action not only against the active circles that motivate and operate the suicide terror. It must also deter the terrorists' families and friends, and effect a change in the consciousness of the Palestinian public, in order to prevent support for this phenomenon. In this connection, various punitive steps are being examined, contingent upon receiving the necessary legal permits. The steps under discussion in this connection are as follows:[2]

The deportation of families from the West Bank to Gaza: This relates to the suicide terrorist's immediate family, in cases where the parents expressed support for their son's action, mainly prior to the suicide (as in the case of the mothers who had their pictures taken with their sons before they left for the attack).

The transfer of those subject to deportation from one area to another in the Palestinian Authority is explained by the fact that the West Bank and Gaza are perceived as one political entity, and thus the restrictions of international law do not apply regarding deportation outside of one's boundaries. There is a difference of opinion as to the effectiveness of this tool. Some maintain that it can serve as a deterrent while others claim that the Palestinians regard this type of exile as a temporary step and therefore do not especially fear it.

Demolition of homes. This step has been implemented in the past, and has already been used several times in the course of 2002-2003. The demolition of houses is perceived as a particularly powerful deterrent, and even today it is possible to illustrate the effect of this step via the reduction of support for suicide attacks.[3]

On the informational level, there is a need for an international campaign against the suicide phenomenon in order to encourage the voices that are beginning to be heard in the Palestinian camp that claim the suicide attacks do not serve Palestinian interests. This campaign should endeavor to recruit moderate entities in the Muslim and Arab world who will denounce suicide attacks and participate in the organization of a global consensus prohibiting the perpetration of these attacks and defining them as a "crime against humanity."

Quite obviously, there is no "magic solution" for the phenomenon of suicide attacks. Therefore, effective, integrated, and systematic handling of this strategic and existential challenge will be required over a long period of time, with Israeli society demonstrating its endurance in the course of the struggle that is being visited against the State of Israel.

On October 16, 2002, Defense Minister Binyamin Ben-Eliezer stated:[4]

The security system succeeded in apprehending 160 terrorists planning to perpetrate suicide attacks. In the course of the interrogation of these terrorists, some of whom were already on their way to carry out their suicide missions, intentions to carry out very grave attacks, including attacks defined by the security system as "mega terror," were exposed.

The combination of steps that Israel has taken has succeeded in significantly diminishing the scope of suicide attacks; testimony to this fact lies in
the number of "suicide attackers" who have been arrested and the attacks that
have been thwarted. However, among the Palestinians there still exists considerable motivation to carry out suicide attacks.

Nevertheless, as the result of Israeli pressure, voices are beginning to emerge
that question the value of the continued use of suicide attacks. An expression
of these questions can be found in a letter written by the father of a suicide
terrorist that was published in the Saudi newspaper *Al-Hayat*.[5] "I write this
letter with a wounded heart and eyes that have not stopped shedding tears,"
so opens the letter by Abu-Saber, father of a Palestinian suicide terrorist. In the
letter, he uses bitter words to express his family's suffering after "the friends of
my eldest son tempted him and lauded the way of death to him." They persuaded him to detonate himself in one of the cities of Israel. "From that day,"
the father (who did not know that his son had joined the military arm of the
Hamas) writes, "I am like a ghost walking the earth, not to mention the fact
that I, my wife, and the rest of my sons and daughters have become uprooted,
after the demolition of the home in which we lived."

Abu Saber, who would not divulge his full name for fear of death, is determined not to speak of his son as a shahid who died in a "Holy War" against
Israel. He stated,

> Yes, I say death and not the "death of a martyr," which is supposedly a nicer term.
> The payment of a few thousand dollars to the family of one who has departed, never
> to return, cannot alleviate the shock or the unquestionable consequence. These amounts
> that are presented to the families of the shahids are more painful than therapeutic.
> They make the families feel that they are receiving monetary payment for their
> children's lives. Can a price be put on our children's lives? Is death (not a martyr's
> death) the only way to reinstate our rights and liberate the land?

Abu-Saber describes what his family has undergone since his son chose
the path of suicide:

> The hardest thing for us was when I learned that the friends of my oldest, dead son
> were starting to circle like poisonous snakes around my other son, so that he would
> detonate himself too to avenge his brother's death. "In any case," so they told him,
> "you have nothing to lose."

The father's bitter accusation is addressed to the recruiters' commanders
and the heads of the Hamas and Islamic Jihad organizations who appear on
the media and threaten in his name, and in the name of hundreds of thousands
of Palestinians, to perpetrate murderous acts of revenge.

"And I ask those sheikhs," writes Abu-Saber,

> that compete among themselves in the publication of aggressive religious rulings and
> declarations in favor of terror attacks: Why don't you send your own sons? Why

don't the leaders, who cannot control their excitement over the satellite waves each time a Palestinian boy or girl goes out on a suicide attack, send their own sons to carry out the attack? Who gave you religious or any other permission to push our children towards their deaths?

This letter written by the father of a suicide terrorist raises a brave question:

Why to this day have we never seen one of their sons or daughters, of those preachers, wearing a belt bomb and going out to make things happen in practice, not just talking, to realize what his father preaches day and night? Does the Jihad, the death of the martyrs, not pertain to the level of the leaders? Does what applies to the children of the general Palestinian public not apply to the individual sons and daughters of the leaders? How long will this patient nation, situated at the front, continue to pay the price with its children's blood?"

And Abu-Saber concludes his letter,

What rends the soul and hurts more than anything else is the phenomenon of those leaders and sheikhs who shirk sending their sons to the war arena. From the moment that the Intifada erupted, Muhammad a-Zaher (spokesman of the Hamas) sent his son Haled to America, Ismail Abu-Shneb (one of the leaders of the Hamas in Gaza) sent his son Hassan to Britain, and the wife of Abd al-Aziz Rantisi announced her refusal to send her son out on a suicide mission. In order to preserve his life she sent her son to Iraq to complete his studies.

Another expression of the success of the Israeli activity can be found in the words of Hamas leader Abd al-Aziz Rantisi. In an interview for the Danish newspaper *Yutland Posten*, he admitted that Israel's recent activities in the territories have been successful, from the aspect that many leaders of the Hamas were killed or arrested.[6] These remarks were made for the first time in an interview with the Western press. Rantisi added that the policy of curfew and closures makes it very hard for the "Hamas fighters" (as he stated it) to penetrate the Green Line boundaries and perpetrate terror attacks. "I cannot deny that the killing and arrest of Hamas leaders has had an effect on our capabilities to act."

Nevertheless, Rantisi promised that the Hamas has a reserve of young men which has now gone underground and which will give birth to what he calls the new leadership of the organization's military arm, "and within several months they will be the known leaders, sought by Israel. The killing of our leaders has only increased our opposition to the conquest."[7]

In the interview, he stated that the conquest of the West Bank cities has created a new situation to which the opposition movement must become accustomed. "After we become accustomed to the state of curfew and closures, we will renew our activities," he promised. In reply to a question as to whether it would not be preferable for the Hamas to adopt the official policy of the Palestinian Authority and restrain from carrying out terror attacks within the Green Line, Rantisi replied that Arafat had requested to stop these attacks in Israel but the Hamas had refused "because Arafat cannot ensure the safety of our children."

The spokesman for the Hamas presented the reporter from the Danish newspaper with a recent opinion poll carried out by an East Jerusalem research institute. In the poll, 64 percent stated that they supported suicide terrorists attacking Israeli citizens within the Green Line.[8]

Can an International Convention be Formulated against Suicide Terror?

The attacks of September 11, 2001, and the U.S. declaration of "a war against terror" represent a historical turning point for the international system regarding the issue of terror and suicide terror in particular. Contending with the phenomenon of suicide terror must occur not only on the military and security levels, but also on the moral, legal, and political levels. International systems have succeeded in formulating international laws that ban the use of certain weapons and prohibit injury to civilians. Suicide terror, which is largely directed as indiscriminate harm to innocent civilians, and the risk of the creation of mega terror by suicide attackers (possibly through the use of non-conventional weapons) necessitate the formulation of an international convention that will ban suicide attacks, like other conventions that ban the use of various weapons and the harming of civilians.

When the United States declared war against terror and the regimes that sponsor it, it created a distinction between countries that fight terror and those that support it. Although a universal definition of terror has yet to be formulated, and despite the controversy regarding the distinction between a legitimate war of liberation and terror is still being waged, the American declaration succeeded in creating an international atmosphere that places pressure on countries to refrain from appearing as supportive of terror, and to pay the political, economic, and sometimes military price as a result of international punishment. An international convention prohibiting all suicide terror, like the ban on the use of chemical or biological warfare, could bring about a significant reduction of the phenomenon's scope.

In July 2002, Amnesty International published an important document in which it analyzed the issue of attacks against Israeli civilians (among others) by Palestinian terror organizations. It reached the conclusion that the indiscriminate attacks against civilians constitute an essential violation of international humanitarian law and a crime against humanity. This type of resolution, anchored in international law, may serve as a sound basis for the formulation of an international convention against suicide terror.

Attacks against Civilians as a Violation of the Basic Principles of
International Humanitarian Law[9]

The claim that international law does not place any restraints on the means used in the struggle against a conquering power violates one of the basic rules of international humanitarian law. According to the Red Cross, the entity with senior authority in interpreting international humanitarian law, "in any circumstances when military force is introduced, the choice of means and methods is not unlimited."[10] International humanitarian law has set standards for humane behavior that apply both to state forces and armed organizations. A basic principle of the international humanitarian law is that the sides involved in the conflict must always differentiate between civilians and fighters, and between civilian and military targets. It is forbidden to direct an attack against civilians, meaning people who are not members of the armed forces of the other party. This principle, which is known as the principle of differentiation, has been established in four Geneva Conventions since 1949 and in two Protocols appended to them since 1977. The principle of differentiation is a basic ground rule of international humanitarian law, and it falls on all sides involved in the military conflict, international or not.[11]

Defining Attacks against Civilians as Crimes According to International Law

If the level of violence in the occupied territories is to be considered a level of violence to which the rules regarding the conduct of hostile acts in armed international conflicts apply, then attacks against civilians will constitute a gross violation of international law and will be deemed as war crimes (clause 85 [3] of the appended Protocol, and clause 8 [2] of the Rome Statute of the International Criminal Court).

The intentional killing of Israeli civilians by armed Palestinian organizations is also considered a crime against humanity. According to the definition of the Rome Statute of the International Criminal Court, crimes against humanity are various acts perpetrated as part of "an extensive or systematical attack against any civilian population which represents the advancement or implementation of the policy of a country or an organization to execute this assault."[12] The specified acts include murder, torture, and "other inhumane acts of similar character that intentionally cause severe suffering or serious injury to its mental or physical health."[13] In the matter of crimes against humanity, a correlation with armed conflict is not mandatory—they may be perpetrated both in times of war and peace. The intentional murder of Israeli civilians by armed Palestinian organizations and intentional manslaughter by individuals are both widespread and systematic, and are implemented as part of a declared policy that turns civilians into targets. Therefore, they comply with the definition of crimes against humanity in the Rome Statute of the International Criminal Court, a definition known to reflect the International Law.

War crimes and crimes against humanity are deemed among the most heinous crimes according to international law, and they represent offenses against all of humanity. Bringing these criminals to court is thus in the interests and the responsibility of the international community. This position is exemplified in the preface to the Rome Statute of the International Criminal Court, adopted in July 1998, which certifies that the most heinous crimes pertaining to all of humanity must not go unpunished and it is important to ensure that charges be brought against them by taking steps on the national level and increasing cooperation on the international level.

Recommendations Made by Amnesty International Regarding the Sides in Israel and the Occupied Territories

Armed Palestinian Organizations

Amnesty International has called upon the leadership of armed Palestinian organizations:

• To publicly denounce any attacks against civilians.
• To instruct all elements under their influence and control not to attack civilians under any circumstances and clarify that these attacks will not be allowed to go unnoticed.

The Palestinian Authority

Amnesty International has called upon the Palestinian Authority:

• To appeal to armed Palestinian organizations and individuals to cease the attacks against civilians, both in the occupied territories and inside Israel.
• To ensure that its criminal court systems act efficiently and diligently to prevent attacks.
• To ensure that all attacks against civilians be investigated swiftly and thoroughly, and that all those dispatching the assailants, organizing these attacks or collaborating with them are brought to trial.
• To ensure that all steps taken against individuals suspected of involvement in attacks will comply with international standards pertaining to human rights. Mainly, that no individual will be incarcerated for a prolonged period without a trial, that the trial will be fair, and that no use is made of torture, maltreatment or the death sentence.
• To initiate a public campaign, including the media, in order to generate opposition in Palestinian society to attacks against civilians.

The Israeli Government

Amnesty International has called upon the Israeli government:

• To ensure that all of its actions against armed groups and individuals suspected of involvement in assaults against civilians, will comply with the standards of international law pertaining to human rights and international humanitarian law.

- To bring to fair trial anyone involved in an attack against civilians, without torture or maltreatment.

Other Governments

Amnesty International calls upon other governments:

- To unequivocally condemn attacks against civilians and at every opportunity when they have contact with armed Palestinian organizations to appeal to them to refrain from attacking civilians.
- To prevent armed organizations from receiving any military aid serving to promote attacks against civilians.
- To assist the Palestinian Authority in improving the efficiency of its criminal law system and its compliance with international standards pertaining to human rights, particularly by dispatching international experts for the purpose of consultation and surveillance of investigations pertaining to attacks against civilians and legal steps taken against the perpetrators.
- To bring to trial anyone suspected of involvement in attacks against civilians, who is under their jurisdiction, and to cooperate with the Palestinian Authority and Israel in their efforts to bring the culprits to justice.

Recommendations of the *Human Rights Watch* Organization

An approach similar to that of Amnesty International can be found in an extensive study published by the Human Rights Watch Association. The study was published under the title:[14] *Erased in a Moment: Suicide Bombing Attacks against Israeli Civilians*. In a media interview granted upon the publication of the study, the organization's director, Kenneth Roth, stated:[15]

> The people who carry out suicide bombings are not martyrs, they're war criminals, and so are the people who help to plan such attacks. The scale and systematic nature of these attacks set them apart from other abuses committed in times of conflict. They clearly fall under the category of crimes against humanity.

The study names four Palestinian organizations that carried out suicide attacks: the Hamas, the Palestinian Islamic Jihad, the Popular Front for the Liberation of Palestine (PFLP), and the Al-Aksa Martyr Brigades. In this connection the study states:

> Each of these four groups has perpetrated attacks against civilians again and again. The scope and systematic nature of these attacks during the years 2001-2002 comply with the definition of crimes against humanity. When these suicide bombings are perpetrated in connection to violent acts which turn into an armed struggle, they are also considered war crimes. The organization "Human Rights Watch" unreservedly condemns these acts of atrocity.

Three of these groups are considered rivals of Arafat and of the Palestinian Authority; the Hamas, the Islamic Jihad, and the Popular Front for the Liberation of Palestine. The fourth group, the Al-Aksa Martyr Brigades, has declared its support for Arafat and the Palestinian Authority. Naturally, the attacks carried out by the Al-Aksa Martyr Brigades caused the most amazement and triggered a stormy discussion as to whether the attacks had been perpetrated with the consent and even under the command of Arafat. This report examines this question, among other issues.

The Palestinian Authority is not a state, and therefore is not a party to the main international conventions of humanitarian law. However, on various occasions it has signaled its readiness to comply with standards set by these conventions. Based on the accepted approach regarding a dispatcher's responsibility, International humanitarian law establishes that whoever holds a position of authority cannot shirk responsibility for war crimes, or for other gross violations of the law carried out by people who are under their jurisdiction, if the said leaders instructed their subordinates to perpetrate these crimes, refrained from taking reasonable action to prevent them, or refrained from punishing the perpetrators of the crimes. This approach is particularly relevant to the chain of military command, but it also applies to political and other leaders who have "effective responsibility and control" over the said perpetrators. According to this outlook, it would appear that the leaders of the Hamas and Islamic Jihad, in particular, must bear criminal responsibility: Many of them have openly praised, encouraged and supported suicide attacks against Israeli civilians, and it seems that they can either renew or put a stop to the attacks at their whim. In the Popular Front for the Liberation of Palestine, which has claimed responsibility for car bombs and several suicide attacks against civilians, there also appears to be a similar scope of internal unity and central authority that makes the organization's leaders bear criminal responsibility.

The greatest failure on the part of President Arafat and the Palestinian Authority—and the heavy responsibility for this must lie on their shoulders—is their decision to avoid the resolute activation of the criminal court system in order to put a stop to suicide attacks. This refers particularly to the year 2001, when it was still within the Palestinian Authority's power to do so. Arafat and the Palestinian Authority also refrained from taking firm steps to ensure that the extreme polarization in the political arena would not serve as justification for carrying out these attacks. Certain steps taken by Israel, such as the demolition of some of the Authority's police stations and security facilities, gradually eroded this entity's capability to take action. But even when their ability to act was almost unrestricted, the Authority and Arafat did not take any practical steps to bring the terrorists from the Hamas, the Islamic Jihad, the Popular Front for the Liberation of Palestine and the Al-Aksa Martyr Brigades to justice for inciting, planning and collaborating in the perpetration of bombings and attacks against Israeli civilians. Instead, Arafat and the Palestinian Authority persevered in their policy according to which if and when suspects were arrested they were never interrogated or charged.

The trials of murderers of Israeli citizens were perceived as subject to negotiation and contingent upon Israeli compliance with obligations that Israel took upon herself in the Oslo Agreements, and not as the unconditional obligation that they really were. The Palestinian Authority tried to explain the release of the suspects from detention under the pretext that the suspects were in danger due to Israel's bombing of the prison facilities. However, the Authority never provided any explanation for the fact that the suspects were never interrogated, charged, or tried—steps that could have been taken without posing almost any risk to the prisoners' well being. Moreover, while Arafat repeatedly and publicly condemned suicide bombings and other attacks against Israeli citizens, he did almost nothing to refute the positive description of the shahid attackers within the Palestinian community or to change this approach. In fact, several position holders in the Palestinian Authority praised the attacks against civilians. It is again worthy of mention that despite the gradual steps taken by Israel against the Palestinian Authority's security and administrative mechanisms, the Authority could have taken steps to delegitimatize the attacks against civilians. And finally, Arafat and the Palestinian Authority refrained from introducing the administrative steps that were at their disposal in order to ensure that there would be no financial incentive to perpetrate attacks against civilians. In several instances, Chairman Arafat approved the transfer of small amounts of money to people who he knew—or he should have known—had carried out attacks against civilians. In most cases, Arafat and the Palestinian Authority did not take the appropriate steps expected of them considering their status as the controlling authority, to stop the transfer of special payments to the attackers and their families, whether by the Authority or others. This lack of action encouraged the creation of an atmosphere that enabled armed Palestinian groups to believe that they could carry out attacks against civilians with impunity.

Armed Palestinian groups have tried to justify attacks against Israeli civilians by pointing to IDF activities during the present skirmishes, in the course of which many Palestinian civilians have been killed, as well as the continued Israeli occupation of areas in the West Bank and large sections of Gaza. However, these arguments are totally unjustified. International humanitarian law leaves no doubt regarding its resolve that attacks directed against civilians constitute war crimes if they are perpetrated in a state of armed confrontation, and when they are carried out systematically—this represents the crossing of a threshold and they are then defined as crimes against humanity, whether carried out during times of peace or war. As the term itself conveys, these crimes are considered the most heinous that can be perpetrated; they are crimes that are under universal jurisdiction and which the entire international community is obligated to prevent and punish.

International humanitarian law, which addresses situations of armed confrontation, even prohibits attacks against civilians that are allegedly perpetrated as reprisals against the civilian population of the assailant. This principle was established both in the fourth Geneva Convention and in the appended Protocol I. But even apart from the international law, a strong inclination has developed in the past two decades to prohibit reprisals against civilians. This ban on reprisals is not contingent upon any mutual adherence to the ban on the part of the opposing forces. Despite alleged Israeli violations of international human rights and the international humanitarian law, armed organizations are obligated to refrain from carrying out reprisals against civilians.

Another claim raised by the Palestinian organizations was that they are embroiled in a "war of independence" against the ongoing Israeli occupation, and for that reason they are exempt from the duty to comply with international humanitarian law. This claim is also unfounded. Protocol I appended to the Geneva Convention, which according to its instructions addresses wars related to national self-definition, establishes that "a civilian population, according to its own definition, as well as individual civilians, will not constitute a target for attack," and in addition, "acts of violence or threats pertaining to acts of violence, whose objective is to spread anxiety in a civilian population—are prohibited." This means that the first Convention that grants recognition of national liberation also reiterates the ban on intentional attacks directed against civilians. Moreover, the basic principles of the Geneva Convention and of the appended Protocols are part of the international law. The implication is that in this regard an extremely high international consensus was achieved, without dependence upon the Conventions' ratification. These principles include one that obligates offensive forces to distinguish between civilian and military targets, the principle of imparting civilian immunity against intentional attack, and the ban on turning civilians into a target for attack. All sides that are party to the conflict are obligated to honor these principles unconditionally.

And finally, Palestinian organizations claimed that due to their very presence in occupied territory, Israeli settlers are not to be considered civilians, and due also to the fact that most adult Israeli civilians serve in the reserve forces they thus should be deemed legitimate military targets. These claims also contradict international humanitarian law. Although the fact that Israel's policy to support and even expand the civilian settlements in the West Bank and Gaza is considered illegal according to international humanitarian law, nevertheless, a person living in the illegal settlement maintains his or her civilian status, unless that individual is involved in hostile acts. With the exception of circumstances involving direct participation in an armed confrontation, these settlers are entitled to full defense as civilians. Similarly, international humanitarian law leaves no doubt regarding its declaration that people serving in the reserves of the army or security forces are not to be considered combat fighters when they are not in active service, and are therefore entitled to protection as civilians.

The claims that have been raised in an attempt to justify or explain suicide attacks and Palestinian attacks directed against civilians are completely unfounded. Those who make these claims either do not understand their obligation according to international humanitarian law, or are intentionally ignoring it. There is and can be no doubt that these attacks constitute grave crimes. In the majority of cases, if not in all of them, these attacks are to be deemed crimes against humanity. International law defines the perpetrators of these atrocities as criminals. This definition applies to anyone dealing in incitement or planning, as well as anyone who assists them.

At the end of the Human Rights Watch study, its authors present a series of recommendations as follows:[16]

To Organizations that are Responsible for the Perpetration of Suicide Attacks and Other Attacks against Civilians

The Human Rights Watch Organization vehemently condemns suicide attacks, deeming them war crimes and crimes against humanity. We call for those responsible to stop them and unconditionally abstain from their use. In particular, the Human Rights Watch Organization appeals to the leaders of the Hamas, the Islamic Jihad, the Al-Aksa Martyr Brigades, and the Popular Front for the Liberation of Palestine:

- To immediately refrain from perpetrating these attacks and publicly announce that attacks of this kind will not be perpetrated in the future, no matter what the circumstances
- To undertake a commitment to honor the basic principles of international humanitarian law, and to instruct all members of their organizations to do the same. This applies in particular to principles relating to the protection of civilians in the throes of an armed conflict, and to the obligation to apprehend and bring to the authorities' custody anyone who avoids doing so, in order to bring them to trial.
- To refrain from recruiting youths under the age of eighteen, or from deploying them in any military activity, including actions that are supportive of combat, and to bring this policy to the attention of anyone who supports the organization.

To President Arafat and the Palestinian Authority

The Human Rights Watch Organization recognizes the fact that during the year 2002 the Palestinian Authority's ability to maintain law and order, and execute legal proceedings, has been seriously impeded. Nevertheless, a significant part of the following recommendations can be implemented immediately, while the other recommendations should be implemented simultaneously with the rehabilitation of the Authority's capability to take action. The Human Rights Watch Organization appeals to President Arafat and other senior members of the Palestinian Authority:

- To announce a clarification whereby suicide bombings and other attacks against civilians constitute grave crimes and anyone who incites, plans, collaborates, attempts to carry out or perpetrates these attacks will be charged with criminal activity, and the Palestinian Authority will take every possible step to ensure that these people are brought to justice.
- To instruct the Authority's law enforcement entities to take all possible measures, according to the accepted international norms vis-à-vis human rights, to identify and bring to justice anyone who incites, plans, collaborates or attempts to perpetrate suicide bombings or other attacks against civilians.
- To inform all people affiliated with the Palestinian Authority's security forces that they are liable to be severely punished if they provide any aid, including intelligence, logistic or any other form of support, to those responsible for the planning, collaboration with or perpetration of suicide bombings or other attacks against civilians. All those who refuse to obey these orders will be punished immediately, arrested and brought torial in a civilian court, according to international standards regarding fair trial, and if they are found guilty will be sentenced to prison terms that reflect the severity of their crimes.
- To appeal to all Palestinians living in the West Bank and Gaza to help the Palestinian Authority to put an end to the suicide bombings and other attacks against civilians. This appeal must include a declaration stating that although the law enforcement capabilities of the Authority itself have been damaged, the Authority is still committed to its responsibility to put an end to these atrocities. The Authority is also required to place "hotlines" at the disposal of the public, which can be used in order to divulge information regarding planned attacks or their perpetrators.
- To make use of the public information systems and all of the media in order to bring these messages to the knowledge of the Palestinians in the West Bank and the Gaza Strip, as well as Palestinian Arabs who are Israeli citizens, and to call for the immediate, permanent and unconditional cessation of all suicide bombings and other attacks against civilians. To clarify that the Palestinian Authority does not consider people who were killed during attacks that were intentionally and indiscriminately aimed at spreading death or terrible suffering among civilians—"shahids."
- To carry out a thorough and independent investigation in order to identify the people, including the members of the Hamas, Islamic Jihad, the Popular Front for the Liberation of Palestine, and the Al-Aksa Martyr Brigades, who are responsible for incitement, planning, collaboration or perpetration of suicide bombings or other attacks against civilians, to arrest these entities, ensure that they are brought to civilian trial, according to international standards regarding fair trial, and if they are found guilty, to sen-

tence them to prison terms that will reflect the severity of their crimes. In the event that these crimes were carried out by the said organizations or sponsored by them, the Palestinian Authority must act immediately to freeze the organization's assets, in order to ensure that these assets can be used for the purpose of reparations in future claims that may be filed by the victims or on their behalf.

- To take every action to prevent the recruitment of young men under the age of eighteen and their employment in armed conflicts, including the adoption of legal tools that will prohibit and make illegal the said recruitment and exploitation.
- To declare before the Swiss Foreign Ministry that the Palestinian Authority undertakes to enforce the guidelines of the appended Protocol I dated 1977 to the Geneva Convention dated 1949, according to the specifications in clause [3] 96 of the Protocol.

To the Israeli Government:

- To ensure that all the steps taken to prevent or provide a response to suicide bombings or other attacks against civilians will comply with international humanitarian law and human rights.
- To cease intentional attacks against police positions and other facilities that constitute part of the Palestinian legal infrastructure, on the condition that these attacks are perpetrated only as reprisal for Palestinian attacks against Israeli targets, and they do not constitute a significant contribution to the military effort.
- To ensure that all restrictions upon freedom of movement will be enforced only in instances and in places where this action is necessary for the prevention of specific violent acts. To provide valid transit permits for use during closures to judges and law enforcement entities, whose role is vital for the function of the Palestinian court system. To instruct Israeli security forces to honor these transit permits at the checkpoint roadblocks and enable the passage of the individuals carrying them.
- To publicly announce that sites that serve the Palestinian Authority for the detention of suspects and the incarceration of prisoners who were found guilty will not serve as a target for military attacks, and to ensure that this policy will indeed be enforced.
- To ratify without delay appended Protocol I dated 1977 to the Geneva Convention of 1949.

To the International Community:

- All governments must refrain both publicly and via diplomatic channels from any action that might be construed as encouragement, support or the expression of consent to suicide bombings or other attacks against civilians, and take advantage of any means of influence at their disposal to influence the organizations perpetrating these attacks to stop them immediately and unconditionally. Particularly, governments in the region must make use of the media means at their disposal in order to clarify that they are opposed to these types of attacks against civilians, and that they regard those who plan or execute them as criminals who must be brought to justice, and not "shahids."

- All governments that provide or approve financing or other aid for organizations that claimed responsibility for suicide bombings or other attacks against civilians must immediately cease providing the said support, as long as these organizations, including the Hamas, the Islamic Jihad, the Al-Aksa Martyrs Brigade, and the Popular Front for the Liberation of Palestine, have not made a public declaration whose reliability can be validated, stating that they no longer support these crimes, and as stated have taken effective steps to ensure that the members of the organizations will cease their involvement in these activities, and anyone who perpetrates these attacks will be brought to justice.
- To provide technical and material support in order to bolster the investigation capabilities of the Palestinian Authority's law enforcement agencies including, if deemed necessary and possible, through the assignment of authorized police investigators as escorts alongside the Palestinian officers, in order to assist them in the apprehension and the bringing to judgment of those responsible for the perpetration of suicide bombings or other attacks against civilians.

Summary

To summarize this issue, I would like to quote Thomas Friedman once again:[17]

> The consequences of the war currently being waged between the Israelis and the Palestinians will have a crucial impact on the security of every American and also, I believe—on the security of civilization as a whole.
>   Why? Because the Palestinians are currently checking out a new form of combat, based on suicide bombers wearing explosive belts and dressed as Israelis, meant to achieve their political goals, and it works.
>   Let it be clearly stated: The Palestinians have adopted the suicide attacks as a strategic choice, not out of desperation, and this phenomenon threatens all of civilization. Because if they let it "succeed" in Israel—then just as in the case of airplane hijackings, the method will spread and culminate with a suicide bomber detonating himself at a nuclear facility.
>   This is why the whole world must ensure that this strategy is defeated.

Terror Threats in the Future International Arena[18]

The suicide attack on September 11, 2001 serves as a source of inspiration for additional terrorist organizations, in light of the "victorious aura" surrounding the suicide attack and the belief that this is a weapon that cannot be combated successfully. Therefore, there appears to be an increasing inclination among other terror organizations, including secular ones, to make use of suicide attacks in order to further their struggle. The success that countries suffering from suicide terror, such as Israel and Sri Lanka, have in effectively contending with suicide attacks may serve as an important touchstone for curbing the phenomenon and diminishing its scope.

Apparently, attacks perpetrated by suicide terrorists are to be expected in the future, instigated by terror organizations in their permanent arenas of confrontation as well as by terror groups and cells from among the Afghan alumni and the organizations affiliated with the Global Jihad Front. The mega terror phenomenon appears to be turning into one of the modi operandi of modern terror, with its goal to perpetrate mass slaughter in unprecedented dimensions. It can be noted that even in the past a significant number of terror attacks causing multiple fatalities has occurred, and others were planned but never took place. These terror attacks that succeeded include the detonation of an Air India aircraft by Sikh terrorists, a bombing that claimed the lives of 329 passengers and crewmembers (June 1985); the detonation of Pan-American flight 103 over the town of Lockerbie, Scotland, where the death toll reached 271 (including passengers, crewmembers and residents of Lockerbie); in Beirut simultaneous suicide attacks claimed the lives of 241 U.S. marines and fifty-eight French soldiers. However, these attacks pale in comparison to the September 11 attacks and in comparison to an even greater toll on human life that future attacks using non-conventional weapons may incur.

The Threat of Non-conventional Terror

The use of non-conventional weapons by a terror organization constitutes one of the gravest threats posed by modern terror.

Despite the fact that the desire to obtain non-conventional weaponry is a recognized fact among various terror organizations, including Al-Qaida, it is possible to list only a very small number of incidents where terror organizations used non-conventional weapons to perpetrate attacks. Here follow several examples in this category:

- The first use of chemical weapons by the Tamil Tigers (LTTE) in June 1990, when a group of fighters from that organization used chlorine gas in an attack on a military camp in Sri Lanka.
- The two most significant and prominent attacks using chemical weapons were perpetrated by the Japanese organization called Aum Shinrikyo:
- On June 27, 1994, the organization attempted to assassinate three judges through the use of sarin gas, which was cleverly introduced into a building in which the judges were present. Seven individuals were killed in this attack.
- On March 15, 1995, the organization perpetrated an attack in the Tokyo subway, again using sarin gas. Twelve people were killed and about 5,000 were injured. This non-conventional attack claimed the highest toll of victims to date from this type of an incident.

- On November 23, 1995, an attack attempt was made by Chechen separatists in Moscow. The terrorists parked a van containing a barrel of radioactive substance at a park in Moscow. There were no known casualties.
- In the months of September-October 2001, envelopes containing anthrax were mailed in the United States. As a result of inhaling the anthrax five people died and twenty-five were injured. To date, it is still not clear who was behind this wave of attacks, though the prevalent suspicion is that an American entity was responsible for them.

A review of the non-conventional attacks that have taken place to date indicates attempts to use three areas of non-conventional weapons: chemical (chlorine and sarin gas), biological (anthrax), and radiological/nuclear. The range of terror organizations that have made use of these means (in Sri Lanka, Japan, Chechnya, and in the United States) indicates that the threat is universal. The organizations do not hesitate to use this weapon, each organization according to its technological and operational capabilities, and according to the adversary that it faces.

Despite the relative infrequency of non-conventional attacks in comparison to conventional attacks, it is clear that the threat of introducing non-conventional weapons into the arsenal of world terror is a significant one and clearly points towards an intensification of the dimensions of the danger that terror poses to the stability of world systems.

The attack on the subway in Japan unmistakably underscores the huge danger of mass attacks that can be perpetrated with chemical or biological weapons, as well as the tremendous difficulty in preventing or thwarting them. In the United States, despite the fact that the anthrax envelopes took a relatively low toll in human life, they created a significant psychological effect that necessitated preparation on the part of various U.S. authorities and which cost a small fortune.

The very precedent created by the use of non-conventional means in terror attacks and by the mass killings of September 11, has instigated a new reality, which may encourage terror organizations to perpetrate mega terror through non-conventional means as well.

The Non-Conventional Terror of Al-Qaida and Additional Islamic Terror Elements

The idea of using non-conventional combat substances had been already examined by Ramzi Yusuf, pioneer of the mega terror, in the 1990s. Yusuf explored the possibility of using a chemical weapon in order to assassinate President Clinton during his visit to the Philippines;[19] he also considered attacking the Twin Towers with toxic gas, but dismissed the idea because it seemed too expensive, and he decided to perpetrate the attack with conventional explosives instead.[20]

During recent years indications have accumulated regarding Bin-Laden's efforts to obtain non-conventional combat substances. Thus, the Americans claimed that Bin-Laden funded the development of non-conventional combat substances in the Shifa pharmaceutical factory in Sudan, which served as a target for an American attack (August 20, 1998), in response to Al-Qaida's attacks at the American embassies in Kenya and Tanzania. The Americans claimed that traces of the production of the nerve gas VX were found at the attack site.[21] According to State Department publications, Mamduah Salem, Bin-Laden's senior deputy who was arrested in Germany in October 1998 and extradited to the United States, was involved in purchasing and logistics, including the procurement of non-conventional substances.

Additional indications of the efforts by Bin-Laden's men to obtain non-conventional weapons came to light in the trials of Al-Qaida members. During the trial of those charged with detonating the American embassies in Africa, the first witness in the trial, Jamal Ahmed Al-Fadel, who was one of the veteran members of Al-Qaida, revealed that Bin-Laden had tried to acquire uranium when he was living in Sudan in the early 1990s.[22] The witness confirmed that he had served as a go-between in the initial attempts to purchase uranium, but he could not verify if the deals went through.

In the trial of Wadia Al-Haj, who had served as Bin-Laden's personal secretary, the charge sheet stated that Al-Haj had taken advantage of the fact that he carried an American passport for travels around Europe in order to purchase chemical weapons.[23]

A rare allusion to training in the use of explosives and non-conventional means at the Abu Habab camp, appeared in the charge sheet brought against Nabil Ukal, a Palestinian from the Gaza Strip, who was arrested in June 2000 by Israeli security forces. The charge sheet stated that in March 1998, Ukal underwent advanced training in the use of chemical explosive charges at the Abu Habab camp. The charge sheet also stated that the camp commander warned Ukal "not to discuss the nature of the training with anyone."

The Algerian, Ahmed Rasem, who stood trial in Los Angeles and was sentenced to 140 years in prison, stated that he had undergone advanced sabotage training at the Darunte training camp in Afghanistan. The training, which went on for six months, included light weapons and explosives, assassination training and intelligence gathering, and special instruction in the use of toxins while practicing cyanide poisoning on dogs.[24] Rasem's testimony was borne out by the findings confiscated in some buildings in Kabul that served Al-Qaida. These findings included traces of chemical substances and documents, including diagrams and explanations on how to assemble nuclear and chemical bombs. Two senior Pakistani nuclear scientists, who were arrested in 2001 by their country's security services and were suspected of leasing their services to Bin-Laden, confirmed Bin-Laden's efforts to obtain non-conventional weapons.[25]

Al-Qaida efforts to obtain non-conventional weaponry for practical use were also corroborated when Abdallah Al-Muhajir was arrested at Chicago's international airport on May 8, 2002. Muhajir, a thirty-two-year-old American citizen, was born in New York as Jose Fediya, and converted to Islam while in prison. Upon his release he found his way to Bin-Laden's training camps in Afghanistan and joined the ranks of Al-Qaida. He is an expert in chemistry and engineering, and in his role in the organization he concentrated on the study and development of capabilities to construct a radiological bomb. According to U.S. attorney general John Ashcroft, Muhajir's arrival in the United States was for the purpose of purchasing radiological substances in order to construct what is dubbed in journalistic terms as "a dirty bomb." Effective detonation of this bomb depends upon the quantity and quality of the radioactive material, but it can instantly cause massive deaths and trigger long-term genetic damage in those exposed to its radioactive fallout. This type of attack can also contaminate a large area, which makes it necessary to seal off the area because of the difficulty in decontaminating it. No less devastating is the morale-psychological damage to the stricken state as well as the event's effect upon the world population.[26]

Muhajir's arrest in Chicago added to a long line of testimony in regard to Bin-Laden's practical intentions to obtain non-conventional weapons. Additional confirmation came from the interrogation of Abu-Zubeida, one of the most senior Al-Qaida personnel under arrest in the United States, as well as from documents found in the organization's safe houses in Afghanistan.[27]

It is reasonable to assume that Al-Qaida and other terror organizations will act to obtain attack capabilities via non-conventional weapons, and this will undoubtedly constitute one of the central challenges with which mostly democratic countries will have to contend. Moreover, the very existence of these means in the possession of terror organizations and their threat to use them may constitute a method of extortion in order to achieve their goals or, alternatively, serve as a deterrent against taking steps to combat these terror organizations.

It is interesting to note that most of the concepts currently in use vis-à-vis non-conventional weapons are based on perceptions connected to the Cold War. The "balance of horror" that characterized this period was founded on a rational policy that was at the behavioral root of the involved countries, and which prevented the use of non-conventional weapons by the various sides. This assumption is not relevant to the behavioral patterns of a terror organization that gets its hands on non-conventional weapons, and so concepts like "the balance of horror," "deterrent capabilities," the "first strike," and the "second strike" are incompatible with the new reality. The West must develop new concepts regarding ways to contend with the non-conventional challenge posed by terror organizations.

Epilogue: How Were Suicide Attacks Halted in
Various Locations Worldwide?

An analysis of confrontation arenas where suicide attacks were perpetrated worldwide indicates various ways that served to stop these attacks. The solutions stemmed from the unique circumstances related to each conflict and its historical context.

Here follows a brief review of these circumstances:

1. *Cessation of suicide attacks due to the termination of the perpetrating entity.* The historical illustration in this case is the Hashishin (Assassin) Order. The suicide attacks of the Hashishins ceased when their reign was terminated; the survivors abandoned this modus operandi.

2. *Cessation of suicide attacks due to the arrest of the terror organization's leader.* An appropriate example is the arrest of the leader of the PKK Ocalan, his standing trial, and the subsequent verdict of a death sentence handed down by a Turkish court. Due to these developments, the PKK decided to cease all suicide attacks in the hope and assumption that this would prevent their leader's execution. This process occurred in the PKK because of its secular nature and due to the blind obedience and belief of the organization's activists in their leader Ocalan.

3. *Cessation of suicide attacks due to a political process or agreement.* A relevant example in this case is Sri Lanka. The Tamil Tigers Organization, which fought for an independent state for the Tamil minority, executed over 160 suicide attacks and fought a guerrilla war that took a toll of over 60,000 victims. As a result of the launching of political negotiations between the organization and the Sri Lanka government, the organization stopped the suicide attacks.

4. *Cessation of suicide attacks as the result of the redeployment of military forces (or a change of military modus operandi).* An example of these circumstances would be Israel's approach to suicide attacks in the Lebanese arena. Two central processes can be indicated in this connection:

*   In the course of the IDF's presence in the security zone in Lebanon, the Hizballah and pro-Syrian Lebanese terror organizations perpetrated suicide attacks against IDF forces and the South Lebanon Army. The number of suicide attacks diminished as a result of the adoption of improved activity and protection patterns by the IDF forces. These made the suicide attacks less effective in comparison to alternative modi operandi (counter-shooting, planting roadside devices, and more.)

    The Hizballah, which was the first organization to execute suicide attacks, believes that martyrdom is justified only on the condition that the results of the attack justify the sacrifice. Thus, when the effectiveness of the suicide attacks diminished, the organization reduced the use of this modus operandi (to a rate of one or two attacks per year).

    The diminishment of the terror and guerrilla activities of the pro-Syrian organizations in the Lebanese arena was accompanied by the cessation of suicide attacks by these entities, which became "marginal players" in the Lebanese arena.

- As a result of the IDF withdrawal from Lebanon and its redeployment along the international border, suicide attacks ceased completely in this arena, due to the lack of relevant military targets for the perpetration of this sort of attack.

  No analogy can be drawn from these examples because in each case the suicide attacks ceased due to different circumstances. However, it is possible to point out several joint characteristics shared by all of the examples:

- The cessation of suicide attacks as the result of a political process or of an informal agreement was achieved in arenas where a government was dealing with secular organizations (the PKK in Turkey and the LTTE in Sri Lanka). These organizations are characterized by a secular and na-tionalist orientation, as well as blind obedience to the organization's leadership, and they do not regard terror, including suicide attacks, as an ideology or religious ruling, but rather as a means for achieving politi-cal goals. Thus, when it is possible to obtain goals through the use of alternative methods, these organizations feel able to give up the suicide terror.
- Suicide attacks are mainly effective against civilian targets, and are less so when military or security forces are involved because the latter can take steps to significantly diminish the effectiveness of these attacks. Therefore, in confrontation arenas where there is "friction" between the army and the terror or guerrilla organizations, and there is little ability to strike out at civilian targets through the use of suicide attacks, the ex-ecution of suicide attacks gradually decreases as a result of cost/benefit considerations on the part of the perpetrating organization (for example, Hizballah and pro-Syrian organizations in Lebanon; relatively few Pal-estinian suicide attacks against IDF forces in the territories).
- A well-protected border that serves as a buffer between the terror organi-zation and the civilian population as well as the army, contributes to a significant, if not complete reduction of the action pattern involving suicide attacks (for example, the Lebanese border or the border fence surrounding the Gaza Strip).

The less optimistic message regarding suicide attacks focuses on Islamic terror organizations. In contrast to secular terror organizations, which ceased the execution of suicide attacks in connection to the above-mentioned cir-cumstances, it is impossible to provide parallel examples regarding Islamic terror organizations. Due to their very nature, these organizations are not inclined towards compromises and political agreements; they regard the Jihad as the way to achieve their goals and the suicide attacks as a major and central component of this Jihad.

Therefore, these organizations, which adopted the modus operandi of the suicide attacks, use this method for a prolonged period, though at fluctuating levels of intensity according to the circumstances. When confronting these organizations, there is a necessity to fight an ongoing and uncompromising battle, while employing every available defensive and offensive means in order to thwart their intentions. Examples of these organizations are Al-Qaida and the other organizations affiliated in the "Global Jihad Front"—the Hamas, the Palestinian Islamic Jihad, and others.

To summarize, despite several "rays of light" in the dark terrain of suicide attacks (such as Turkey and Sri Lanka), it would appear that in the foreseeable future suicide attacks will continue to constitute the central threat posed by radical Islam against its adversaries in the Muslim world, the West, and at any other confrontation points of Islam versus other cultures (India, Russia, and more). The combination of suicide attacks along with the use of non-conventional means (mega terror) may become the gravest threat to public security throughout the Free World.

Notes

1. This figure is accurate for December 2003.
2. Based on the article by Amos Harel, *Ha'aretz*, July 16, 2002.
3. *Ha'aretz*, Tel Aviv, August 27, 2002; *Yediot Aharonot*, Tel Aviv, August 27, 2002.
4. *Maariv*, Tel Aviv, October 16, 2002.
5. *Yediot Aharonot*, Tel Aviv, October 9, 2002.
6. *Yediot Aharonot*, Tel Aviv, October 6, 2002.
7. Ibid.
8. Ibid.
9. Based on the document of Amnesty International, "The Occupied Territories and the Palestinian Authority: Without Promise—Attacks against Civilians by Armed Palestinian Organizations," July 2002.
10. A declaration made by the International Conference of the Red Cross, Geneva, December 5, 2001. This basic rule is clearly expressed in several principles of the humanitarian international law including clause 22 of the regulations appended to the Ninth Hague Convention, which addresses the laws and rules of war on land (1907), and clause 35 (1) of Protocol 1 of the Geneva Convention (1977).
11. A case that applies to military and para-military activity against Nicaragua (*Nicaragua vs. the United States*).
12. Clause 7 (1) and (2) (a) of the Rome Statute of the International Criminal Court dated 1998.
13. Ibid.
14. Human Rights Watch Report, "Erased in a Moment: Suicide Bombing Attacks against Israeli Citizens," November 2002.
15. Human Right News, http://hrw.org/press.
16. Ibid.
17. Thomas Friedman, quoted in *Ha'aretz*.
18. This chapter is based on the book by Yoram Schweitzer and Shaul Shay, *The Globalization of Terror*.
19. Simon Reeve, *The New Jackals*, Boston, Northeastern University Press, 1999, p. 76.
20. Ibid., p. 108.
21. www.cnn.com, November 19, 1998.

22. Uwad Salach, *Al-Sharq al-Awsat*, Internet, February 8, 2001.
23. Ibid.
24. Josh Meyer, "Terrorist Says Plot Didn't End with LAX," *Los Angeles Times*, Internet, July 4, 2001.
25. *Ha'aretz*, Tel Aviv, June 11, 2002.
26. Ibid.
27. Ibid.

Appendices

Appendix A
Development of Islamic Suicide Attacks

Hassan al-Sabah - The Assassins (Tenth century)	→	*Objective*: Eliminating political enemies through suicide attacks. *Weapon*: A poison-tipped dagger.
Moro attacks against the Spanish and subsequently against Americans in the Philippines (Fifteenth-twentieth centuries)	→	*Objective*: Suicide attacks against colonial forces and Christian population. *Weapon*: Dagger (Kris); guns; pistols.
Shiite terror attacks (Twentieth century, 1983 onwards)	→	*Objective*: Suicide attacks against foreign forces in Lebanon (the Americans and French), and against IDF forces. *Weapon*: Explosives (belt bombs, car bombs).
Sunni suicide attacks (Twentieth and twenty-first centuries)	→	*Objective*: Palestinian suicide attacks against civilian population and military targets in Israel. *Weapon*: Explosives (belt bombs, car bombs).
Suicide attacks by Bin-Laden "Mega Terror" (Twenty-first century)	→	*Objective*: Striking out at "qualitative" targets in the U.S. September 11, 2001 (Twin Towers and the Pentagon, over 3000 killed). *Weapon*: Hijacking aircraft and crashing into the target.
Non-conventional suicide attacks (Twenty-first century)	→	*Objective*: Mass killing for strategic objectives. *Weapon*: Radiological weapons – "dirty bombs"; chemical weapons; biological weapons.

Appendix B
Trends in the Development of Terror

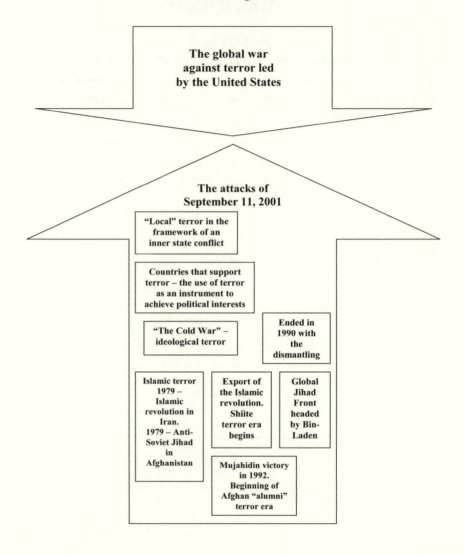

The global war
against terror led
by the United States

The attacks of
September 11, 2001

"Local" terror in the
framework of an
inner state conflict

Countries that support
terror – the use of terror
as an instrument to
achieve political interests

"The Cold War" –
ideological terror

Ended in
1990 with
the
dismantling

Islamic terror
1979 –
Islamic
revolution in
Iran.
1979 – Anti-
Soviet Jihad
in
Afghanistan

Export of
the Islamic
revolution.
Shiite
terror era
begins

Global
Jihad
Front
headed
by Bin-
Laden

Mujahidin victory
in 1992.
Beginning of
Afghan "alumni"
terror era

Appendix C
A List of Suicide Attacks
October 2000-December 2003

Date	Description of the attack	Responsible organization
October 26, 2000	A suicide attacker riding a bicycle and carrying an explosive device in a backpack, detonated himself near an IDF outpost about a kilometer north of "Gush Katif." Casualties: An IDF soldier was lightly wounded.	The Islamic Jihad
November 6, 2000	A boat exploded near a "Dabur" vessel of the Israel Navy, near the Israel/Egyptian border at Rafiah.	Hamas
December 15, 2000	A suicide terrorist attempted to detonate a bomb belt he was wearing against a security force at the "Magen 12" outpost (near the Erez roadblock), and he then tried to stab one of the security guards at the outpost. The terrorist was shot and killed. No casualties.	Hamas
December 22, 2000	A suicide terrorist detonated a bomb belt he was wearing on his body at a kiosk in Mehola, in the Jordan Valley. The terrorist was killed: 3 soldiers were wounded.	Hamas
January 1, 2001	A car bomb exploded in Netanya: 35 Israeli civilians were wounded, the majority lightly.	Hamas

Date	Description of the attack	Responsible organization
March 1, 2001	A terrorist carrying an explosive device in a bag detonated it while seated in a taxi, near the Mei-Ami intersection. One Israeli civilian was killed and 10 were wounded.	Hamas
March 4, 2001	A suicide terrorist carrying an explosive device in a bag detonated it in a central Netanya street. Three Israeli civilians were killed and 53 were wounded.	Hamas
March 27, 2001	A suicide terrorist detonated an explosive charge in a backpack that he was carrying on his body near an Israeli bus at the French Hill intersection in Jerusalem. The terrorist was killed; 21 Israelis were wounded.	Hamas
March 28, 2001	A terrorist detonated an explosive device near the gas station at Neva Yemin/Kfar Saba. The terrorist was killed. Two civilians were killed and four were wounded.	Hamas
April 22, 2001	A terrorist detonated an explosive device near a bus standing at the bus stop on Tchernikowsky Street in Kfar Saba. One Israeli civilian was killed and about 50 were wounded.	Hamas
April 29, 2001	A suicide terrorist detonated a car bomb near a school bus at the Tsir Sharaf intersection. No casualties.	Hamas
May 18, 2001	A suicide terrorist detonated an explosive device that he was carrying on his body at the entrance to a mall in Netanya. Five Israeli citizens were killed and 86 were wounded.	Hamas

Date	Description of the attack	Responsible organization
May 25, 2001	A suicide terrorist detonated an oil truck bomb containing 48 kg. of fuel and 3 gas balloons at the Netzarim/ Gaza Strip intersection. No casualties.	Hamas
May 25, 2001	Two suicide bombers detonated a car bomb at the central bus station in Hadera. Sixty-six Israelis were wounded.	The Islamic Jihad
May 29, 2001	Two suicide terrorists attacked an IDF outpost at the "Tapuach" roadblock. One detonated a bomb that was strapped to his body and the other, who lobbed hand grenades, was shot and killed. Two soldiers were wounded.	Hamas
June 1, 2001	A suicide bomber detonated an explosive device that he was carrying on his body at the entrance to the "Dolphinarium" in Tel Aviv, near midnight. Twenty-two citizens were killed including twenty Israelis and two tourists, and eighty-three were wounded.	Hamas
June 17, 2001	A suicide terrorist in a cart drawn by a donkey detonated an explosive device near the IDF outpost at Badahania/Rafiah. No casualties.	The Islamic Jihad
June 22, 2001	A suicide terrorist detonated a car bomb near an IDF patrol at the Shikma beach near the Alei Sinai settlement. Casualties: two soldiers were killed and one was lightly wounded.	Hamas

Date	Description of the attack	Responsible organization
July 9, 2001	A suicide terrorist detonated a car bomb near an IDF vehicle in the Gush Katif area. An IDF soldier was lightly wounded.	Hamas
July 11, 2001	A terrorist was apprehended in Afula when he unsuccessfully tried to detonate a device that he was carrying in a bag. No casualties.	The Islamic Jihad
July 16, 2001	A suicide terrorist detonated an explosive device strapped to his body at a bus station near the train station in Binyamina. Two soldiers were killed and 8 civilians were wounded.	The Islamic Jihad
July 22, 2001	A terrorist was apprehended in Haifa after unsuccessfully trying to detonate a belt bomb strapped to his body. No casualties.	The Islamic Jihad
August 2, 2001	A suicide terrorist was caught while trying to board a bus near Beit Shean with the aim of detonating it. No casualties.	Hamas
August 8, 2001	A car bomb driven by a suicide terrorist exploded near the Bekaot roadblock. One soldier was wounded.	Hamas
August 9, 2001	A suicide terrorist detonated an explosive charge that he carried in a bag at the "Sbarro" restaurant on the corner of King George and Yaffo Streets in Jerusalem. Fifteen civilians were killed and 110 were wounded.	Hamas
August 12, 2001	A suicide terrorist detonated a belt bomb strapped to his body at the "Wall Street" café in Kiryat Motzkin. Sixteen civilians were wounded.	The Islamic Jihad

Date	Description of the attack	Responsible organization
September 4, 2001	A suicide terrorist detonated an explosive device that he was carrying in a bag on Haneviim Street in Jerusalem. Thirteen Israelis were wounded.	Hamas
September 9, 2001	A suicide terrorist detonated an explosive device that he was carrying in a bag at the Nahariya train station. Three fatalities (two soldiers and one civilian) and forty-six were wounded.	Hamas
October 7, 2001	A suicide terrorist detonated a belt bomb on his body near the car of a member of Kibbutz Shluchot, right near the entry to the kibbutz. One Israeli citizen was killed.	The Islamic Jihad
October 17, 2001	A suicide terrorist detonated an explosive device that he was carrying in a bag near an IDF jeep about 3 km. southeast of the "Karni" pass, 400 m. east of the border fence, inside the "Green Line." Two IDF soldiers were lightly wounded.	Popular Liberation Front of Palestine (PLFP)
November 8, 2001	A suicide terrorist detonated an explosive device that he was carrying in a bag on his way to perpetrating a suicide attack in Israel. Two Border Guard policemen were wounded.	Hamas
November 26, 2001	A suicide terrorist detonated a belt bomb strapped to his body at the Erez roadblock. Two Border Guard policemen were lightly injured.	Hamas

Date	Description of the attack	Responsible organization
November 29, 2001	A suicide terrorist detonated an explosive charge strapped to his body on a bus near Mahaneh 80. Three civilians were killed and eight were wounded.	The Islamic Jihad
December 1, 2001	Two suicide terrorists detonated explosive devices that were either in bags or strapped to their bodies at the Ben Yehuda pedestrian mall. Subsequently, a car bomb exploded nearby. Eleven civilians were killed and about 170 were wounded.	Hamas
December 2, 2001	A suicide terrorist detonated a belt bomb on a bus on Yad Lebanim Street in central Haifa. Fifteen civilians were killed and thirty-five were wounded.	Hamas
December 4, 2001	A suicide terrorist detonated a backpack that he was carrying on his body, apparently after he missed a bus near the Holiday Inn Hotel at the Memila intersection in Jerusalem.	The Islamic Jihad
December 9, 2001	A suicide terrorist partially detonated an explosive device that he was carrying on his body at the Checkpost intersection in Haifa. The terrorist was seriously wounded and was shot to death. Thirty Israelis were wounded.	The Islamic Jihad
December 12, 2001	Two suicide terrorists detonated explosive devices that they were carrying in bags near two Israeli vehicles near Ganei Tal/Gush Katif. At the same time a road bomb was detonated near one of the vehicles. Three civilians were lightly wounded.	Hamas

Date	Description of the attack	Responsible organization
December 15, 2001	A suicide bomber detonated a belt bomb near a roadblock south of Tul Karem. No casualties.	Fatah/ Martyrs of the Al-Aksa Brigades
January 25, 2002	A suicide terrorist detonated an explosive device strapped to his body on Neveh Sha'anan Street in Tel Aviv. Twenty-three civilians were wounded, including two foreigners. Another terrorist who was supposed to shoot a gun was apprehended.	The Islamic Jihad
January 27, 2002	A female suicide bomber detonated an explosive charge strapped to her body on Jaffa Street in Jerusalem. One civilian was killed and 127 were wounded.	Fatah/ Martyrs of the Al-Aksa Brigades
January 30, 2002	A suicide bomber detonated himself near Taibeh. Two civilians were wounded.	Fatah
February 6, 2002	A suicide terrorist was apprehended on his way from Jerusalem to Maaleh Adumin when he unsuccessfully attempted to detonate a belt bomb strapped to his body.	Hamas
February 16, 2002	A suicide terrorist detonated an explosive device that was strapped to his body at a shopping center in Hashomron Mall. Three Israeli civilians were killed and 22 were wounded.	The PLFP

Date	Description of the attack	Responsible organization
February 17, 2002	Two suicide terrorists on their way in a car to perpetrating an attack were killed near Mahaneh (Camp) 80. One was shot dead by IDF security forces and the other detonated the belt bomb. Two policemen were slightly wounded.	Fatah/ Martyrs of the Al-Aksa Brigades
February 18, 2002	A suicide terrorist detonated a car bomb near the Alzaim roadblock in Jerusalem. One Israeli policeman was killed and two were wounded (a policeman and a civilian).	Fatah/ Martyrs of the Al-Aksa Brigades
February 19, 2002	A suicide terrorist detonated a belt bomb near a bus that he attempted to board at the Mehola intersection. No casualties.	Fatah/ Martyrs of the Al-Aksa Brigades
February 22, 2002	A suicide terrorist detonated a belt bomb strapped to his body at a supermarket in Efrat (the Etzion Bloc). The device partially exploded. Three civilians were lightly wounded.	Fatah/ Martyrs of the Al-Aksa Brigades
February 27, 2002	A suicide terrorist detonated herself near the Macabim / Modiin roadblock. Two Arab Israelis who drove her were shot and wounded. Three Israeli policemen were lightly wounded.	Fatah/ Martyrs of the Al-Aksa Brigades
March 2, 2002	A suicide terrorist detonated an explosive device strapped to his body on Haim Ozer Street in Jerusalem. Ten Israelis were killed and forty-six were wounded.	Fatah/ Martyrs of the Al-Aksa Brigades

Date	Description of the attack	Responsible organization
March 5, 2002	A suicide terrorist detonated a device strapped to his body on a bus in Afula. One civilian was killed and twenty were injured.	The Islamic Jihad
March 7, 2002	A suicide terrorist was caught when he attempted to detonate an explosive device that he was carrying in a backpack at the "Kafit" café on Emek Refaim Street in Jerusalem. No casualties.	Hamas
March 7, 2002	A suicide terrorist detonated a belt bomb strapped to his body at the "Eshel Hashomron" Hotel in the settlement of Ariel. There were nine injuries.	The PLFP
March 7, 2002	A suicide terrorist who arrived in Carcur with a belt bomb and an explosive device concealed in a birdcage was apprehended after arousing the suspicion of a local resident and fled in the direction of Um El-Fahem.	The Islamic Jihad
March 9, 2002	A suicide terrorist detonated an explosive device strapped to his body at the entrance of the Moment café on Azza Street in Jerusalem. Eleven Israelis were killed and 58 were wounded.	Hamas
March 17, 2002	A suicide terrorist who attempted to board a bus at the French Hill intersection in Jerusalem detonated the device on his body. Twenty-five civilians were lightly wounded.	The Islamic Jihad

Date	Description of the attack	Responsible organization
March 20, 2002	A suicide terrorist detonated a belt bomb strapped to his body in a bus at the Musmus intersection in Wadi Ara. Seven Israelis were killed (including 4 soldiers) and twenty-eight were wounded.	The Islamic Jihad
March 21, 2002	A suicide terrorist detonated an explosive charge strapped to his body at entrance to a café in Jerusalem. Three civilians were killed and eighty were wounded.	Fatah/ Martyrs of the Al-Aksa Brigades
March 22, 2002	A suicide terrorist detonated an explosive device strapped to his body at the Salem/Zebuba roadblock in Jenin. One soldier was wounded.	Fatah/ Martyrs of the Al-Aksa Brigades
March 26, 2002	A suicide terrorist unsuccessfully tried to detonate a belt bomb that he was carrying on his body at the Hares/Kalkilya roadblock, left the belt and fled.	The PLFP
March 27, 2002	A suicide terrorist detonated a belt bomb strapped to his body at the Park Hotel in Netanya. Twenty-nine civilians were killed and 144 were wounded.	Hamas
March 29, 2002	A female suicide terrorist detonated an explosive device strapped to her body at the entrance to a supermarket in Kiryat Yovel, Jerusalem. Two Israelis were killed and 22 were wounded.	Fatah/ Martyrs of the Al-Aksa Brigades

Date	Description of the attack	Responsible organization
March 30, 2002	A suicide terrorist detonated a belt bomb at the "My Coffee Shop Café" on Allenby Street in Tel Aviv. One Israeli was killed and twenty-nine were wounded.	Fatah/ Martyrs of the Al-Aksa Brigades
March 30, 2002	A suicide bomber detonated a belt bomb in a car and an additional terrorist, who shot at Border Guard policemen, was shot and killed at Baka al-Garbiah/Nazlat Issa near Tul Karem. A policeman was killed and another was wounded.	Fatah/ Martyrs of the Al-Aksa Brigades
March 31, 2002	A suicide terrorist detonated a belt bomb at the "Matzah" restaurant in Neveh Sha'anan, Haifa. Fifteen Israelis were killed and thirty-one were wounded.	Hamas
March 31, 2002	A suicide terrorist detonated a belt bomb near an infirmary in Efrat. Six civilians were wounded.	Fatah/ Martyrs of the Al-Aksa Brigades
April 1, 2002	A suicide terrorist detonated a belt bomb in a car near a police roadblock at the intersection of Haneviim and Shivtei Yisrael Streets in Jerusalem. One policeman was killed.	Fatah/ Martyrs of the Al-Aksa Brigades
April 10, 2002	A suicide terrorist detonated a belt bomb on a bus at the Yagur intersection. Eight individuals were killed and seventeen were wounded.	The Islamic Jihad
April 12, 2002	A suicide terrorist detonated a belt bomb at the entrance to the Mahaneh Yehuda market in Jerusalem. Six Israelis were killed and sixty-four were wounded.	Fatah/ Martyrs of the Al-Aksa Brigades

Date	Description of the attack	Responsible organization
April 19, 2002	A suicide terrorist detonated a car bomb near an IDF outpost at the Gush Katif intersection. Two soldiers were lightly wounded.	The Islamic Jihad
April 20, 2002	A suicide terrorist detonated an explosive device strapped to his body near the 108 Kalkilya roadblock. No casualties.	Hamas
May 7, 2002	A suicide terrorist detonated a belt bomb and an additional explosive device in a bag at a billiard club in Rishon Lezion. There were sixteen fatalities and fifty-one wounded.	Hamas
May 8, 2002	A suicide terrorist was seriously wounded when an explosive device strapped to his body detonated at a bus stop at the Megiddo intersection. Three civilians were wounded.	The Islamic Jihad
May 19, 2002	A suicide terrorist wearing an IDF uniform detonated an explosive device that he was carrying in a backpack on his body on Zangwill Street in the Netanya market. There were three fatalities and 60 injured.	The PFLP
May 20, 2002	A suicide terrorist detonated an explosive device that was strapped on his body near the roadblock at the Ta'anachim intersection. There were no casualties.	The Islamic Jihad

Date	Description of the attack	Responsible organization
May 22, 2002	A suicide terrorist detonated an explosive device that he was carrying in a bag in the Rothschild pedestrian mall in Rishon Lezion. Two civilians were killed and 36 were injured.	Fatah/ Martyrs of the Al-Aksa Brigades
May 24, 2002	A suicide terrorist in a car bomb was shot and killed near a club on Kibbutz Galuyot Street in Tel Aviv. The car partially exploded. Seven civilians were injured.	Fatah/ Martyrs of the Al-Aksa Brigades
May 27, 2002	A suicide terrorist detonated himself near a café outside of the "Em Hamoshavot" mall in Petach Tikva. Two women were killed and thirty were injured.	Fatah/ Martyrs of the Al-Aksa Brigades
June 5, 2002	A suicide terrorist detonated a car bomb alongside Egged bus no. 830 near the Megiddo intersection. Seventeen individuals were killed and 42 were wounded.	The Palestinian Islamic Jihad
June 11, 2002	A suicide bomber detonated a belt bomb at the entrance to a restaurant on Sokolow Street in Herzlia. One girl was killed and twelve were wounded.	Fatah/ Martyrs of the Al-Aksa Brigades
June 17, 2002	A suicide bomber detonated a belt bomb near Marja / Yarkon. There were no casualties.	Fatah/ Martyrs of the Al-Aksa Brigades
June 18, 2002	A suicide terrorist detonated an explosive charge that he was carrying in a bag on a bus on Dov Yosef Street in Gilo, Jerusalem. Nineteen civilians were killed and fifty were wounded.	Hamas

Date	Description of the attack	Responsible organization
June 19, 2002	A suicide terrorist stormed the area of the bus stops at Jerusalem's French Hill and detonated an explosive charge that he was holding in a bag. Seven individuals were killed and thirty-nine were wounded.	Fatah/ Martyrs of the Al-Aksa Brigades
July 17, 2002	Two suicide terrorists detonated bags that they were carrying in the Neveh Sha'anan pedestrian mall in Tel Aviv. Five individuals were killed (including two foreigners) and thirty-three were wounded.	Fatah/ Martyrs of the Al-Aksa Brigades
August 4, 2002	A suicide terrorist detonated himself on a bus near the Merion intersection. Nine individuals were killed, 48 wounded.	Hamas
August 6, 2002	A suicide bomber detonated himself in a vehicle in Umm el Fahem (apparently a work accident), The driver was wounded.	Hamas
September 18, 2002	A suicide terrorist detonated himself prior to boarding a bus in Wadi Arra. A policeman was killed.	The Palestinian Islamic Jihad
September 19, 2002	A suicide terrorist detonated himself on a bus at the corner of Allenby and Rothschild Streets in Tel Aviv. Six individuals were killed and 58 were injured.	Hamas
October 9, 2002	A suicide bomber attempted to board a bus near Bar Ilan University. He tripped and failed to board it. After struggling with the driver and a passenger he detonated himself near a group of people. One woman was killed and 35 were injured.	Hamas

Date	Description of the attack	Responsible organization
October 11, 2002	A suicide bomber tried to detonate himself near the "Tayelet" coffee house in Tel Aviv. Security guards overpowered him and caught him.	Hamas
October 21, 2002	A car bomb with 2 suicide attackers exploded near a bus at the Karkur intersection. Fourteen individuals were killed and 50 were injured.	The Palestinian Islamic Jihad
October 27, 2002	A suicide bomber exploded while struggling with soldiers who tried to stop him at the gas station in Ariel. Three people were killed, 16 were injured.	Hamas
November 4, 2002	A suicide terrorist detonated himself at the entrance to the "Arim" mall in Kfar Saba. Two individuals were killed and 37 were wounded.	PFLP
November 21, 2002	A suicide terrorist detonated himself on a bus (line 20) in Kiryat Menahem. Eleven people were killed and 51 were wounded.	Hamas
November 23, 2002	Two suicide terrorists detonated themselves in a boat near the IDF navy's Dabur. Four soldiers were wounded.	The Palestinian Islamic Jihad
November 27, 2002	A car bomb with a suicide driver detonated near the offices of the DCO at the Erez roadblock. No one was hurt.	PFLP
December 28, 2002	A car bomb exploded at the Russian Compound in Jerusalem. No one was hurt.	Perpetrator unknown

Date	Description of the attack	Responsible organization
January 5, 2003	Two suicide attackers detonated themselves at the pedestrian mall in Neveh Sha'anan in Tel Aviv. Twenty-three were killed and 105 were injured.	Fatah/ Martyrs of the Al-Aksa Brigades
February 9, 2003	A suicide terrorist detonated himself near the Orhan outpost in Gaza. Four people were injured.	The Palestinian Islamic Jihad
February 18, 2003	A suicide attacker detonated himself near an Israeli tank in Gaza's Sujaia neighborhood. No one was injured.	Hamas
March 5, 2003	A suicide terrorist detonated himself on a bus in Haifa. Seventeen individuals were killed and 60 were injured.	Hamas
March 30, 2003	A suicide attacker detonated himself at the London coffee house at Kikar Ha'atzmaut in Netanya. Fifty-four were injured.	The Palestinian Islamic Jihad
April 26, 2003	A suicide attacker detonated himself at the train station in Kfar Saba. One person was killed and fourteen were injured.	Fatah/ Martyrs of the Al-Aksa Brigades
April 30, 2003	A suicide attacker detonated himself at the entrance to a club on the Tel Aviv promenade. (A second terrorist escaped.) Three people were killed and about 50 were injured.	Hamas
May 8, 2003	A car bomb with a suicide driver exploded near a tank in the Gaza Strip. No one was injured.	Fatah/ Martyrs of the Al-Aksa Brigades
May 17, 2003	A suicide terrorist who was disguised as a settler detonated himself in Hebron. Two Israelis were killed.	Hamas

Date	Description of the attack	Responsible organization
May 18, 2003	Two suicide attacks were perpetrated in the Jerusalem area: A suicide attacker detonated himself on a bus. A suicide attacker detonated himself at the Ram intersection. (No one was hurt in this attack.) Seven Israelis were killed and over 20 were wounded.	Hamas
May 19, 2003	A female suicide terrorist detonated herself at the entrance to a mall in Afula. Three people were killed and 52 were injured.	The Palestinian Islamic Jihad possibly in co-operation with Fatah
May 19, 2003	A suicide terrorist on a bicycle detonated himself near an armored IDF jeep. Three soldiers were slightly wounded.	Hamas
June 11, 2003	A suicide terrorist detonated himself on a bus in Jerusalem. Seventeen people were killed and more than 100 wounded.	Hamas
June 19, 2003	A suicide terrorist detonated himself in a shop in Sde-Trumot. One man was killed.	The Palestinian Islamic Jihad
July 7, 2003	A suicide terrorist detonated himself in a house in Kfar Yavez. One woman was killed and three wounded.	The Palestinian Islamic Jihad
August 12, 2003	A suicide terrorist detonated himself in a shopping mall in Rosh Haayn. One man was killed and 9 wounded.	Fatah/ Martyrs of the Al-Aksa Brigades

Date	Description of the attack	Responsible organization
August 12, 2003	A suicide terrorist detonated himself near Ariel Intersection. Two were killed and two wounded.	Hamas
August 19, 2003	A suicide terrorist detonated himself on a bus in Jerusalem. Twenty-three people were killed and 120 wounded.	Hamas and The Palestinian Islamic Jihad claimed responsibility
September 9, 2003	A suicide attacker detonated himself near a bus station in Tzrifin. Nine people were killed and ten wounded.	Hamas
September 9, 2003	A suicide terrorist detonated himself in a coffee shop in Jerusalem. Seven people were killed and seventy wounded.	Hamas
October 4, 2003	A female suicide terrorist detonated herself in a restaurant in Haifa. Twenty-one people were killed and fifty wounded.	The Palestinian Islamic Jihad
October 9, 2003	A suicide attacker detonated himself near the DOC office in Tul Karem. Two soldiers and one Palestinian were wounded.	Fatah / Tanzim
November 3, 2003	A suicide attacker detonated himself near an IDF patrol in Azun village. One soldier was wounded.	Fatah / Tanzim
December 25, 2003	A suicide terrorist detonated himself near a bus station in Bne-Brak Intersection. Four people were killed and fifteen wounded	PLFP

To these numbers one can add an additional attack on May 14, 2002 regarding which there is some doubt whether it was an act involving self-sacrifice or an actual suicide attack.

Index

DATE DUE